O'Shaughnessy - Frey Library
University of St. Thomas
St. Paul, MN 55105

584923

"Steel for the Mind"

Samuel Johnson and Critical Discourse

Charles H. Hinnant

Newark: University of Delaware Press
London and Toronto: Associated University Presses

© 1994 by Associated University Presses, Inc.

All rights reserved. Authorization to photocopy items for internal or personal use, or the internal or personal use of specific clients, is granted by the copyright owner, provided that a base fee of $10.00, plus eight cents per page, per copy is paid directly to the Copyright Clearance Center, 27 Congress Street, Salem, Massachusetts 01970. [0-87413-492-7/94 $10.00 + 8¢ pp, pc.]

Associated University Presses
440 Forsgate Drive
Cranbury, NJ 08512

Associated University Presses
25 Sicilian Avenue
London WC1A 2QH, England

Associated University Presses
P.O. Box 338, Port Credit
Mississauga, Ontario
Canada L5G 4L8

The paper used in this publication meets the requirements of the American National Standard for Permanence of Paper for Printed Library Materials Z39.48–1948.

Library of Congress Cataloging-in-Publication Data

Hinnant, Charles H.
"Steel for the mind": Samuel Johnson and critical discourse / Charles Hinnant.
p. cm.
Includes bibliography references (p.) and index.
ISBN 0-87413-492-7 (alk. paper)
1. Johnson, Samuel, 1709-1784—knowledge—Literature.
2. English literature—18th century—History and criticism—Theory, etc.
3. Criticism—England—History—18th century. I. Title.
PR3537.L5H56 1994
828'.609—dc20 93-766
CIP

PRINTED IN THE UNITED STATES OF AMERICA

The mind once let loose to enquiry, and suffered to operate without restraint, necessarily deviates into peculiar opinions, and wanders in new tracts, where she is indeed sometimes lost in a labyrinth, from which though she cannot return, and scarce knows how to proceed; yet, sometimes, makes useful discoveries, or finds out nearer paths to knowledge.

—Samuel Johnson, *An Essay on the Origin and Importance of Small Tracts and Fugitive Pieces*

Contents

List of Abbreviations

From *The Yale Edition of the Works of Samuel Johnson* (New Haven and London: Yale University Press):

Idler, Adventurer	Vol. 2. *The Idler and the Adventurer,* eds. W. J. Bate, John M. Bullitt, and L. F. Powell (New Haven and London: Yale University Press, 1963).
Rambler	Vols. 3–5. *The Rambler,* eds. W. J. Bate and Albrecht Strauss (New Haven and London: Yale University Press, 1969).
Rasselas	Vol. 16. *Rasselas and other Tales,* ed. Arthur Sherbo, with an Introduction by Bertrand Bronson (New Haven and London: Yale University Press, 1990).
Shakespeare	Vol. 7. *Johnson on Shakespeare*, ed. Arthur Sherbo, with an introduction by Bertrand H. Bronson (New Haven and London: Yale University Press, 1968).
Lives	*The Lives of the English Poets,* ed. G. B. Hill, 3 vols. (Oxford: Clarendon Press, 1905).
Works	*The Works of Samuel Johnson, L.L.D. With an Essay on his Life and Genius,* by Arthur Murphy, 12 vols. (London: J. Nichols and Son, 1810).

Citations from *A Dictionary of the English Language* are from a facsimile reprint of the 1755 edition.

Acknowledgments

In writing this book, I have been helped enormously by the encouragement of a number of friends. I have especially benefited from Catherine Neal Parke's detailed readings of an early version of the manuscript, from John Richetti's broad and constructive suggestions for revision, and from the shrewd and exacting appraisal of the second draft by a reader for the University of Delaware Press. Steve Adams gave the manuscript a detailed and thorough proofreading before it was submitted to the press for final approval. A University of Missouri Curator's Fellowship made it possible for me to complete the initial working draft of the manuscript.

"Steel for the Mind"

1
Introduction: Between Theory and Practice

This book is an attempt to reexamine Samuel Johnson's literary criticism in the context of current critical debates. Through juxtapositions of Johnson with such movements as poststructuralism, reader-response criticism, and the New Historicism, I hope to create a justification for reexamining conventional assumptions about his writings; more ambitiously, I hope to demonstrate the importance that Johnson's work might possibly hold for anyone concerned with issues in present-day literary criticism.

Yet it is precisely this aspiration and its theoretical assumptions, even more than the conclusions it reaches, that will likely provoke resistance today. Putting aside the widespread tendency to perceive theory as "merely" theoretical and to understand practical criticism in terms of an antitheoretical criticism of intuitive observation and judgment, there is also the view, perhaps not as explicitly stated, that Johnson's theoretical formulations are uninteresting, if not hopelessly antiquated. To show where his work impinges on the interests of present-day critical theory is thus to run the risk of exposing its pastness, its difference from the present, its utter remoteness from contemporary critical concerns. Yet it is equally out of the question for criticism to seek to demonstrate Johnson's relevance, for this is to read present preoccupations back into the past and then claim to discover that Johnson's ideas once held something like their current significance. Through such assertions of parallel meaning, criticism will only be making common cause with oppression, with a totalitarianism of the same. To avoid both pitfalls, I have tried to adopt a perspective which accepts the fact, as Roland Barthes once argued, that "critical work," inevitably "contains within itself a dialogue between two historical situations and subjectivities, those of the author and those of the critic."[1]

Barthes is by no means unique in this use of the term "dialogue"; the formulation is Mikhail Bakhtin's, from whom Barthes probably borrowed the concept, and Bakhtin also used the term to criticize what he regarded as a myth of objectivity. Culture for him was a spectrum of different voices, and dialogic discourse was its most sensitive medium.[2] For Barthes, the critic is still trying to analyze and understand an author, like the historian who seeks to capture the whole picture of an age, person, or institution. But at the same time, the critic is also ready to acknowledge resistance, invisibly present but detectable by the interpreter, a stubbornly resistant reading that might constitute a genuine challenge to prevailing critical norms. This double orientation can be understood as taking hold through a process in which the interpreter enters into a conversational "exchange" with the past, rather than simply trying to understand it. Yet such a process will not take place if one treats an author—as William R. Keast treats Samuel Johnson in his otherwise distinguished essay on Johnson and the metaphysical poets—as if Johnson's concerns were distinguished solely by their distance from those of present-day critics. According to Keast,

> Johnson's examination of the metaphysical poets, like his criticism in general, is marked by the prominence in it of questions which, if they have not entirely disappeared from modern critical discussion, have been relegated to a position so subordinate as to amount effectively to their disappearance. At the same time Johnson fails to give any serious or extended consideration to those questions with which modern critics have been occupied. Johnson is not much interested in the development and cross-fertilization of metaphor, the structural employment of ambiguity, or the formative use of irony and paradox. His primary concern is with the pleasure which literature is capable of producing. He wants to know chiefly whether poems interest readers, engage their attention, and move them emotionally.[3]

What Keast failed to recognize—perhaps necessarily so given his priorities—is that the issues that preoccupied Johnson cannot simply be relegated to a kind of historical limbo, even if they pose no difficulties (and indeed appear entirely unreal) at the level of commonsense, practical awareness. It is not sufficient to contend that the question of the extent to which "pleasure" should be taken into account in the analysis of literary texts has disappeared from modern criticism. Keast's essay sets out to address this and other questions by dealing with Johnson's theoretical principles solely on their own terms, in accord with canons of internal coherence and consistency. More specifically, he argues that the disagreements between Johnson and the New Critics arose through a failure to distinguish between Johnson's criticism of "the characteristic manner of a school" and a criticism that concentrates on a few individual poems. It was the former practice, according to Keast, that makes Johnson's strictures concerning the metaphysical poets seem much more sweeping than they actually are. Nowadays critics are apt to make their judgments in interpretive terms, as for instance by focusing on particular aspects of a certain privileged group of texts.[4] But the theoretical problem is still there—unavoidably there—no matter what area of agreement is introduced by way of easing the gulf between Johnson and modern critics. Quite simply, we are unable to enter into a conceptual universe so remote from our own unless we undertake something like the dialogue recommended by Bakhtin and Barthes. We cannot hope to grasp the import of Johnson's criticism unless we are willing to enter into something like an engagement with its central critical ideas.

It is important to stress two further points about Barthes's argument. First, this perspective does not imply that there is an absolute, categorical distance between past and present. Barthes believes that we can come to terms with the beliefs, ideas, and interests that characterize discourses other than our own. In using the word "subjectivities," he is not espousing the kind of relativism that argues that there is no possibility of shared understandings on basic assumptions about poetry, representation, or affects. But Barthes also does not want to commit the fallacy of suggesting that an eighteenth-century critic and moralist and his modern interpreter are engaged in the same enterprise or that they need not disagree on some basic matters of principle and method. Nothing will have been gained if one begins by assuming that Johnson's criticism and modern critical theories have a common (e.g., Aristotelian) structure or that the assumptions of one will necessarily be identical with those of the other.

It is possible to discern a similar dialogic impulse at work in the text of Johnson's own criticism. I will propose an interpretation of Johnson's dialogism in chapter 2 and chapter 5. Here I would stress that this interpretation goes far beyond a discussion of critical ideas. One can find support in Johnson for Bakhtin's dialogic view of the world; it is as if Johnson thought of his critical writings as gesturing toward the thought of others, so that we could see in them an argument and even polemic—both with others and with himself. One thing that can be learned from Johnson is the need to distinguish between different orders of utterance, those that offer arguments—and invite counterarguments—and those that depend upon an appeal to divine revelation, scriptural authority, and a truth beyond rational understanding. There is a tendency among some of Johnson's admirers to treat all of his theoretical statements as if they belong to the latter category. Johnson's critical principles could then be dispensed with as if they were part and parcel of the same stock of common ideas that seem to inform many of his sermons and moral essays. What drops out in this simplified account is the fact that the critique of pastoral or devotional poetry (in Johnson) or the denial of dramatic illusion are projects carried through by dint of his disagreements with the arguments of others. These disagreements invite one to approach Johnson's criticism as the disclosure of difference. They are intrinsic to a mode of discourse that, in its most self-conscious form, stands at the opposite extreme from the kind of bland commonplaces that Johnson ridicules in his portrayal of Dick Minim.

This aspect of Johnson's critical writings deserves emphasis since many readers take his criticism for just another variant of the same assumptions that inform Dick Minim's pronouncements. But this view is radically mistaken as one can see not only from his various essays on pastoral poetry but also from those texts in which Johnson displays what Jean Hagstrum described as an "impatience" with the "romantic absurdities, puerile enchantments, and outmoded pagan mythology" that characterized much eighteenth-century poetry.[5] At issue is the nature of poetry as an art of pure fiction, lacking any claim to reality. Whether one considers Johnson's critique of pastoral and devotional poetry, his advocacy of the advantages of rhyme over blank verse, his denial of dramatic illusion, or his privileging of truth over fiction, one finds, behind his robust common sense and impatience with fashionable cant, a distrust of the kind of poetry that is content to gloss over the gap between words and experiences, signs and reality in poetry. Much of what Johnson has to say on this subject stands in opposition to William Hazlitt's idea of poetry as "a fiction, made up of what we wish things to be, and fancy that they are." One can see Johnson, therefore, as advocating a mode of poetry in which the disparity between desire and its object is the structuring principle, the kind of poetry that will take issue with the desire to be "transported" through art to "elysian regions" and will contest an idea of poetry in which "descriptions" when "seen through the fine medium of passion . . . are identical with the things themselves."[6] Appropriately enough, the anti-illusionistic stance of Johnson's criticism also implies a preference for dramatic and narrative modes that present the self in interaction with other characters and events. Johnson's interest in nonfictional genres like travel, history, biography, and autobiography, as well as his admiration for Shakespeare as the poet of "nature" and unmediated observer of men and manners, are perfect examples. Such an admiration is supported by Johnson's conviction that the poet must not assert himself as a self-enclosed subject but "must find the means of flying from himself . . . must adopt the joys and pains of others, and excite in his mind the want of social pleasures and amicable communication" (*Rambler,* IV: 107).

Of course, it might be objected that this stance is mainly evidence of Johnson's critical limitations, his literal-minded unwilingness to acknowledge a realm of fictive recreation without bearing on reality. But what is striking about this position is that it is formulated in opposition to the conventional theories of his day. This opposition, which involves regarding poetry as the representation of truth, leads him to formulate a distinctive critical terminology. In place of a language that focuses on the workings of the poetic process, Johnson employs terms—e.g., "endeavour," "composition," "performance"—that highlight the most self-conscious aspects of the act of writing. To accept this inversion of received priorities—to abandon an epistemology that refers to a self-contained realm of appearance—is to take the first step (so Johnson almost seems to imply) toward a resistance to the seductions of a delusory and demonic imagination. The only effective means of resistance is an opposing perspective, one that rejects all forms of delusion, that insists upon the absolute primacy of truth, and that consequently aligns itself with ironic rather than sentimental forms of poetry.

So there is clearly no question of Johnson's critical principles being somehow rendered commonplace or marginal by the demonstrable fact that he rejected contemporary notions of poetry as having to do with much more than truth telling. In fact, one could argue that Johnson's repudiation of a poetry of wish fulfillment is inseparable from his rejection of the kind of ambitious system building exemplified by Edmund Burke's *A Philosophical Enquiry into the Origin of Our Ideas of the Sublime and the Beautiful* or Lord Kames's *Elements of Criticism.* There comes a point at which judging according to abstract principles is tantamount to dwelling in a purely imaginary realm where the critic is able to play with the semblance of texts, rendering verdicts without being genuinely engaged, exempt from the responsibility of being attentive and fair-minded. But to repudiate critical principles altogether is equally unsatisfactory. Indeed, it is one of Johnson's main points in his discussion of Dryden's criticism that the only alternative to critical standards is a reliance upon "chance" or "instinct." It is precisely this condition of ignorance, coupled with an uncertain reliance upon "genius," that prevailed in "the days of Elizabeth" (*Lives*, I: 411). Thus the upshot of Johnson's argument is to question both the assurance (characteristic of critical theory) that critical principles can be formulated in a realm apart from local perceptions and the notion (common to all forms of empiricist or inductivist thinking) that these perceptions count for everything and that the critic has no need for the sort of ideas that philosophy has mistakenly regarded as essential to its own calling.

All the same it is difficult to avoid this dualistic habit of thought, one that treats critics as either engaged in a quest for systematic truths, a priori concepts, definitions, axioms, propositions, etc., or as close readers whose work reveals a detailed engagement with specific texts. Such is the assumption that governs Leopold Damrosch's *The Uses of Johnson's Criticism.* Damrosch insists that critical ideas do not translate directly into local perceptions, that Johnson's finest criticism cannot be understood as a one-way application of theoretical principles, and that a great deal besides critical theory went into the construction of Johnson's critical texts. Hence it should not be surprising that Damrosch has little patience with the old-fashioned theory-to-practice model. Indeed he goes so far as to argue that "the much-quoted *Ramblers* and the *Preface* to Shakespeare where he is most theoretical, do not show him at his best" and that a precise formulation of the fundamental axioms of Johnson's thought runs the risk of distorting or omitting what is most important to an understanding of Johnson.[7]

To some extent the tone of these remarks can be explained by Damrosch's commitment to the empirical mode, by his own resistance to critical theory in whatever form. But it also shows very clearly how the emphasis in Johnson's criticism has shifted in the thirty or so years since Keast, Hagstrum, and René Wellek sought to provide a more rigorous formulation of Johnson's critical ideas. For Keast, the crucial lesson to be gained from a reading of Johnson's criticism was the need to infer "general views" from "particular lines of argument," an approach that would respect the relative autonomy of different critical spheres and thus not take Johnson's theory for "the whole of his argument." Where we run the risk of confusing the issue, Keast maintains, is in thinking that Johnson's assumptions might vary from one work to another or be tailored to fit specific contexts. In fact this amounts to a dilution of Johnson's thought, one that need not come about if his critical ideas were taken more seriously. Thus, for Keast, the value of Johnson's thought lies in its rigorous application of its theoretical principles; only by recognizing this rigor can one make sense out of some of Johnson's most controversial assessments. For Damrosch, on the contrary, what marks out Johnson as a valuable critic is his total distrust of "abstract theory," his "broad conception of literary history," his intelligence, and his moral seriousness. In Johnson's case, it is the merest of delusions to think of theoretical principles as exerting an interest apart from his practical judgments. Quite simply, there is no distinguishing one from another, no means of knowing for sure what might be the limits of Johnson's critical theory or how far these merely reflect a desire to salvage some of Johnson's more outrageous verdicts from the censures of his detractors.

Curiously enough, one can argue that Johnson anticipates this debate point by point in his "Life of Dryden." The section of the life devoted to Dryden's criticism was aimed at the presumption—apparently common among Johnson's contemporaries—that "he who, having formed his opinions in the present age of English literature, turns back to peruse [the *Essay on Dramatick Poetry*], will not find perhaps much increase of knowledge or much novelty of instruction" (*Lives*, I: 411). Johnson sets out to rescue Dryden from this complacent assumption by arguing that Dryden's criticism is "the criticism of a poet; not a dull collection of theorems, nor a rude detection of faults . . . but a gay and vigorous dissertation" (*Lives*, I: 412). Johnson's praise results from his persuasion on the one hand that Dryden's criticism makes logical sense, i.e., that it offers a coherent and compelling theory, and on the other that it remains first and foremost a practical theory, one whose authority cannot be assessed apart from Dryden's own "power of performance." It is here—in a further distinction between Dryden's "general precepts, which depend upon the nature of things and the structure of the human mind" and "occasional and particular positions," which are "sometimes interested, sometimes negligent, and sometimes capricious" (*Lives*, I: 413)—that Johnson makes his preference for the former apparent.

In the background of this argument, one detects not only Johnson's respect for Dryden's immense critical achievement but also Johnson's sense that he was writing for an audience—a community of readers who believed themselves to have advanced well beyond Dryden and his age in critical sophistication. Johnson writes as a self-conscious defender, one for whom the value of Dryden's criticism can only be a matter of attentive, close reading and of momentary glimpses of that which must elude more conventional expectations. Behind Johnson's defense, one can detect a certain degree of scepticism concerning the critical skills of his audience. But there is a crucial difference between scepticism and rejection, since Johnson shows no desire to see criticism revert to that stage of uninformed response when instinct was the only guide to critical judgment and when ignorance placed absolute limits on the exercise of critical speculation.

What thus seems apparent is that Johnson shares none of the hostility to theory that characterizes some of his modern admirers. He advocates a broad critical approach that combines general precepts and particular observations, instruction and delight. The object of this exercise is not to compose ever more recondite treatises on abstract topics but, on the contrary, to rescue criticism from precisely that kind of misapplied labor. That general precepts may turn out to be "scattered over all" an author's works is what one ought to expect, given the circumstances under which they were formulated. But this need not be thought to impugn the validity of these precepts, so long as we think the questions they raise worth our close attention. For such precepts have their own authority, one that derives from their power to "assist our faculties when properly used" (*Rambler*, V: 166–67). Johnson makes this point—the distinction between an appropriate and an unskillful application of the rules of criticism—in connection with a discussion of the relation between author and critic. But the same argument applies to the kind of general precepts that can be found scattered throughout Johnson's essays, prefaces, and lives—definitions, axioms, propositions, corollaries, etc. that solicit assent on an intellectual level and not simply by means of their application to particular texts. What Johnson hoped to achieve was at once a technique for avoiding the tedium and aridity of systematic theory and yet a method of subjecting his own specific judgments to the tribunal of enlightened reason.

In Johnson, this approach is conjoined with the implicit claim that the highest form of human knowledge consists in perceiving "the nature of things and the structure of the human mind." It is remarkable that Johnson should find this kind of knowledge accessible to empirical observation. But in fact he takes this whole rationalist metaphysics on board, including the notion that its insights are not susceptible to time and change. Thus he declares in the final *Rambler* that "arbitrary decision and general exclamation I have avoided, by asserting nothing without reason, and establishing all my principles of judgment on unalterable and evident truth" (*Rambler*, V: 319). From this, it follows that criticism is itself but one part of a broader science of nature, that criticism has no reality outside this science and, therefore, that the end of all rational inquiry is to uncover a structure of stable and certain truths. Such truths are accessible to reason alone and are in no way dependent on the fallible signs of passion or the caprices of fancy.

It is precisely this aspect of Johnson's criticism that has struck some readers as a species of rationalistic delusion, the result of his assuming that the task of the critic was to teach readers "to determine upon principles the merit of composition" (*Lives*, I: 410). For it is the aim of criticism, in Johnson's account, "to establish principles

. . . criticism reduces those regions of literature under the dominion of science, which have hitherto known only the anarchy of ignorance, the caprices of fancy, and the tyranny of prescription" (*Rambler*, IV: 122). To theorize is to move beyond the realm of gothic superstition and tyranny, to establish a critical distance from the unreliable data of subjective thinking. For Johnson, it is a chief virtue of criticism that it enables the mind to survey this progress beyond the partial and perplexing evidence of the fancy, to gain access to a realm of "unalterable and evident" truths where critical judgments are reduced to order and reason. To many modern readers, this appears nothing more than a striking instance of the errors to which Johnson was prone whenever he accepted uncritically the prevailing critical assumptions of an outmoded neoclassicism. Johnson's mistake was to confuse his own distinctive contribution to criticism with these conventional statements about the rules.

Such is Damrosch's argument in *The Uses of Johnson's Criticism*: to point out the difficulties that arise when Johnson's claims are taken too literally, when his "statements about theory" are taken for the "theories themselves," and when general pronouncements are allowed to override the concerns that actually preoccupied Johnson as a critic. Otherwise there is no defense against the arguments of those who contend that Johnson is indifferent to the prevailing theoretical issues of his time—e.g., the issues of genre theory, the nature of artistic creation, or the connections between the various arts. Damrosch's answer of course is that this emphasis is wholly misconceived and that Johnson's practical criticism is actually the obverse of neoclassical theory. Thus commentary should concern itself with Johnson's criticism not "as a body of doctrine and adjudications" but as "an act in which the reader shares." This would bring two main benefits according to Damrosch. One the one hand, it would show that what fascinated Johnson was "literary history, not the internal dynamics of form but the successive performances of a host of human beings." On the other, it would suggest that Johnson's criticism is best understood as the embodiment of a kind of natural or precritical attitude that accepts what is given in common sense and finds no reason to go beyond the grounds of an immediate response. This attitude is explified most of all in Johnson's mature critical writings, the *Lives*, though not (Damrosch argues) in those texts that predate that work, the *Rambler* essays, *Rasselas*, and the *Preface* to Shakespeare, texts that still bear traces of an earlier—neoclassical or theoretical—mode of understanding.[8]

* * *

So one can see why it would be no exaggeration to say that the entire project of coming to terms with Johnson's criticism comes down to the issue of Johnson the theorist versus Johnson the practical critic, or the interest of a Johnsonian science of criticism as opposed to an empirically centered interpretation of biography, history, and specific literary works. In the remainder of this book, it will be argued that the one is inseparable from the other. There are problems in Johnson's work that have less to do with his theoretical assumptions than with his prejudices. Yet these problems are only compounded if Johnson's criticism is not read in the context of his poetics. His notorious attack on *Lycidas* cannot be divorced from his sense that the self is defined by its relation to an other who is a separate voice and not an echo, or from his perception of Milton and Shakespeare as monologic and dialogic poets. This kind of critical thinking involves a rich but largely tacit dimension of enabling motives and assumptions. Its model is not the ambitious theories projected in writings of his Scottish contemporaries but the much more provisional arguments of Dryden, Addison, or Pope. The task of the commentator is to explain where those arguments come from, to expose them to rational critique, and to demonstrate their structural genealogy.

It is this kind of approach that my book invokes in seeking to account for Johnson's apparently conflicting statements about "particularity" and "generality." Its premise is that all the comments on "particularity" that disturb the conventional view of Johnson's commitment to the grandeur of generality can be reinscribed within an entirely different but nonetheless rigorously argued form of discourse. It is not necessary, moreover, to assume that Johnson was consciously aware of this second, implicit level of discourse. His comments on genre are widely scattered and often ad hoc in character, yet when they are assembled, they constitute much more, I believe, than a merely negative aspect of his analysis of literary texts. What we discover in Johnson's criticism is the outline of a preliminary, but nonetheless distinctive, revision of genre theory, one that is in keeping with his privileging of dramatic and narrative forms over monologic genres like pastoral, didactic, and devotional poetry.

The argument of this book is thus more closely related to the earlier studies of William R. Keast, Jean H. Hagstrum, and Walter Jackson Bate than to the monographs of Damrosch or Paul Fussell. Against the attempts of an older generation of scholars to establish the "theoretical foundations" of Johnson's criticism, more recent commentators have given emphasis to his undoubted achievements as a practical critic as well as to his distrust of what is sometimes misleadingly called "abstract theory." Yet I would argue that Johnson's unique combination of moral and critical analysis cannot be disengaged from theoretical assumptions and that a focus upon practical judgments invariably carries with it a conviction that the critical values behind these judgments are irrelevant. It is significant, in this connection, that Johnson invariably uses the word "performance" instead of "practice" in specific judgments of individual poems and poets. As the product of a calculated "design" or "intention," the term "performance" conveys the suggestion of a practice that is connected to theory in the sense that it may be a kind of enactment of what has already been conceived in advance. Even more important, what Johnson actually attacks in his writings is not so much theoretical principles as theoretical systems; like so many other thinkers of his time, he ridicules the great metaphysical structures of Descartes, Leibniz, Spinoza, and Hobbes. It is perhaps in keeping with this antimetaphysical posture that Johnson often seems to resist the conventional metaphysical hierarchies that characterize eighteenth-century thought. Thus we find a whole series of opposed valuations—nature versus art, poetry versus prose, presence versus representation—undergoing scrutiny and revaluation in his criticism. This may also be why Johnson puts forward most of his criticism in essays, prefaces, and notes—forms of discourse whose authority is tentative rather than absolute and whose mode of argument, although emphatic in expression, is much more dialogic, inconclusive and provisional than that of the formal treatise. Even if the reasoning in these texts proves, upon close analysis, to be quite rigorous, it is articulated with a brevity and force that can easily conceal its theoretical implications.

This reasoning is characteristically embodied in two different forms. The first possesses the concision as well as the generality of the aphorism. Because of its condensed and sometimes elliptical cast, the Johnsonian aphorism often requires elucidation and extended explanation. One of the hazards confronting the modern student of Johnson is that the explication of this kind of compressed utterance entails the speculative reconstruction of assumptions and implications. The second form includes more extended statements; these may run from several lines to several paragraphs but are never longer than what we might expect to find encompassed within the scope of a single periodical essay. It could be argued that these statements are often attached to judgments of particular poets and poems and, thus, deserve to be seen as generalizations of specific instances. Yet this is not always the case. Johnson's critique of devotional poetry in the "Life of Waller," for example, is not linked to comments on any individual poems of Waller and takes a disproportionately larger amount of space than Waller's relatively few "divine poems" would actually seem to warrant. Johnson's remarks thus appear to provide the occasion for a general statement about sacred poetry, one that will not only serve as a background for subsequent comments in the *Lives* but will also serve to define Johnson's general position on the subject. Johnson's comments on pastoral or on the "advantages" of rhyme over blank verse are not quite so obviously positioned as his critique of religious poetry, but they serve a similar purpose: they are clearly meant to stand as formulations whose validity extends beyond the particular instances they support.

Johnson's preference for short forms—the brief essay and still briefer aphorism—is accompanied by two other characteristics that help to mask the full implications of his criticism. The first is his obvious reluctance to enter into polemical debate. Even though he became the subject of vigorous controversy during his lifetime, Johnson's own practice was to couch his arguments in general terms, to adopt a stance that appeared to elevate him above the quarrels of petty disputants. Johnson sometimes professed to believe that his age had entered into an era of good manners and, thus, had moved beyond the kind of ill-tempered polemics that had disfigured the writings of earlier critics like Rymer, Settle, Dennis, and Milbourne. Yet this posture should not lead us to assume that Johnson repressed his differences with his contemporaries. The larger world of eighteenth-century criticism is already present within Johnson's critical discourse, but the latter is engaged in a dialogue with this world even as it seeks to minimize purely ad hominem disagreements. The second feature of Johnson's criticism, which can make it difficult for us to grasp all of its theoretical nuances, is Johnson's lifelong endeavor to make his arguments accessible to the nonspecialist reader, sometimes by explaining his ideas in simple and homely ways. For all Johnson's obvious delight in Latinate words and phrases, he consistently simplifies his critical terms and firmly holds in check any desire to fit his ideas into the standard framework of neoclassical polemics. To Johnson's way of thinking, such a framework would be unhelpful—or even unintelligible—since nothing can make sense in isolation from its impact on the common reader. Thus Johnson's aim is to seek to make things plain, while consistently minimizing any larger claims to speculative consistency.

This may help to explain the persistent misreading of Johnson, which takes him to deny all commerce between theory and practical common sense. It is the critic's proper business, as Johnson sees it, to pass back and forth between the detailed local perception and generalized statements of method and principle. One can see how a work like the *Lives of the Poets* conforms to this ideal. On the one hand, there are those passages of "minute" and particular criticism that aroused such controversy among Johnson's contemporaries. On the other hand, there is the constant practice of dropping statements of an offhand nature on such general questions as the difference between simile and exemplification, the nature of poetry, and the limits of allegory. What is excluded in the process is any kind of reasoned theoretical linkage between the various passages. There is something slightly disingenuous about Johnson's statement that the criticism of Pope's poetry as too uniformly musical is "the cant of those who judge by principles rather than perception" (*Lives*, III: 248). In fact, Johnson's criticism consistently moves back and forth between principle and perception, although relating the two in such a way as to avoid the larger ground of rational system. Johnson can thus get on with the business of making specific judgments, while the *Lives* make their larger claims about poets without becoming entangled in the filiations of systematic argument.

This is why the following chapters refuse the temptation to collapse theory into practical criticism, or a version of practical criticism that excludes "theory" as just one more futile attempt to "rescue" Johnson's critical opinions from his detractors. Thus the second chapter begins by examining the contention that Johnson was a dogmatic critic, seeking to demonstrate that his claim to interpretive authority did not rest upon the exclusion of dialogue but was rather located within a contentious space of argument and debate. A corollary of this argument is the insistence that Johnson's poetics is dialogic rather than monologic and that something very much like this distinction guides his sharply contrasting evaluations of Shakespeare and Milton. Johnsonian dialogism is not merely reflected in a particular conception of poetry, moreover; it is also internalized, as it were, in a divided and conflicting idea of literary and cultural history. Far from projecting a naïve and unreflective view of progress, Johnson's account of the evolution of Augustan versification from Denham and Waller to Dryden and Pope can be shown, from the start, to be a simultaneous movement toward progress and retrogression. The view of prose that emerges in Johnson's criticism appears as similarly divided and thus differs from both the view that Johnson inherited and from the one implicit in Wordsworth's criticism of eighteenth-century poetic diction. Early eighteenth-century critics postulated a unitary "plain style," a zero degree of figuration in which prose becomes the transparent vehicle of truth and hence poetry's oppositional limit. By contrast, Johnson comes to see prose as governed by the same Horatian imperative of pleasing and instructing and thus by the same tropes and figures as poetry. But unlike

Wordsworth, who also sought to redefine the relation between prose and poetry, Johnson does not see prose as providing a naturalized norm for poetry, so that an irreducible difference between the two is preserved.

Chapter 2 also raises the question of the way Johnson views the classical relation between author, text, and audience. Chapter 3 tries to show that the apparent simplicity with which Johnson handles these terms—which were given wide currency in Meyer Abrams's *The Mirror and the Lamp*—is deceptive. The underlying relation Abrams posits takes for granted the unity and identity of the authorial and reading subjects, but what is actually presented in Johnson's criticism is a subject that is neither unified nor identical to itself. Johnson clearly accepts a pragmatic and rhetorical model of poetry in which the text serves as a vehicle of communication and persuasion. But alongside this rhetorical model goes a rather different set of emphases, a vein of thinking that treats the subject as decentered and subject to delusion. This moralizing strain is most evident in the *Rambler*, *Idler*, and *Adventurer* essays, but it also appears in the *Lives of the Poets*. It postulates the existence of an inevitable disparity between authorial intention and achievement which, it contends, is further duplicated in a discrepancy between critical judgment and understanding. The text fails as a mediating term to overcome these two lacunae, for it is subject, both within and without, to a temporal erosion that renders its status as an empirically effective unity problematic.

The fourth chapter focuses on the relation between the text and the external world. In contrast to the views of many eighteenth-century critics from Addison to Lord Kames, Johnson maintains that mimesis necessarily implies the absence of what it purports to represent and thus can never achieve what Kames calls "ideal presence." This argument provides the basis for Johnson's contention in the *Preface* to Shakespeare that "it is false" to think that "any representation is mistaken for reality." It is precisely because he examines the structure of presence and representation in terms of difference as well as identity, moreover, that Johnson argues against the notion that poetry can be confined to a realm of fictive recreation without bearing on reality. As the site of a limited reappropriation of presence, a poem can achieve credibility only as a representation of a prior reality, not as the invention of an imaginary golden world.

The source of this difference between presence and representation can be traced with some precision in Johnson's moral psychology. His contention that "the present . . . ceases to be present before its presence is well perceived" starts out from the assumption that the present moment is not an undivided unity of perception but a complex process in which reinscriptions of the past are combined with anticipations of the future. The lesson of this internal division within perception, as the fifth chapter will try to demonstrate, may be figured for Johnson in the argument that "the mind can be captivated only by recollection, or by curiosity, by reviving natural sentiments, or impressing new appearances of things" (*Lives*, I: 312). As a result of this temporalization of the reader's response, Johnson is led to view the familiar and the new, not as complementary facets of the same originally present "experience," but rather as products of recollection and curiosity, past memories and future anticipations. What complicates matters in Johnson's criticism is the sense that each norm is in implicit opposition to the other and that the two cannot easily be conceived to exist in a peaceful state of harmonious integration. There remains an irreducibly epistemological conflict between the natural and the new, a conflict that can only be resolved by an appeal to the higher, synthetic ground of the *consensus gentium*.

The sixth chapter deals with the issue of intertextuality and rhetorical imitation. It argues that the insistence on the priority of an original presence to representation gives rise to a similar insistence on the temporal priority of original to copy, which, in turn, yields to a division among poets between precursors and latecomers. The latter division, which makes itself felt in what Harold Bloom called the "anxiety of influence," is apparent in Johnson's discussion of poets and critics in the *Lives* in terms of a vocabulary of power, rivalry, competition, and dissimulation. This predicament is most fully explored, however, in *Rasselas*. There Imlac evokes images of a lost past, a Golden Age in which the possibility of achieving mimesis was not intertwined with the rewriting of materials from texts that had already taken possession of nature.

It may be asked if Johnson sees a way out of the inbred puzzles and problems of intertextualist thinking. Chapter seven attempts to answer this question in terms of Johnson's interest in the nonfictional prose genres of history, biography, travel, autobiography, and the personal letter. Certainly Johnson is opposed to any theory that treats of literary forms as wholly comprised within a fixed and immutable hierarchy of genres. To an extent that has not been sufficiently appreciated, his is a realist theory of literary kinds, seeking to make variety and novelty a firmer grounding for the claims that specific forms can lay upon the reader's attention. It is this side of Johnson's thinking—his apparent provision for a theory of affects as a part of a theory of genre—that might be considered as an antidote to the malaise of influence and intertextuality in his criticism.

The subject of the last chapter is language and style. Special attention is devoted to Johnson's interpretation of the classical doctrine that language is the dress of thought, to be amplified or compressed at the poet's discretion. It is perhaps this aspect of Johnson's criticism that seems most resistant to modern theory, which takes it as axiomatic that thought is always already enmeshed in the signifying codes of language. Yet where the classical emphasis lies upon the signified concept, Johnson's focus is clearly upon the more ample sequences of the signifier. That "words, being arbitrary, must owe their power to association, and have the influence, and that only, which custom has given them" is a notion that Johnson accepts as an article of faith. Yet it is precisely because of this notion that it sometimes becomes difficult, in Johnson's reasoning, to disentangle sense from sign, since the two may be bound up in a way that prohibits any easy distinction between them. Thought is never able to subjugate language, on account of its involvement in linguistic forms and categories that are at least partially outside an author's control. Thus if Johnson shows a premodern concern with language as the dress of thought, it is because he sees language as the foundational ground of thought, not because he sees thought as the ground and determining origin of language.

2
Tradition and Critical Difference

Johnson's critical writings comprise a mansion with many rooms, most of them linked by their access to a central chamber of reason and judgment. Only the most blinkered polemicist could nowadays attack Johnson's criticism as if it presented the monolithic unity that was attributed to it in the popular tradition of Johnsonian commentary. This book, like other recent studies of Johnson, presupposes a wide margin of difference between the assumptions that guided his criticism and the views that were ascribed to him within this tradition.[1] Thus it accepts, up to a point, the arguments commonly adduced in Johnson's defense: namely, that his works were subjected to a crude and benighted reading, encouraged in part by the brilliant portrayal of Johnson as a conversationalist in Boswell's *Life*. But it also asks a further question: why did Johnson's writings lend themselves to treatment in this manner? Here it argues that the answer is to be sought in Johnson's intense engagement with contemporary critical opinion. The nineteenth-century tradition of Johnsonian interpretation was an extension of the contemporary response to his texts, and this response, in turn, was engendered by Johnson's own combative posture. Thus many of his most familiar critical positions—his view of genius as a mind of "large general powers," his advocacy of rhyme over blank verse, and his notion of the affiliations between poetry and prose—took their rise in the context of his opposition to other points of view. These points of view, moreover, are not necessarily to be thought of as preromantic or romantic, for they encompass positions—the vogue for pastoral, the supposed coincidence of sound and sense in poetry—that have customarily been viewed as neoclassical or Augustan. In this sense, they confirm Wellek's recent perception that "there is no evolution in the history of critical argument, that the history of criticism is rather a series of debates on recurrent concepts, on 'essentially contested concepts'."[2]

What this chapter presents, therefore, is the possibility that Johnson's engagement with contemporary critical opinion is an integral part of his critical orientation. The point can best be made by returning to the nineteenth-century tradition of Johnsonian commentary, since it is here that we find the claim that Johnson's critical premises are nothing more than the product of dogmatism, prejudice, sensibility, or mere taste.[3] Such a claim acknowledges the force of Johnson's convictions, but it comes up against the obvious objection that Johnson's criticism is quite plainly dialogic and confrontational rather than dogmatic and exclusionary. Indeed, Johnson appears to have been quite comfortable with the notion that his arguments were controversial and thus susceptible to attack, ridicule, and caricature. Far from seeking to disclaim all responsibility for his ideas, Johnson was more than willing to take full credit or blame for what was made of his critical legacy. Thus, his writings, in their very willingness to court difference and disagreement, actually demand to be interpreted with an eye to their misreading by his opponents. In different ways, the *Rambler*, *Idler*, and *Adventurer* essays, the *Preface* and *Notes* to Shakespeare, and the *Lives of the Poets* all assume a model of discourse in which the critic, instead of seeking to achieve full mastery over his subject, is inscribed within the intersubjective space of literary discussion and debate. It is impossible, for instance, to read the periodical essays without noticing that they are a collection of short pieces, composed at different times and on a wide variety of topics and, moreover, composed anonymously and sometimes by other authors. The heterogeneous nature of the collection inevitably forces us to read the individual essay, whether it is on the comic romance, the literature of travel, personal letters, biography, or Shakespeare's language, as part of a network of differences and to regard it as a tentative exploration that establishes a distance, however marginal, from the commonplaces of received opinion. By the same token, the *Preface* to Shakespeare, which has frequently been taken to represent a brilliant summation of the views of the age, can more appropriately be seen as self-consciously striking out new positions on decorum and generic purity, the unities and dramatic illusion, but also as placing them in the context of a large body of existing commentary and thereby making it more difficult for the reader to define its relationship to a newly emerging "tradition" of Shakespearean criticism and scholarship.[4] In an even more radical form, the *Lives of the Poets* internalizes within itself an implicit, if necessarily one-sided, dialogue with opposing perspectives. This is undoubtedly because it is embodying, as John Wain has suggested, "a point of view" that "Johnson understood well enough to be no longer dominant in literary circles."[5] In the process, however, it also exposes Johnson's apparently dogmatic obiter dicta to the implied dissent of another voice already present within the supposedly monolithic fabric of his critical discourse. The dialogizing of critical judgment at work in all of the lives is most explicitly seen in his strictures on Gray's sister odes, where the critical voice assumes the presence of an alternative voice that makes us feel that the attitudes which inform the contemporary replies to Johnson's criticisms already existed even before the "Life of Gray" was composed.

Thus it seems to me that there do exist grounds for the claim that there is a qualitative difference between dogmatic criticism and a criticism that invites the reader to view its positions as occasions for contention and argument. Dogmatic reasoning, as a rhetorical mode, is marked by the suppression of other voices through which we become aware of differences in critical opinion. This may be a defining feature of such theoretical treatises as Lord Kames's *Elements of Criticism* or Alexander Gerard's *Essay on Taste*, but Johnson's judgments present the critic in an immediate and "personal" interaction with other readers. The adoption of a "personal" voice is of course a prominent and widely recognized feature of Johnson's critical writings, but its presence may have something to do with the ideal Johnson set forth in a conversation with Boswell on 1 October 1773. According to Boswell, Johnson

> remarked, that attacks on authors did them much service. 'A man who tells me my play is very bad, is less my enemy than he who lets it die in silence. A man, whose business it is to be talked of, is much helped by being attacked . . . . Every attack produces a defence; and so attention is engaged. There is no sport in mere praise, when people are all of a mind'.[6]

Here Johnson conceives of understanding as a dialogical process but one that culminates in disagreement rather than consensus, the disagreement being due both to the process of exchange and the implied failure of the parties to the controversy to arrive at a common ground of agreement. When the dialogic elements of a text are acknowledged, it is read as rhetorical disputation rather than logical argument. Thus Johnson observes to Boswell of the reception of *Taxation, No Tyranny:* "I think I have not been attacked enough for it. Attack is the re-action; I never think I have hit hard unless it rebounds."[7] In this explosive dialectic of action and re-action, any controversial discourse finds the objects of its concern always charged with value, open to dispute, and exposed to possible condemnation or ridicule.

One can thus understand Johnson's obvious reluctance to cast his ideas in any form that might be characterized as a "dull collection of theorems" (*Lives*, I: 412). The obvious unwillingness of Johnson's nineteenth-century critics to recognize this aspect of his thought contributed to their tendency to prefer his conversation, as recorded in Boswell's *Life*, to his writings. According to Coleridge, "Dr. Johnson seems to have been really more powerful in discoursing *viva voce* in conversation than with his pen in hand. It seems as if the excitement of company called something like reality and consecutiveness into his reasonings, which in his writings I cannot see."[8] For neither of these statements does Coleridge give any evidence. They rather seem to presuppose—in an opposition fundamental to nineteenth-century criticisms of Johnson—an assumed difference between oral and written modes of discourse, no matter what their contents.

To a certain extent, this misunderstanding can be traced to Johnson's refusal to adopt the strident, abusive voice of an earlier and outmoded neoclassicism, exemplified, for example, in the opinions of Dennis, Rymer, and Voltaire. In Johnson's critical writings, no one appears to speak, and no one appears to dissent; the arguments seem to unfold without Johnson's massive presence as a speaker and conversationalist. As Leslie Stephen complained, "we are overhearing a soliloquy in his study, not the vigorous discussion over the twentieth cup of tea."[9] Such is the effect of a particular notion of the "written"—of writing defined as a monologic form of exposition—in which language signifies the total absence of both the author and listener and thus in which there may be a decline in the capacity for consecutive reasoning and even the loss of a sense of reality as a consequence of this absence. The model for privileging the Boswellian Johnson over Johnson as the author of his own texts is a theory of language that views language primarily as oral discourse and sees the "written text" as a secondary and substitutive mode of communication.

There can be no doubt of course that Johnson prefers conversation over all other forms of social activity, but this preference is closely related to his view of discourse, whether written or oral, as an essentially dialogic mode that exposes the lie behind every formal, systematic attempt to monumentalize the quest for truth. Thomas De Quincey, whose own preference is clearly monologic, describes dialogism "as a *conditio sine qua non*" of Johnsonian conversation: "he did not absolutely demand a *personal* contradictor by way of 'stoker' to supply fuel and keep up his steam," De Quincey argues, "but he demanded at least a *subject* teeming with elements of known contradictory opinion."[10] But what De Quincey fails to understand is that for Johnson a mode of communication in which there are no "others" whose difference constitutes a challenge to the authority of certitude assumed by the speaking or writing subject overlooks the "struggle for emulation" in and through which most discourse originates. Interestingly, Johnson does not argue that dialogism leads to truth, only that it makes explicit the "contest for superiority" that is masked in monologic forms of discourse. Boswell's contention that while Johnson "sometimes talked for victory . . . he was too conscientious to make errour permanent and pernicious, by deliberately writing it" probably makes too sharp a distinction between Johnson's oral and written statements.[11] Although Johnson was obviously unwilling to engage in theological disputation, he was certainly not reluctant to enter into the lists in other fields of doubt and disagreement. Indeed, what Johnson appears to be calling for in his numerous comments to Boswell on conversation is a perspective that wholly abandons any pretensions to neutrality or objectivity in favor of creatively attempting to exploit the irremediable facts of cultural division and difference. In this respect, Johnson approximates the position of thinkers like Michel Foucault who argue that knowledge can never be totally disengaged from the power interests that affect its production.This may be the reason why Johnson never seeks to transform conversation or controversial writing into forms of consensus building that would resolve doubts or incorporate points of opposition into a truth that is developed rather than imposed. Where the rhetoric of consensus transforms otherness into identity, the rhetoric of Johnsonian dialogism is troubled by questions of partiality and autonomy that preclude any attempts to integrate self and other.

It is precisely this aspect of Johnson's criticism that drops out of sight when he is treated as the magisterial spokesman for a homogeneous tradition of eighteenth-century poetry. This view is reinforced by the assumption that, since tradition is based on a hermeneutics of agreement which allows the critic to reproduce a consensus, criticism communicates to a reader who is an echo of the author and not a separate voice. Nevertheless, as shall later be seen, there is good reason to suppose that Johnson's attitude toward tradition, which is clearly intended to encourage the give-and-take of attack and defense, is always already within an oral/written world of difference, of disagreement rather than consensus. Critical judgments are shown as enmeshed in a larger context beyond them, the context of conflicting viewpoints present in the "living world" outside the text. As Bakhtin argues throughout his work, the living world is already present within this kind of critical utterance, because the latter is oriented toward the complexity of this world, even as it seeks to anticipate its replies.[12]

The difference between the dogmatic prejudice attributed to Johnson by his nineteenth-century critics and his own dialogic discourse can be seen if one examines his remarks on Gray's sister odes. There are two factors that undermine the claim that Johnson's criticism embodies the monologic voice of tradition. The first is the clear indication, set forth in Johnson's prefatory appraisal of the current reputation of the poems, that he is engaging in a debate with their proponents. At a time when such friends of Gray as Walpole and Mason were discovering the beauties of the two odes, Johnson pointedly observes that while the poems were "at first universally rejected . . . many have been since persuaded to think themselves delighted. I am one of those that are willing to be pleased" (*Lives*, III: 436). Equally important, perhaps, is the fact that Johnson's shifts back and forth between the third person of an implied *consensus gentium* and the first person of an author/critic result in a criticism that is conscious of its audience and therefore calls upon the reader to assent or deny its claims. At least in part, the usage assumes that it is the reader's option in the verbal drama to either give or withhold this assent. As Johnson examines Gray's *The Progress of Poesy*, differences emerge in his question as to whether the poet confounds the images of "spreading and running water" in the first stanza, whether the conclusion of the second ternary stanza arises from its premises, or whether the poet is correct in affirming that "Poetry and Virtue go always together" (*Lives*, III: 437). The emergent dialogism may seem to be repressed by the vigor of Johnson's strictures, which often assume the closure of aphorism: "an epithet or metaphor drawn from Nature ennobles Art; an epithet or metaphor drawn from Art degrades Nature" (*Lives*, III: 436–37). Yet the very organization of the argument militates against dogmatism because it is structured as a series of discrepancies among the critic, poet, and reader. Thus of the third stanza we read,

> Gray is too fond of words arbitrarily compounded. 'Many-twinkling' was formerly censured as not analogical; we may say *many-spotted*, but scarcely *many-spotting*. This stanza, however, has something pleasing. (*Lives*, III: 437)

The last line catches attention, for it reveals a disparity within the judgment rendered. Such disparities invite us to approach Johnson's "minute" criticisms of particular passages as the disclosure of difference. They are intrinsic to a critical stance that, at its most characteristic, stands at the opposite extreme from the bland pronouncements of a Dick Minim, Johnson's parodic personification of the voice of consensus.

How the intertextualization of argument and counterargument awakens the trace of difference from itself can be seen if one examines Johnson's criticism of Gray's odes in the context of a contemporary reply. There is a certain appropriateness in viewing Johnson's criticism of Gray's odes in this way because it enables us to see how Johnson's peers initially responded to the dialogic elements in his criticism. William Fitzthomas's reply to Johnson's strictures—republished in part in James Boulton's *Critical Heritage* volume—reveals his bewilderment at what might be called Johnson's insistence on the intertextuality of Gray's odes—his self-conscious foregrounding of commonplaces, imitations, and a wide range of rhetorical effects, in conjunction with his highlighting of a proposition that, simply by being examined, becomes subject to question. Fitzthomas is even more clearly bothered by what he regards as the self-conscious theatricality of Johnson's criticism of the poems:

> after all these remarks, these severe strictures, I much suspect, that the Doctor offers us but an *artificial copy* of his sentiments, with regards to this truly elegant and original writer. Is it reasonable to imagine, considering the well-known taste and discernment of Dr. Johnson, that he should *really* be so callous to that beautiful simplicity which runs through many of Gray's productions? Or, considering his just, and truly discriminated decisions on the merits of every other writer, that he should really be so insensible to the inexpressible dignity and animation which reign in these particular odes?—It seems most probable, therefore, that the Doctor, looking upon the great, and almost unexampled reputation of this writer as somewhat superior to his real merit, might think that he was doing the public a piece of service by 'bending the wit the contrary way'; and, by confining Gray's fame within its proper bounds, render it more solid and durable.—If this were his design, it must be, I think, the general opinion, that he has greatly over-acted his part in the critical drama.

Here Fitzthomas's notion of critical discourse as the expression by the critic of his true feelings stands in implicit opposition to Johnson's view of criticism as a focus of contention and debate. The concept of sincerity, a naturalization of discourse by which words become identical with the sentiments they represent, assumes that language can, by divesting itself of all pretence, overcome the difference between author and reader, intention and expression. Fitzthomas's well-founded suspicion that Johnson is only offering an "*artificial copy*" of his sentiments betrays more than a conviction that Johnson is seeking to expose the derivative, artificial character of Gray's odes; it also reveals a sense that Johnson is self-consciously adopting a dramatic posture rather than expressing his opinions candidly. The sincere critic, seeking to arrive at "just and truly discriminated decisions on . . . every writer," can disregard his readers and dismiss their views as irrelevant whenever their opinions of the "merits" of a poet do not coincide with his own. The simplifications of discourse that this encourages is not available to a highly self-conscious critic like Johnson who must act out his part before a large and necessarily diverse audience.[13]

The susceptibility of Johnson's criticism to Fitzthomas's strictures on its artifice and dissimulation can be traced, then, to Johnson's conviction that the sign is less the expression of an autonomous and self-coincident subjectivity than a site of struggle and contradiction. Rather than seeking to enforce a consensus that he believes could only be achieved, at most, over a long period of time, Johnson openly courts difference and disagreement. The *Lives of the Poets* exemplifies this dialogic conception of the sign, inasmuch as it locates the individual prefaces within a world of textuality. The narrative of each of the lives remains unfractured only as long as it is read *in vacuo*, for the convention of the Johnsonian Life, which, among other things, asks us to respond to the criticism of the poetry separately from the account of the life, allows the narrative to unfold in a continuous sequence. But the incorporation of letters, extracts from earlier critics, poetical testaments, sections contributed by other writers, and adaptations of earlier works, abruptly changes the perspective. It compels us to reexamine the assumption that the life is a self-identical, self-enclosed textual system. Not only does the intertextual nature of the *Lives* problematize the mode by revealing the presence of other voices alongside or within the seemingly monologic narrative voice, there is also the sometimes jarring sense, as many scholars have noticed, that the *Lives* were meant to be read in the context of their implicit relation to other, rival lives of the poets.[14] Hence it is one thing to claim that earlier lives are "superseded" by the discovery of additional facts about a poet and quite another to hold that the *Lives* are engaged in a process of challenging and questioning. This distinction is vital since, otherwise, it might seem that Johnson's achievement rests on his accomplishments as a researcher. The point is rather that, because of the presence of other lives, the text as a whole and even the individual events within it become a perpetually shifting intersection of contending viewpoints rather than something fixed and final. To put it somewhat differently, the dialogic mode of

Johnson's criticism foregrounds the subtext by creating not simply spaces on the margin of the text but also spaces within the discourse that makes up the text, spaces that make us aware of other, different texts. The implicit dialogue within the life, in turn, conditions the interpretive constraints through reading. It becomes the model for the interpretative process in which the life mediates a series of differences between Johnson and the reader, between Johnson and earlier biographers and critics, and between these biographers and critics and the reader.

Thus Johnson's running debates with earlier biographers need not be judged by the standards of what Lawrence Lipking called a "perpetual commentary." This is because Johnson's intentions are clearly at variance with the undertaking of an exhaustive and scrupulous enumeration of sources characteristic of the antiquarian scholar or universal historian.[15] Matters of expediency undoubtedly played a role in dictating the suppression of many sources, but what remains is shaped into a hidden polemic in which the contemporary reader is clearly invited to take sides. Thus the biographical section of Johnson's "Life of Cowley" is described as "a slender supplement" to Thomas Sprat's well-known and highly admired *Account of the Life and Writings of Abraham Cowley* (1668), but it is a supplement only in the sense in which Johnson defines it in *The Dictionary*: that is, as an "addition to any thing by which its defects are supplied." This means that it is not only an amplification of Sprat's account, but, in some sense a substitution that seeks to expose the deficiency in Sprat's methods and conclusions. There is a certain appropriateness in looking at this life, because not only is it a brief encapsulated biography, it is also about biography: about different ways of interpreting the same event. In this case, the event in question was Cowley's decision, in Sprat's words, "to [forgo all public employments and to] follow the violent inclinations of his mind, which, in the greatest throng of his former business . . . represented to him the *true* delights of solitary studies" (*Lives*, I: 15). Johnson's insertion of citations from other authors—a quotation from a satirical poem by Suckling, a passage from a brief life by Anthony Wood, and an unpublished letter from Cowley to Sprat shortly before his death—make us aware that Cowley's decision may possibly have been errant rather than exemplary: a story about misery, frustration, and disappointment rather than a panegyric to Cowley's stoic renunciation of society in favor of the delights of rural life. Johnson had already made his opinion of Cowley's decision emphatically clear in *Rambler*, number 6. But if Johnson's life is read without taking the earlier essay or his polemic against Sprat into account, the meagerness of the sources available to him thrusts it back into the recesses of a distant past, thus muting our awareness of the different interpretations to which the same action are susceptible. The passages that Johnson incorporates into his life may not make us change our minds about Cowley, but they force us to reconsider what Sprat has asserted by shifting our frame of reference from a monologic one, in which we consent to the authority of a single voice, to a dialogic framework, in which we are exposed to divergent perspectives. In other words, they disturb the closure of a literary hagiography which previously had been sealed to alternative points of view.

The edition of Shakespeare provides an even more obvious example of the intertextualization of Johnson's criticism, as an event that actually occurred in the early history of Shakespearean scholarship. The edition of Shakespeare was originally published, as Johnson's hostile reviewer, William Kenrick, pointed out, with "the several prefaces of Pope, Theobald, Hamner and Warburton, as also the dedication and preface of Heminge and Condell, and Shakespeare's life by Mr. Rowe. Of Mr. Pope's notes, the Editor hath retained the whole."[16] The addition of earlier prefaces and dedications must have radically changed the contemporary reader's view of the edition, without Johnson's having altered a single word of the individual texts and simply by changing the interpretive conventions in which his own criticism and commentaries on the plays were read. Reading the edition of Shakespeare monologically as we must if, as most of us do, we read Johnson's *Preface* and *Notes* in isolation, is quite different from reading it intertextually in such a way that the complementary and conflicting prefaces and notes become part of a broad field of contention. The intertextual reading is plainly manifest in both the *Preface* and *Notes*: in the *Preface*, ten pages are devoted to a complex mixture of praise and censure of Johnson's predecessors; in the *Notes*, Johnson conducts a running commentary and debate with William Warburton. Walter Raleigh believed that, while Lewis Theobald was a better Shakespearean scholar, Warburton "was a man of large general powers, who wrote an easy and engaging style."[17] By choosing to reproduce Warburton's notes along with his own commentary and replies, Johnson, in effect, makes a monologic, scholarly reading difficult, if not impossible. The "disappointment" that some of Johnson's contemporaries are reported to have voiced at the publication of his edition of Shakespeare may have been due as much to its intertextuality as to the numerous and highly publicized delays in its publication. In place of a clearly delineated and demarcated "original" body of criticism and commentary, they found a text woven out of several discourses, some of which were explicitly inserted, others of which were present only by acknowledgement. There is no doubt that many readers were inclined to attribute this phenomenon to Johnson's indolence. Yet by compelling the contemporary reader to read other voices as well as his own, to read Warburton alongside his own replies, Johnson may have been attempting to make the reader see the reading process as the discovery of differences around a text that cannot always be paraphrased or made to coincide with itself. Moreover, in this respect, Johnson's interchange with Warburton can also be seen as the subtext of an earlier interchange between Warburton and Theobald, which the contemporary reader must now reread dialogically rather than monologically. Once the reader does this, he discovers the gap in the supposed articulation of a steadily improving and improved Shakespearean text. The presence of other voices, an explicit feature of Johnson's edition of Shakespeare, is intended to make the eighteenth-century reader aware that all utterance is incipiently intertextual, a discourse that bears within itself the traces of other discourses.

Of course one reason why this intertextual dimension of Johnson's edition has often been overlooked has to do with the homogeneous, monolithic consensus seemingly evoked in the opening pages of the *Preface*. What becomes of the dialogic nature of Johnson's criticism if controversy can always be surmounted by an appeal to the *consensus gentium*? There are of course many passages in which Johnson adopts the perspective of the *consensus gentium*—the introductory section of the *Preface* to Shakespeare, the estimates of *L'Allegro* and *Il Penseroso*, *The Rape of the Lock*, and the *Elegy in a Country Churchyard*. Yet these passages are always situated among other passages that are not at one with them. Thus Johnson's estimates of Gray's poems as they stand mutually qualify each other within a larger framework that cannot be grasped in its entirety from the standpoint represented by any one poem, whether it be the *Elegy* or one of the odes. Indeed Johnson takes popular opinion as the basis for the construction of an interpretation of Gray's poetry in which the elitist views of Walpole and his friends are condemned. Moreover, the *consensus gentium* itself is fissured, consisting as it does of a union of critical and popular points of view. When one of the elements is missing as in the contrasting instances of Gray's sister odes (which had achieved a belated critical success) or of Gay's *The Beggar's Opera* (which had achieved a great popular success), the reputation of the text becomes divided, subject to implications that contradict what it supposedly affirms. Finally, even in instances like *The Rape of the Lock* where the voice of the *consensus gentium* appears to be overwhelming, a dissenting voice (in this case, that of John Dennis) is allowed to be heard. Johnson's arguments may defend the poem from the implications of the minority viewpoint. But the very fact that the dissenting voice is allowed to intrude places the *consensus gentium* in a context that opens up the possibility of its becoming different from itself.

* * *

Johnson's dialogic conception of discourse goes far beyond the example established by his own critical writings. It is also embodied in what can fairly be described as a dialogic conception of the human mind. In repudiating the authority possessed by monologic signs in given literary and theoretical contexts, Johnson is also opposing a view of the mind in which these signs are assumed to have their origin. Mid-eighteenth-century understanding posited the existence of an original genius, an autonomous power whose "peculiar" gift is marked by the exclusion of other gifts. Johnson's well-known observation to Boswell in Edinburgh indicates the extent to which he opposes this conception of genius:

> one man . . . may, by accident, see the success of one kind of study, and take a desire to excel in it. I am persuaded that, had Sir Isaac Newton applied to poetry, he would have made a very fine epick poem.[18]

Here Johnson's observation forces one to question the notion of "peculiarity" that is central to the eighteenth-century notion of genius, as a power that expresses a single mood or achieves originality by its "deviation" from the common track. Not only does his estimate of genius as a general capacity deny the swerve that such critics as Edward Young and William Duff portrayed as characteristic of "original" genius, it also exposes genius to the world of difference embodied in the notion of established disciplines of thought. Within this world, genius necessarily becomes exposed to the opposition of other minds, discovering its difference from them, not through a "detour" from the beaten "path," but in the common playing fields of conflict and competition.

It is evident that Johnson cannot envisage the exercise of genius exempt from conflict: exempt from the internal and external obstacles through which we become aware of the difference of the mind from itself. The danger posed by an inflated conception of original genius, he argued in *Rambler*, number 25, is that it may actually discourage the young from undertaking ambitious enterprises, in

> an opinion that every kind of knowledge requires a . . . mental constitution, framed for the reception of some ideas, and the exclusion of others; and that to him whose genius is not adapted to the study which he prosecutes, all labour shall be vain and fruitless, vain as an endeavour to mingle oil and water, or, in the language of chemistry, to amalgamate bodies of heterogeneous principles. (*Rambler*, III: 139)

What is false about this notion of originality is that it promises a redemption of the mind from its limitations through a unique adaptation of a particular subject to a particular object. Johnson rather envisages genius as a generalized power, a power that "like fire in the flint" is "produced by collision," not by congruity (*Rambler*, III: 139). Such a collision is dialogic rather than monologic for it is organized in terms of the discovery of limitations as well as strengths. To overlook these limitations is to ignore what Johnson's writings most forcefully proclaim: the liberation of genius from the illusion that it does not have to depend on anything outside of itself, anything foreign to its own self-coincident spontaneity.

Ken Frieden has recently described the development of the term "genius" in the writings of Shaftesbury, Addison, Gerard, Young, and Duff as a "turn to subjectivity and monologue," transforming it "from an externalized divine guide" to an enclosed and autonomous power.[19] Johnson's opposition to this monologic idea of genius stems less from a desire to restore it to the quasi-divine status it possessed in earlier eras than from a wish to subject it to the space of difference. The hypothetical power described by Young and Duff is one that "may reign arbitrarily over its own empire of Chimeras" and "will naturally discover itself in visions."[20] In this sense, it resembles the enclosed process described by Johnson in one of his sermons as occurring in "the gloom of solitude and the stillness of retirement." Johnson holds that such a process will "neither extinguish the passions, nor enlighten the understanding," for true knowledge can only be "advanced by an intercourse of sentiments, and an exchange of observations," by a disburdening of the "bosom" through a "communication of its cares."[21] In a similar vein, Johnson insists in *Rambler*, number 89, that "when a man shuts himself up in his closet," he will find himself giving in to an "invisible riot of the mind," a "secret prodigality of being" (*Rambler*, I: 105–6). In order to free himself from this captivity, he "must, in opposition to the Stoick precept, teach his desires to fix upon external things; he must adopt the joys and the pains of others, and excite in his mind the way of social pleasures and amicable communication" (*Rambler*, IV: 107). It follows that a monologic idea of "unassisted genius" is an impossibility: the activity of genius, even if it does not have to go through the external detour of observation and intercourse with others, must still submit itself to the internal detour of study and ratiocination. If we fail to take either of these two detours, we are likely to remain enclosed within a narcissistic world of auto-affection and auto-admiration. As Johnson puts it in *Rambler*, number 154,

> when we have once obtained an acknowledged superiority over our acquaintances, imagination and desire easily extend it over the rest of mankind, and if no accident forces us into new emulations, we grow old, and die in admiration of ourselves. (*Rambler*, V: 56)

Johnson's view of the way monologic and dialogic conceptions of genius differ from one another can perhaps be best seen in his contrasting attitudes toward Milton and Shakespeare.[22] For Johnson, Milton and Shakespeare represent two different impulses taken to their extremes. Both resisted the seductions implicit in the notion of "unassisted genius" that Johnson deplores in *Rambler*, number 154, but whereas Milton "saw Nature . . . through the spectacles of books" (*Lives*, I: 178), "there is a vigilance of observation and accuracy of distinction" in Shakespeare "which books and precepts cannot confer" (*Shakespeare*, VII: 88). Johnson believes that "Milton would not have excelled in dramatic writing," for "he knew human nature only in the gross," whereas Shakespeare was "able to obtain an exact knowledge of many modes of life, and many casts of native dispositions; to vary them with great multiplicity; to mark them by nice distinctions; and to shew them in full view by proper combinations" (*Shakespeare*, VII: 89). Hence, while Milton was a poet of sublimity whose delight "was to sport in the wide regions of possibility" (*Lives*, I: 177–78), Shakespeare's dialogue seems "scarcely to claim the merit of fiction, but to have been gleaned by diligent selection out of common conversation, and common occurrences" (*Shakespeare*, VII: 63). Johnson assumes that common conversation is a characteristic of comedy and, through an examination of Shakespeare's dialogue, arrives at the conclusion that Shakespeare must have excelled in comedy rather than tragedy. Johnson's obvious preference for a dialogic conception of genius does not mean that he scorns Milton's sublimity, but it does lead him to insist that the "images and descriptions" of Milton's imagination are without human similitude and therefore excite "little natural curiosity and sympathy." Thus, while the reader is not excluded from Milton's text, his potentially negating presence emerges from its failure to offer "transactions in which he can by any effort of imagination place himself" and, as such, reflects back on a conception of reading itself as a "transaction." Of crucial importance to this conception is the expectation that the reader will place himself in the transactions of the characters within texts instead of identifying himself with the mind of the author behind the text. Furthermore, Johnson means characters not merely in their relation to themselves but also in their reciprocal "transactions" with other characters.

So described, the opposition between Johnson's view of Shakespeare and Milton seems almost schematic in its simplicity, but it helps to distinguish Johnson's perspective from that of Milton's nineteenth-century admirers. Thus Hazlitt praised *Paradise Lost* precisely because "there are none of the every-day occurrences, contentions, disputes, wars, fightings, feuds, jealousies, trades, professions, liveries, and common handicrafts of life."[23] What Hazlitt praises for being excluded is what Johnson censures for being absent. The insistence on dialogism, moreover, clearly shapes Johnson's estimate of Milton's minor poems. He acknowledges that "every man that reads" *L'Allegro* and *Il Penseroso* "reads them with pleasure," but also holds that "both Mirth and Melancholy are solitary, silent inhabitants of the breast, that neither receive nor transmit communication; no mention is therefore made of a philosophical friend or a pleasant companion" (*Lives*, I: 165–66). The dramatic poet must "study the shades of character," but the distinctions that this permits are not available to Milton and "the colours of diction" in *L'Allegro* and *Il Penseroso* "seem not sufficiently discriminated," the characters not "kept sufficiently apart" (*Lives*, I: 167). In a similar manner, the prologue to *Comus* is addressed to the audience, "a mode of communication so contrary to the nature of dramatick representation, that no precedents can support it" (*Lives*, I: 168). Johnson acknowledges the presence of dramatic elements within the masque, but he insists that they lack "the spriteliness of dialogue animated by reciprocal contention" and are therefore "rather declamations deliberately composed and formally repeated on a moral question" (*Lives*, I: 168).

In Johnson's notorious strictures on *Lycidas*, too, there is an insistence on the enclosed subjectivity of the monologic genius and its inability to dramatize the experience of grief in such a way that it will make both the passion and its object accessible to the reader. Johnson's harsh judgment of *Lycidas* has been subject to more commentary, pro and con, than any of his other estimates, and it is unecessary to review all the arguments that have been advanced.[24] Nonetheless, it is important to emphasize that Johnson insists upon the referential nature of the genre and defines this nature in terms of a relation between self and other. Thus the vocabulary required to memorialize an absent friend must be very different from the kind of "mythological imagery" that "a College easily supplies" (*Lives*, I: 164). The flocks, copses, flowers, and heathen deities, a residue of a dead tradition that makes do without the other because it can respond to him or her in a shopworn fiction, seem to image the limitations of the monologic consciousness. This consciousness mourns, but excites "no sympathy" and heralds a life beyond itself, but "confers no honour" because it does not make that life present except as an echo. One might be tempted to think that Johnson has failed here to recognize the complex dissonances and harmonies of the poem, but he is rather demanding a shift from a narrowly "poetical" to a referential standard of value. *Lycidas*, because of its proximity to pastoral, is associated with a fictive convention that ruptures the link between language and what it signifies, where elegy should be mimetic, because it seeks in some sense to revivify "the presence of the dead" (*Idler, Adventurer*, 140). This is not to affirm that Milton's pastoral fiction wholly ignores the dead Edward King, only that, unlike Abraham Cowley's elegy on his friend William Hervey or Johnson's own *On the Death of Dr Robert Levet*, it fails to give sufficient credence to his reality.[25]

Johnson's remarks on *Lycidas*, then, are one instance of a larger movement in his criticism toward construing understanding from a dialogic point of view. What this engenders, as has been seen, is an attitude that is quite different from what is found in the writings of Addison, Young, or Duff. Commentators have sometimes carelessly assimilated Johnson's encomium on Alexander Pope's gifts to this mid-eighteenth-century conception of genius:

> Pope had likewise genius; a mind active, ambitious, and adventurous, always investigating, always aspiring; in its widest searches still longing to go forward, in its highest flights still wishing to be higher; always imagining something greater than it knows, always endeavouring more than it can do. (*Lives*, III: 217)

The philosophical implications of this passage are quite different from the views of such critics as Addison or Young. While Johnson shares their conviction that genius is central to artistic achievement, he refuses to hypostasize it. Hence instead of reducing it to an enclosed, teleological form of self-expression, he sees Pope's genius manifest in poetry only in the sense that there is within it the power of "imagining something greater than it knows," of "endeavouring more than it can do." Far from engendering an identity between subject and object, such a power invariably produces a gap between desire and accomplishment, present and future. Its goals once attained, moreover, are invariably disappointing and are often spoiled by the very act of attainment, so that they in turn recreate an initial void or absence, thus furnishing grounds for ever-renewed desire and investigation.

Genius is active and spontaneous, to be sure, but only to the extent that it is restless and unappeasable. Johnson's description of Pope's genius has little to do with singularity and everything to do with non-coincidence. As long as a difference can be charted between one self and other selves, or between one's past achievements and future aspirations, one possesses the conditions for the exercise of genius. One needs a sense of the limitations of one's own past and of the achievements of others. It is in this sense that one may understand Johnson's remark about Milton that

> the appearances of nature and the occurrences of life did not satiate his appetite of greatness . . . . Milton's delight was to sport in the wide regions of possibility; reality was a scene too narrow for his mind. He sent his faculties out upon discovery, into worlds where only the imagination can travel, and delighted to form new modes of existence, and furnish sentiment and action to superior beings, to trace the counsels of hell, or accompany the choirs of heaven. (*Lives*, I: 177–78)

* * *

Johnson can redefine genius as aspiration rather than fulfillment because he rejects the outlook that sees texts as the simple expression or extension of an author's feelings. This is also Johnson's main reason for quietly insisting that criticism continue to respect the distinction between endeavor and composition, or between composition and performance. The implications of the term "performance" are discussed at greater length in chapter 3, but it is sufficient to note here that it differs from simple communication or expression in being openly dialogic. A performance requires both a speaker and a listener (or a writer and a reader). The word is never highlighted in Johnson's criticism, yet it manages to convey Johnson's sense of the inherently dramatic or histrionic character of a text, its inherently unstable relation to the "endeavour" of the author who brought it into being. The relationship between "endeavour" and "performance" is not organic or expressive in the preromantic or romantic sense of those terms, because a performance is the product of artful design and premeditation, not an organism related to an originary expression as a plant is to a seed. Thus Johnson suggests that a performance may conceal as much as it reveals of the intention that produced it. Indeed, it is a firm sense of the disparity between hidden intention and public performance that guides many of Johnson's practical judgments, and this disparity is often broad enough to permit a critical reading that exposes what the original had wished to hide. What this means, given that performances are personally and biographically variable, is that poems are open to interpretations that, as performances, they might wish to suppress. Johnson's comment on Pope's *Epistle to Dr. Arbuthnot* is a case in point for it suggests something of his awareness of the complex relation between aspiration and enactment in poetry:

> The *Epistle to Arbuthnot*, now arbitrarily called the *Prologue to the Satires*, is a performance consisting, as it seems, of many fragments, wrought into one design, which by this union of scattered beauties contains more striking paragraphs than could probably have been brought together into an occasional work. (*Lives*, III: 246)

Here as elsewhere, Johnson's criticism disarticulates, it "undoes" the original, revealing that what appeared to be a unity is actually a composite. Yet Johnson's verdict is not invariably negative: it is the prerogative of poets, he implies in this passage, to exercise a certain arbitrary discretion in their reworking of earlier texts, in other words, to produce a palimpsest of lines and passages rather than allowing them to grow as organic unities. Thus the capacity of a poem to suppress alternative performances is the source of its momentary authority, but also of its vulnerability, for it means that any performance is susceptible to an evaluation that will judge it somewhat differently than its author may have anticipated.

It is in such passages that Johnson's criticism comes closest to approximating the basic activity of deconstructive criticism. If there is a principle that serves to unify this otherwise disparate movement, it is a determination "to reveal the existence of hidden articulations and fragmentations within assumedly monadic totalities."[26] The effect of such readings—as seen in Johnson's various judgments on specific poems in the *Lives*—is to challenge the idea that the poem should enjoy a privileged status as an organic unity. That the unfolding of a dramatic action is also a performance that cannot be reified into an organic form governed by its own laws is a corollary of this point of view. Thus Johnson, despite his evident admiration for Shakespeare, clearly believes that Shakespeare's habits of composition were too time-bound, too mired in the rifts of expediency for him to be able to make full use of the opportunities available to him or even "fully to comprehend his own design." One may argue that Johnson, like other critics of his age, was perhaps too ready to ascribe Shakespeare's supposed dramatic faults to carelessness, but it is not so much with particulars as with the general issue of intention and performance that romantic critics such as August Wilhelm von Schlegel appear most uneasy, most eager to claim Shakespeare for the tradition of romantic poetry. When Schlegel accuses Johnson of altogether mistaking "the rights of poetry and the nature of the romantic drama," it is necessary for him to insist that "the Fancy lays claim to be considered as an independent mental power governed by its own laws."[27] A shift in focus from judgment to imagination, from intention to expression, is crucial to Schlegel's belief that if Shakespeare's dramaturgy is to be protected from adverse criticism, it must be protected as organism or expression, not as performance.

The disparity between the performative and the organic implicit in Johnson's notion of "performance," then, prevents a work from automatically coinciding with the rules that govern its composition. Indeed one can argue that the term "performance" moves the problem of organic unity beyond the simple dyadic relation of parts to whole by introducing the reader as an essential part of the evaluative process. Such a process entails not only an interaction between the text as a public performance and the reader, but also a transaction between the reader and other readers, between one performance and other performances. The necessary presence of other readers and other texts, a necessary condition of public performances, makes it difficult, as will be seen in chapter 4, for one to suppose that "any representation is mistaken for reality" (*Shakespeare*, VII: 76). It also makes one aware that the reading process is incipiently dialogic: a communication with an other that forces a text to pass through the external detour of comparison and judgment and thus become decentered. Or to put it rather differently, performance is Johnson's term for what allows a text to become an identity through its relation to alterity.

For Johnson, the notion of performance thus means that the text can never be apprehended solely from the point of view of the subjective intention of the author but must also encompass the point of view of the audience. This is not the same thing as saying that the audience constitutes the meaning or value of the text. It is instead a way of saying that an author cannot expect to constitute the worth or unity of his text except from a perspective outside of himself. Such a perspective is not necessarily identical with that of the audience, for the term performance also implies the notion of an arena or theater, a site of unremitting struggle between the competing interests of the author and his critics, of the author and other authors. In this arena, "an author places himself uncalled before the tribunal of criticism, and solicits fame at the hazard of disgrace" (*Lives*, III: 241). What the term performance thus allows to appear is a system of values in which the possibility of a writer's glorification is balanced by the possibility of his failure. It follows that a recognition of both possibilities must be inscribed within the text itself: "dullness or deformity are not culpable in themselves, but may be very justly reproached when they pretend to the honor of wit or the influence of beauty" (*Lives*, III: 241). Any performance must, therefore, incorporate within itself an awareness of the possibility of its own disappearance, an awareness that prevents it from ever resting secure in the stability of its self-enclosed organic unity.

* * *

Thus Johnson also follows Horace (and most neoclassical critics) in regarding poetry—by virtue of its status as performance—as grounded in the knowledge that it must delight as well as instruct if it is to win the approval of its audience. But this also leads him to argue, unlike them, that *all* texts—including prose texts—are performances and, thus, must be subject to the same demands as poetry. Johnson, to be sure, once seemed to deny this unity of purpose when he declared in the *Preface* to Shakespeare that "the end of writing is to instruct; the end of poetry is to instruct by pleasing" (*Shakespeare*, VII: 67). Here the insistence that pleasure is restricted to poetry makes it possible to view prose and poetry in terms of an opposition in which prose as seen as a purely instrumental vehicle of communication, devoid of the figural characteristics that invest poetry with its power of giving delight. But Johnson's subsequent insistence in the "Life of Swift" that Swift's prose "instructs, but does not persuade" (*Lives*, III: 52) seems to move beyond this opposition of prose and poetry and the teleology that orients it to an argument that, at the very least, seems to complicate the relation between the two modes.

In Chapter seven, we will consider in some detail how this line of thought appears to have led Johnson to repudiate the plain style. Here we would like to consider the broad implications of what he sees as the strengths and limitations of Swift's decision to cultivate a simplicity of manner. Johnson argues that Swift's

> style was well suited to his thoughts, which are never subtilised by nice disquisitions, decorated by sparkling conceits, elevated by ambitious sentences, or variegated by far-sought learning. He pays no court to the passions; he excites neither surprise nor admiration; he always understands himself, and his reader always understands him: the peruser of Swift wants little previous knowledge; it will be sufficient that he is acquainted with common words and common things; he is neither required to mount elevations nor to explore profundities; his passage is always on a level, along solid ground, without asperities, without obstruction. (*Lives*, III: 52)

In the carefully measured criticisms advanced in this passage, Johnson implies that there is no form of discourse that is exempt from the Horatian imperative: to be committed to prose, therefore, is to be committed to the same system of tropes and figures that governs the composition of poetry. Instead of being situated within a conceptual space that stretches from the organic to the instrumental, poetry and prose are governed by a unity of intention that precludes any valorization of prose as a transparent medium of communication. Here as elsewhere, Johnson's approach is guided by a sense of the link between the demands that he imposes on prose and his view of discourse as performance. Specifically, it derives from his moral vision, his opposition to systematic reasoning and, especially, his dialogism. It follows that for Johnson the relation between poetry and prose can never attain the hierarchical structure that organizes it in much modern criticism (including Bakhtin's). The extent to which the two were linked in an interlocking and mirrorlike relationship can be seen in Matthew Arnold's well-known view of the eighteenth century as an age of prose. While prose may often be said to define poetry—to function as its point of reference and construction, the twinned estimates of poetry and prose adopted by Arnold particularly insist upon their dramatically constrasting, virtually symmetrical qualities. Arnold's contention that "we did well to return in the present century to the poetry of the Elizabethan age for illumination, and to put aside, in a great measure, the poetry and poets intervening between Milton and Wordsworth" is thus balanced, in an exact reversal, by his belief that "the prose of Milton and Taylor is cumbersome, unavailable, impossible."[28] A poetry that returns to the Elizabethans for inspiration renounces the poetry of the eighteenth century but concedes the advantages of its prose—and vice versa: a prose that returns to the eighteenth century in order to appropriate what it finds to be a "serviceable" modern "prose style," renounces the "old English prose" but concedes the superiority of its poetry. It is of course entirely possible that Arnold could be shown to have been right, yet what is noteworthy about this passage is the way in which what is included in this system of oppositions is also inscribed within the system in an enclosed and symmetrical form, as its negative key, its excluded other.

It is precisely this essentially hierarchical system of oppositions that is threatened if Johnson's understanding of the term of performance is taken in its broadest possible sense. It is no new discovery that Johnson was seen by his nineteenth-century detractors as a prosaic critic in an age of prose. But what they may have actually been responding to was the extent to which Johnson's criticism calls into question the bipolar schema upon which such strictures are based. As soon as one ceases to believe in the efficacy of the plain style, a zero degree of figuration that can serve as a vehicle of communication and instruction and still make the familiar seem new, the very idea of an absolute oppositional limit between the two modes is endangered, and the possibility of a hierarchically superior (or inferior) poetic language from which it might take its meaning breaks down. It is instructive, in this connection, to recognize that many of the same critics who disparaged Johnson for his inability to judge poetry also condemned him for failing to achieve a natural style in prose. Coleridge characterizes what he sees as the artificiality of Johnson's prose style and the prose style that it inspired in the following manner:

> the essence of this style consisted in a mock antithesis, that is, an opposition of mere sounds, in a rage for personification, the abstract made animate, far-fetched metaphors, strange phrases, metrical scraps, in every thing, in short, but genuine prose.[29]

One cannot but be struck by the kinship of this account with Johnson's own criticism of the metaphysical poets. While the modern reader would probably not concur with the precise terms of Coleridge's estimate of Johnson's style, it does seem clear that what Horace Walpole calls its "hardness of diction" and "muscular toughness" arises out of a deliberate repudiation of the opposition between the natural and the artificial in language.[30] What Coleridge and Walpole find artificial about Johnson's prose style—its antithetical constructions, Latinate vocabulary and density of imagery—is partly meant as a demonstration that discourse need not be reduced to a pristine, transparent structure of sense. The style probably goes along with a rooted desire to find a middle ground somewhere between the excesses of Sir Thomas Browne and the metaphysicals and the limitations of the school of prose writers who followed them. Thus Sir Edmund Gosse—in a passage quoted by William K. Wimsatt, Jr.—observes that "where his early verse owes so much to the teaching of Pope, his early prose shows no tincture of Steele or Swift." This omission lends support to Wimsatt's contention that the origin of Johnson's prose is to be found not in earlier prose models but in the "rhetoric of the neoclassical couplet."[31] Indeed, it may be the purpose of Johnson's writing to show how ubiquitous are the purposes of figurative language in discourse and how easily they subvert any simple distinction between different kinds of verbal propriety. To regard such writing as merely symptomatic of artifice or rigidity is to write off the hope that there are alternatives to the ideal of a pure, undistorted medium of communication.

So what remains of the distinction between poetry and prose, if both are seen as two analogous but different manifestations of the same notion of performance? Johnson addresses the issue most forcefully in his argument on the advantages of rhyme over blank verse. Here once again it is necessary to go behind the popular tradition of Johnson commentary in order to uncover the link between Johnson's position and opposing points of view. Within the popular tradition of Johnsonian criticism, Johnson's preference for rhyme was sometimes explained in terms of his "tin ear," but this argument was in turn part of a polemic that ontologized blank verse on the basis of an essential superiority and relation to nature and auditory truth. The tendency of such a polemic was to counter what was considered to be Johnson's natural deficiency in hearing with an authentic experience of musical rhythms that is assumed to be open to all. What it overlooks, however, is the extent to which its reasoning can be turned against itself. That reversal is worth examining in some detail.

Johnson's argument here is a subtle one and refers here to a distinction between oral and written modes of discourse and the use of this distinction by eighteenth-century critics to justify the superiority of blank verse over rhyme. Typical of their increasing tendency to privilege speech over writing, as the medium of passion rather than reason, is John Dennis's sense of a poetic discourse that is "every where extremely pathetick" on the one hand and a discourse "that is writ in very good Numbers" on the other; if the latter "wants Passion," Dennis wrote, "it can be but measur'd Prose."[32] In defining poetry as performance, Johnson appears to endorse this definition of it as utterance rather than written text, but this similarity should not obscure the differences between Johnson and Dennis. In contesting the superiority of blank verse to rhyme, Johnson insists that "the music of metre" rather than mimesis or passion has been the criterion by which poetry has been distinguished from prose "in all languages." Whether that music is understood in terms of rhyme, blank verse, or some other form, one is still speaking of the priority given to the ear over the eye in distinguishing poetry from prose. Johnson thus implicitly adopts the point of view of proponents of blank verse. According to their perspective, poetry is the province of public readers whose mode of presentation is that of oral performance and who must therefore "enable their audience to perceive where the lines end and begin" (*Lives*, I: 193), rather than that of private readers who apprehend verse silently and, as it were, through the eye. In reading every other line of a passage from Thomson's *Seasons* to Robert Shiels without Shiels recognizing it as such, Johnson was almost certainly testing the limits of this assumption. Blank verse, like Dennis's "Poetry without Numbers," can achieve the "variety" necessary to poetry but only at the cost of becoming indistinguishable from oratory, the prose equivalent to poetry as an oral performance in a literary culture.

Johnson's reference to a generalized "music of metre" suggests a further difference between his view and that of his opponents. In affirming the superiority of a single verse form—unrhymed iambic pentameter—they were adopting an argument that was as much theological as it was critical. Thus when Edward Young characterized blank verse as "verse unfallen, uncurst; verse reclaim'd, reinthron'd in the true *language of the Gods*," it seems clear that he was suggesting that blank verse had not yet fallen from the purity of being it expresses.[33] It is this nostalgic yearning for a purely poetic, extra historical language, far removed from the contingencies of everyday life, that Johnson may be addressing when he refuses to exempt blank verse from contamination by the impurities of prose. Far from standing at the opposite extreme from prose, a poetry defined by blank verse can be distinguished from oratory only by the introduction of "bold figures and striking images" (*Lives*, I: 237). By contrast, a poetry that is defined by rhyme is a poetry that depends only on itself, only on its own essential characteristics as poetry.

Having stated this argument, however, one must also recognize Johnson's willingness, in life after life, to make exceptions to his general contention. This follows from his well-known doubts—enunciated very clearly in the *Rambler* essays—concerning the essentialist implications of critical definitions.[34] His argument in favor of rhyme is initially Drydenian and rationalistic but may finally be sceptical. In which case Johnson could fairly be regarded as contending that the reader may ultimately be unable to command the difference between poetry and prose and that the two modes are subject to a homogeneity that definition may mask but cannot dispel. Any definition may overlook not only the aural resemblance of the one and the other but also their possible similarity in nature. What is distinguished only with difficulty by the ear may thus be distinguished only with difficulty ontologically as well.

All this may seem to lend further grist to the contention, urged by Johnson's nineteenth-century critics, that he was constitutionally incapable of distinguishing poetry from prose. This may of course prove to have been the case. Yet it is important to notice that what Johnson actually insists upon is not the total dissolution of a boundary line separating poetry from prose but the reduction of this line to a single, conventional distinction. In elaborating the advantages of rhyme over blank verse, Johnson holds that what he calls the "music of metre" is the only yardstick by which "poetry has been discriminated in all languages" (*Lives*, I: 192). In its performative function as "a distinct system of sounds," the "music of metre" thus provides the condition of difference between poetry and prose, serving, at least by way of public testimony, as its primordial constitution. By insisting upon this one agreed-upon difference among all the other possible differences between poetry and prose, Johnson refuses, as Joseph Wood Krutch recognized, to reduce them to a "clearly definable and absolute qualitative difference" that could then be organized into a hierarchically determined opposition.[35] Thus even though the "easiness" of prose is contrasted to the "brevity and compression" required of poetry (*Lives*, III: 358), it is situated beyond the common opposition of variety and regularity of sounds and thus is not allowed to become the basis for a binary system in which either poetry or prose takes precedence over the other. Moreover, the "music of metre" is an economical distinction in the sense that it can encompass a configuration of different systems of sounds from a plurality of languages. Indeed, it is not even a homogeneous unity of heterogeneous features, since it can even extend to languages, like English, where "metre is scanty and imperfect." Rather, it is a kind of minimal difference within discourse, the only difference that can distinguish poetry from prose without seeking for a foundation outside of itself.

There is of course one obvious danger in this reduction of a hierarchically determined system of oppositions between poetry and prose to a minimal difference. It may threaten to submerge all limits and distinctions in an undifferentiated play of textuality. Yet if Johnson's reasoning works to complicate the system of priorities set up to distinguish poetry from prose, it does not thereby collapse them. Johnson may deride Gray for believing that "his language" was "more poetical as it was more remote from common use" (*Lives*, III: 435), but he is not necessarily seeking, as has sometimes been supposed, to approximate the Wordsworthian belief that "there neither is, nor can be, any *essential* difference between the language of prose and metrical composition."[36] Even if one concedes that Wordsworth's position is close to that of Johnson on this issue, it remains that such a purported reduction amounts to nothing more than a romantic reversal of values. Its tendency is to locate prose outside culture, to define it in terms of an absolute exclusion of artifice and consequent innocence with respect to rhetorical figures and poetic diction. Reproducing the classical split between nature and art, it assumes that the poet can shed a supposedly vicious style adopted from the outside and begin speaking to other men in an authentic, unmediated voice. But prose never occupies anything remotely resembling this position in Johnson's criticism; it is not coterminous with common usage but rather reacquires some of the figural characteristics that, in the age of the plain style, had been assigned exclusively to poetry. To mistake this revaluation of prose for an argument that erases the differences between the two is to confound different levels and modes of discourse, to overlook "those happy combinations of words which distinguish poetry from prose" (*Lives*, I: 420). Even if Johnson's intention, in the last analysis, is to contest the system of priorities and oppositions that governed the difference between poetry and prose in eighteenth-century criticism, his point of departure remains an acute awareness of those "happy combinations of words," which, even though they can never be formulated into a simple rule like the "music of metre," still affirm an irreducible difference between the two modes. Taken together, "the music of metre" and a happy combination of words correspond to "those means of pleasing which depend," on the one hand, "upon known causes and rational deduction" and, on the other, to "the nameless and inexplicable elegancies which appeal wholly to the fancy, from which we feel delight, but know not how they produce it" (*Rambler*, IV: 122).

* * *

This discussion of the relations between poetry and prose is enough to indicate that it is consistent with Johnson's dialogism, his view of discourse as a force field of contending interests, and his implicit rejection of theoretical systems as an enterprise premised on false ideas of what criticism ought to be about. Yet what has not yet been addressed is the fact that all these considerations would normally have been answered in the nineteenth century by pointing to Johnson's seemingly highly visible role as a confident and unquestioning apologist for a narrowly Augustan tradition of poetry. Whatever independence might have been acknowledged in specific critical judgments would have been countered by an emphasis upon his endorsement of a general teleology of poetic progress. Thus Macaulay declared that

> Johnson repeatedly laid it down as an undeniable proposition that during the latter part of the seventeenth century, and the earlier part of the eighteenth, English poetry has long been in a constant progress of improvement. Waller, Denham, Dryden, and Pope, had been, according to him, the great reformers.[37]

This account of Johnson's enthusiastic embrace of a specifically eighteenth-century poetic tradition, moreover, clearly survived the twentieth-century revaluation of Johnson as a critic. Thus Leavis wrote that Johnson "found" what had now become the "Augustan" tradition "so congenial that he was able, quite naturally, to adapt its idiom and conventions to the needs of his own sensibility." Yet this represents an equally low estimate of Johnson's critical acumen, inasmuch as it assumes that a critic who has adapted the idiom and conventions of an outmoded tradition to his own needs is a critic whose views of poetry are likely to seem remote from our own. Hence Leavis also found Johnson "representative in his inability to appreciate the more creative uses of language." Implicit in this judgment is the notion—typical of modernist adaptations of romantic poetics—that "the method" of Johnson's criticism is "that of prose statement, the only use of language Johnson understands." Leavis differs from nineteenth-century critics in shifting from psychology to discourse, from inside to outside. Johnson is no longer seen as deficient in perception and imagination but rather in his ability to appreciate, for instance, "the Shakespearean handling of language."[38] Yet the underlying premises remain the same: Johnson, whether as limited in perception or in his ability to respond to the language of poetry, is equally distant from the perspective of our own age.

At first glance, this view of Johnson's estimate of the tradition of late seventeenth- and early eighteenth-century poetry appears to rest on solid ground. The lives of Cowley, Denham, Waller, Dryden, and Pope seem to trace a stylistic evolution from rudeness to refinement and to demonstrate this movement in terms of a development from "Donne's or Jonson's ruggedness"—"the Poets of Elizabeth" having "attained an art of modulation, which was afterwards neglected or forgotten" (*Lives*, I: 293)—to the "language and skill" of Pope's "versification." A similar, if less discernible, movement can be detected in the evolution of poetic diction from the inelegancies of Cowley and the metaphysicals to the proprietary systems of Dryden and Pope. In so far as Johnson's argument could be still said to represent a dominant viewpoint, he might indeed be seen as the upholder of what Leavis termed "the Augustan tradition." Yet a more careful analysis raises a number of questions about Johnson's attitude toward this tradition. Quite apart from the issue of the extent to which this thesis about the evolution of eighteenth-century poetry was still held by a majority of Johnson's educated contemporaries, the indication that he did not wish it to be so viewed comes in the curiously cautious way in which the internal debate between rhyme and blank verse is conducted in the *Lives*. Johnson's well-known willingness to make an exception for the blank verse of Milton, Thomson, and Young directs the reader to the possibility of a countertext existing outside the enclosure of the *Lives*. Moreover, despite Johnson's admiration for the perfection of the couplet, the reader is made aware that it can be subject to a tedium that is the inevitable outcome of a repetition of the same. Thus Johnson, frequently more tentative and cautious than later critics have been willing to allow, notes that Denham "taught his followers the art of concluding their sense in couplets, which has perhaps been with rather too much consistency pursued" (*Lives*, I: 81).

Indeed, if one looks more carefully, one finds that Johnson's attitude toward the development of late seventeenth- and early eighteenth-century poetry, far from being naïve and complacent, is in fact highly equivocal. For Johnson, the very triumph of this poetical revolution, a revolution that virtually ended with Pope, is what constitutes the chief threat to it. Pope acquired "sufficient power of language and skill in metre to exhibit a series of versification which had in English poetry no precedent, nor," Johnson goes on to insist, "since has had an imitation" (*Lives*, III: 224–25).

The sense of tradition here is resolutely that of progress towards an ever-increasing harmony of versification. Yet the point of insisting that Pope's couplets can be read as the culmination of such a tradition is that its very perfection inevitably leads to its own eclipse and that to acknowledge its history is also to announce its end. Opposed to the sense of accomplishment, therefore, is also the contention that "any further improvement of versification will be dangerous. Art and diligence have now done their best, and what shall be added will be the effect of tedious toil and needless curiosity" (*Lives*, III: 251). It is precisely because the achievement is so complete that there is no clear sense of any future direction that the tradition might take. The point of view of Johnson's nineteenth-century critics, of course, is that there was an alternative line, a succession of transcendencies that originated with Milton, progressed through Thomson, Gray, and Collins, and culminated in the poetry of the romantics. The fact that

Johnson was obviously unwilling to entertain this alternative should not be taken to mean that he endorsed its antithesis, a naïve teleology that celebrated the progress of Augustan poetry. It is significant, in this connection, that, in *Rasselas* at least, Johnson projected a much broader model of literary decline, a model in which "the early writers" are seen as being "in possession of nature, their followers of art," the former excelling in "strength and invention," the latter in "elegance and refinement" (*Rasselas*, X, 40). One could of course read this passage as a general statement, having nothing to do with English poetry. Yet one could also find warrant in it for an argument that undermines the historical myth of English Augustan poetry, both because the poets in question are seen as followers and because the progress they achieved falls so obviously into the category of "elegance and refinement."

If the latter interpretation seems strained, it nevertheless communicates something of the uncertainty, the ambivalence that characterizes Johnson's attitude toward progress in the arts. This ambivalence becomes apparent if Johnson's attitude toward culture in *Idler*, number 63, is considered; here he explicitly reflects on the problem at the heart of the matter: that of whether any progress in the arts is not inevitably accompanied by degeneration. This account of "the natural progress of the works of men" produces a fissured interpretation of tradition that resembles what Jacques Derrida described in Rousseau's *Essay on the Origin of Languages*: "beginning with an origin or a center that divides itself and leaves itself," writes Derrida, "an historical circle is described, which is degenerative in direction but progressive and compensatory in effect."[39] Johnson's idea of cultural development in *Idler*, number 63, might well be described as progressive in direction but degenerative in effect. Thus it portrays progress in the arts as a movement from "elegance" to "nicety" or "luxury" (*Idler, Adventurer*, 196), but clearly views this movement as double-edged. Luxury or nicety, like elegance, is seen as the product of an endeavor "to excel others in accuracy, or outshine them in splendour of style," but it cannot really surpass them and thus produces something superfluous and substitutive in place of the "refinement" it seeks to achieve. Hence it comes about, in Johnson's words, that "Ionick and Corinthian columns are soon succeeded by gilt cornices, inlaid floors, and petty ornaments, which shew rather the wealth than the taste of the possessor" (*Idler, Adventurer*, 196–97).

That the *Lives* also project a divided conception of tradition, one that views progress as a corruption as well as an improvement, is evident from Johnson's account in the "Life of Pope"

> of a time when nations emerging from barbarity, and falling into regular subordination, gain leisure to grow wise, and feel the shame of ignorance, and the craving pain of unsatisfied curiosity. To this hunger of the mind, plain sense is grateful: that which fills the void removes uneasiness, and to be free from pain for a while is pleasure; but repletion generates fastidiousness; a saturated intellect becomes luxurious, and knowledge finds no willing reception till it is recommended by artificial diction. Thus it will be found, in the progress of learning, that in all nations the first writers are simple, and that every age improves in elegance. One refinement always makes way for another; and what was expedient to Virgil was necessary to Pope. (*Lives*, III: 239)

Here the appearance of "artificial diction" is presented as a supplement to a plenitude ("leisure") that is also a lack or absence ("a hunger of the mind"), so that the historical process consists of an origin that divides itself and a progress that is also a decline. Johnson's evaluation of minor poets in the *Lives* may be an expansion of this trajectory. If they project any kind of pattern, it may be an implicit movement in poetic diction from rudeness through refinement to degeneration. Or to put it rather differently, Johnson's lack of enthusiasm toward the midcentury poets may rest, as David Perkins shrewdly observed, "on the same misgivings" that "he had about much neo-classic poetry, and that he may even have regarded both of them as sharing some of the same limitations."[40] In this light, one can read Johnson's account of progress in poetic diction as the discovery of a difference within a tradition that cannot be made to coincide with itself. "Repletion generates fastidiousness," which, nevertheless, will give way to a new luxuriance, which, in turn, will call for a new internal stringency, a new supplementary compensation (which might consist, for example, in a new system of terminations to check the luxuriance and harshness of diction that Johnson sees in the poetry of Thomson, Gray, and Collins). Only by understanding that the seemingly unilinear trajectory of progress is in fact an oscillation between two different poles, one negative, the other positive, can one grasp its import and, with it, the precise significance the argument possesses in Johnson's criticism.

We may note that it is the impulse toward refinement that finally triumphs here. But the discovery that poetic evolution is both progressive and degenerative makes it impossible hereafter to read the *Lives* monologically. A monological reading of Johnson's account of English poetry remains feasible only if one ignores Johnson's highly problematical estimates of the major figures. John Denham's *Cooper's Hill* is given qualified praise, but the poetry of Edmund Waller is treated very severely, much more severely than the poetry of Thomson or even Gray. Dryden and Pope are given their just due, but in both accounts praise is blended with censure. This has always and rightly been attributed to Johnson's rugged independence in critical judgment, but it also needs to be related to his internally dialogized conception of poetic tradition. In this respect, Johnson's evaluations of individual texts stand in striking contrast to the writings of apologists for romantic poetry. Constantly escaping the constraints of symmetry and poetic ideology, Johnson's local perceptions trace out a series of triumphs and failures that belie the telos of a would-be program of reform.

What is central to Johnson's conception of tradition is probably best comprehended in the term performance. Here critical examination must begin from the fact that a performance can never really be viewed as a self-enclosed, self-subsistent organism, disengaged from the concerns of the author on the one hand and the reader on the other. The notion of performance inevitably engenders the rhetorical and communicative sequence to which Meyer Abrams has given the term "pragmatic poetics." In this sequence, the work as the reader apprehends it might be said to stand in relation to the work as the author intends it as a dramatic performance stands in relation to the "script" that elicits it. Yet the sequence, as Johnson envisages it, is not necessarily a continuous one because the dualism between script and performance is duplicated by a dualism of author and text, reader and text. In the next chapter, we shall see how Johnson's understanding of these divisions acts to complicate and problematize any notion of pragmatic poetics as a simple, linear process of persuasion and communication.

3
Author, Work, and Audience

The opening chapter of Meyer Abrams's well-known study of romanticism, *The Mirror and the Lamp*, presents a comprehensive survey of poetic theories and raises the question of Johnson's relation to them. According to Abrams, the artist, work, universe, and audience can be seen as constituting the four coordinates of all critical discourse, and each coordinate can be related to a particular kind of critical theory: the artist can be associated with expressive theories, the universe with mimetic theories, the work with objective theories, and the audience with pragmatic theories. Among other consequences, it follows that different coordinates came into prominence at different times and different places: in the ancient world, the central category was the universe with a resulting emphasis upon mimetic theories; from the Renaissance through the eighteenth century, it was the audience with an implied view of "the work of art as a means to an end, an instrument for getting something done," and an evaluation of the work in terms of "its success in achieving that aim." The equivalence of these two coordinates is also a possibility in Abrams's schema: the function of a work in pragmatic theories is Horatian rather than Aristotelian—to please and instruct and to instruct by pleasing. Yet mimesis is still the characteristic means of achieving that end, for by imitating nature the artist chooses the surest way of pleasing an audience.[1]

What is especially useful about Abrams's approach is that it offers a broad framework into which any poetic theory can supposedly be fit. This gives it a significant bearing on the issue of Johnson's position with respect to critical theory. Given the unification of mimetic and rhetorical functions characteristic of much eighteenth-century criticism, it is not surprising that Abrams regards Johnson as an admirable example of a critic whose method is pragmatic. Although he notes Johnson's distrust of "rigid and abstract theorizing" and his application of "the method with constant reference to specific literary examples," Abrams holds that Johnson habitually evaluates poetry in terms of its end and affects. For Johnson, Abrams maintains, Shakespeare is the preeminent instance of an author who succeeded in pleasing many and in pleasing long, but "since the powers and excellence of an author can only be inferred by the nature and excellence of the works he achieves," Johnson's energies are devoted to a general examination of Shakespeare's works. The consequence, however, is not to lead back from the audience to the work as an end in itself, since Shakespearean drama is seen as a limit point, an exemplary instance of mimetic art. Thus Abrams quotes Johnson to the effect that Shakespeare "knew how he should most please," that is to say, by holding up "the mirror to general nature."[2]

On the face of it, Abrams's acknowledgement of the richness and flexibility of Johnson's "own expert response to the plays" would seem to bring his analysis close to that of many recent students of Johnson. Most readers would agree with Abrams's view that Johnson adheres to a pragmatic or rhetorical outlook in which the success of a work of art is measured by its ability to please many and please long. Jean Hagstrum argued that "most of Johnson's definitions of poetry are couched in the language of psychology, of education, and of communication"; W. R. Keast similarly held that "Johnson wants to know chiefly whether poems interest readers, engage their attention, and move them emotionally"; and, according to Paul Fussell, "Johnson fully understands that the relation between poet and poem is not the relation between penitent and confessor: it is rather the relation between barrister and client."[3] But there are limits to this agreement, limits that emerge most clearly if one looks into the reasons for Abrams's emphasis. For while modern commentators on Johnson find his focus on the audience a positive feature of his criticism, Abrams views it as evidence that Johnson, like other eighteenth-century critics, subscribes to an implicitly external and thus inferior conception of art. The general tenor of *The Mirror and the Lamp* is to affirm the relative priority of romantic as opposed to eighteenth-century theories of poetry. It is easy to see, in such a context, how one could form the project of relating the four coordinates, not to four coequal points, but to a central opposition that privileges expressive over pragmatic theories, objective over mimetic theories. Even if Abrams was not himself aware of this emphasis, the subsequent argument of his book makes it apparent. In pragmatic theories, the work is seen as serving a wholly instrumental purpose, possessing no interest except insofar as it produces a desired effect in the reader. In the so-called expressive and objective theories of the nineteenth and twentieth centuries, Abrams finds the artist and work of art assuming an intrinsic value denied in earlier theories.

This results in the kind of drastic antinomy to be found not only in Abrams's opposition between the mirror and the lamp but also in the notion that the author has no bearing in rhetorical or pragmatic theories. For Abrams's case will only seem convincing—will only have the impact it was intended to possess—if one accepts his implicit confinement of pragmatic theories to art in its suasive or purely affective aspects. Yet if it stands to reason that if the means by which a work moves an audience is a major center of concern in a rhetorical poetics, then an even more important center of concern in this mode of criticism must pertain to the author's conscious aims. The attention devoted to an author's "powers and training" may vary from one kind of poetics to another, but it seems clear that the writer's authority must be central in any rhetorical model governed by the principle of intentionality. The author is of course considered by Abrams to be a calculating rather than a spontaneous, expressive subject in pragmatic theories, but the subject still seems to be dominant, even if this dominance is not necessarily total and is constrained by the imperative of pleasing and edifying an audience. No matter how secondary he finds this authority—the authority of the author as an originating subject—Abrams has not completely succeeded in displacing it.[4]

What is the bearing of all this on Johnson and pragmatic theories of poetry? One can begin by pointing out that failure to observe the role of the author in a rhetorical theory can give rise to an important sort of confused understanding. This is the assumption that rhetorical techniques serve as the means by which intentions are translated directly into persuasive effects. It might be argued that this is precisely the point at which an author's character, temperament, innate capacities, training, and attitudes have to be taken into account and that these could threaten the integrity of any rhetorical schema at the very moment when authorial intention is required to make it work. Abrams tends to assume a pattern in which calculated ends are brought into being by the considered intention of an author or work. In this sense, his pragmatic theory corresponds to George Campbell's definition of "eloquence" as "that art or talent whereby the discourse is adapted to produce the effect which the speaker intends it should produce in the hearer."[5] This is where Johnson comes in, so to speak, as a critic who directed attention to the discontinuities that might trouble such a sequence and who did so, moreover, in particular cases that gave his arguments an added urgency and force. In examining Johnson's criticism, Abrams makes do with a commonsense empirical theory of language that effectively ignores Johnson's acute awareness of the problems involved with negotiating the transmission of a text from author to reader. The relationship among author, work, and audience is not simple, determinative, or continuous in Johnson's criticism but one in which there are ruptures at every point in the chain.

* * *

This is not to say that Abrams would ever endorse such a reading of his own arguments. In fact, as I have mentioned, he does make a case for regarding Johnson's critical assumptions as capable of at least some generalized adjustments in the realm of concrete examples. But what Abrams overlooks are the complex mediations, the structures of unmasterable contingency that open up in Johnson's accounts of the always error-prone activity of authorial composition. Indeed, the issue of intentionality is related in Johnson's criticism to his unusual use of the term "performance" in order to refer to an author's poems—a usage that points to the disparity that can always arise between an author's original intention and the reader's response, which always occurs after the fact. In the absence of the author's immediate presence, Johnson finds that a poem's intention is not always easy to discern. Thus of Waller's "Battle of the Summer Islands," he notes that "it seems not easy to say whether it was intended to raise terror or merriment; the beginning is too splendid for jest, and the conclusion too light for seriousness" (*Lives*, I: 289). In this context, the term "performance" not only suggests a composition designed to produce certain effects in the audience, much in the manner of a stage play, but also carries with it the possibility that during the course of time the intention behind a particular performance may have become obscured or forgotten. Johnson's remark is of course meant to be taken as an indication of the failure of the "Battle of the Summer Islands" to fulfill whatever intentions Waller may have had for the poem, but Johnson makes it clear in many other instances that there is no way in which the category of intention can ever fully govern or master the performance of a work of art. Because of the mind's capacity for self-deception, an author's intentions will always be open to challenge and exposed to the errors and dangers of presumption. Thus in commenting upon a passage from Cowley's "Olympionick," Johnson avers that "it is hard to conceive that a man of the first rank in learning and wit, when he was dealing out such minute morality in such feeble diction, could imagine, either waking or dreaming, that he imitated Pindar" (*Lives*, I: 44). In the phrase "waking or dreaming," Johnson implies that poets—even poets of wit and learning—are deceiving themselves if they fail to recognize that their mastery over their own performances is far from complete. Although aspiring to be the intentional source or origin of their own texts, poets are dependent upon an activity that is at least partially outside their control. Even a major poet, moreover, is not exempt from this limitation. In estimating Pope's achievement in inventing a new poetical mythology in *The Rape of the Lock*, Johnson observes that "those performances which strike with wonder, are combinations of skilful genius with happy casualty; and it is not likely that any felicity, like the discovery of a new race of preternatural agents, should happen twice to the same man" (*Lives*, III: 104).

The category of "intention," therefore, is highly problematical in Johnson's criticism, even when an author's intention is clearly discernible and manifestly realized. Nonetheless, it is important to realize that an awareness of the discrepancy between initial project and finished product does not lead Johnson, as it has led some modern critics, to seek to replace the category of intention with a perspective that affirms the autonomy of the work as a self-contained entity. In the twentieth century, criticism has tended to oscillate between two extremes. On the one hand, the poet is an ideal subject who is fully responsible for all of the effects he has produced. This idea can be traced back to T. S. Eliot and his distinction between the "man who suffers" and "the mind that creates." But its real apotheosis came in works like Cleanth Brooks's *The Well-Wrought Urn*, a series of interpretive essays on texts by poets from Donne to Yeats, each chapter reaching a similar conclusion, namely that "the poet knows precisely what he is doing" and that we as readers need to be certain "that we are completely aware of what he *is* doing."[6] On the other hand, there is the death of the author and the subsequent opening up of the text to the interminable play of the sign; a claim brought about by an all-embracing theory of language that would leave no room for the individual subject as origin and locus of meaning. Johnson, it seems clear, cannot be seen as going along with either extreme. He never asserts that the writer is an original genius, creating aesthetic objects outside of history, nor does he suppress the importance of difference and agency in the response of poets to particular issues and dilemmas. He rather appears to conceive of the poet as an empirical subject who, in a performative act, is held accountable for the effects he seeks to produce in an audience but who is nonetheless blind, in crucial respects, to the disparity between his own intentions and achievements.[7] What this means in practical terms is that the poet becomes accessible to the kind of biographical and evaluative criticism found in the *Lives of the Poets*. He remains autonomous, but his autonomy is defined as material, biographical and relative rather than as ideal, transcendental, and absolute.

In rejecting the assumption of an idealized author-subject, Johnson is also repudiating the prevailing conventions of panegyrical biography. In contrast to earlier forms of biographical preface—whether appreciative or debunking—Johnson seeks to offer carefully balanced accounts of the strengths and weaknesses of specific poets. There is of course no evidence, as Krutch argued, "that Johnson himself aimed at anything which he regarded as original so far as intention or method were concerned."[8] Yet he set forth specific opinions about biography, emphasizing, for instance, that the biographer/critic cannot take it for granted that a great work must be the product of a good man and use this assumption as a pretext to show "his favourite at a distance decorated and magnified like the ancient actors in their tragick dress" and "hide the man that he may produce a hero" (*Idler, Adventurer*, 262). Once this act of concealment is prohibited, it is no longer possible to suppress specific details, so that "scarcely any thing is distinctly known" and "all is shewn confused and enlarged" (*Lives*, I: 1). The poet can no longer be ghettoized as being different from other individuals. This view, Johnson believes, holds for major as well as minor poets—it is indeed more manifestly applicable to major poets because of the greater interest their lives hold for readers. Yet it also imposes a constraint upon the evaluation of works, for, as we have seen, they cannot be judged as the immediate product of an author's intention. The interval between invention and judgment disrupts the coincidence of process and product in the text. We never grasp an author's subjectivity directly but grasp only its difference from others and from ourselves. As a result of this limitation, the text escapes the kind of critical/biographical gaze that seeks to "read" authors' lives in their works and thereby reinstate the author as the genetic origin of a work whose characteristic features, whether good or bad, can all be traced directly back to his or her "character" and life.[9]

This distinction could be put in slightly different terms by saying that at the center of Johnson's pragmatic conception of poetry is an author who is still behind a work but whose consciousness, if it appears at all, appears like the consciousness of the critic only after the fact. The blindness of the author at the point of origin is a recurring motif in Johnson's criticism. Thus he observes in the "Life of Prior" that while

> tediousness is the most fatal of all faults . . . unhappily this pernicious failure is that which an author is least able to discover. We are seldom tiresome to ourselves; and the act of composition fills and delights the mind with change of languages and succession of images; every couplet when produced is new, and novelty is the great source of pleasure. Perhaps no man ever thought a line superfluous when he first wrote it, or contracted his work till his ebullitions of invention had subsided. (*Lives*, II: 206)

An author, like other people, is "always present to himself" and is thus utterly incapable of discerning whether his or her effusions will seem tedious or novel to others. Any poem may come to seem tiresome, as the intentions of poets, their consciousness of their own minds in the act of composition, is never a certain measure of its quality. The limitations of the poet's mind, his or her capacity for self-absorption and self-deception, all lead to a decentering of the concept of intention and, by implication, of the rhetorical model it supports.

No doubt such warnings are common enough in treatises and handbooks aimed at neophytes. But Johnson's argument appears to go considerably beyond the kind of wisdom embodied, for example, in the Horatian advice that the poet keep a work nine years before publishing it. Indeed, even when poets are blessed with invention and learning, they are susceptible to the kind of blind spots and limits of vision that afflict all persons as they seek to estimate the value of their own endeavors. Johnson locates this blindness at the very moment of composition, understood as a habitual activity that can be reconstructed through inference from the extant texts. Thus when Johnson reproaches Dryden for his readiness to "enjoy fame on the easiest terms," he declares that Dryden "did not keep present to his mind an idea of pure perfection; nor compare his works, such as they were, with what they might be made" (*Lives*, I: 464). This follows, in Johnson's view, from the assumption that "an idea of pure perfection" ought to be the ultimate goal of any author. To attain this goal, which invariably differs from an inaugural intention, however, poets must recognize that the latter is always insufficient. They must never be satisfied with the intention behind the initial project but only with the distant goal behind and at the center of the final product. At this point, one must suppose that Dryden's laxity is being seen as the blindness that prevents him from aspiring to the peaks reached by Pope.

Johnson's author-centered criticism seizes upon precisely such symptoms of inattention and laxity. Dryden's blindness to the limitations of his poems, his readiness to acquiesce in his first thoughts, does not distinguish him from other writers, for the control of every author is relative and limited at each moment of the act of composition. Thus Cowley's "versification seems to have had very little of his care; and if what he thinks be true, that his numbers are unmusical only when they are ill read, the art of reading them is at present lost; for they are commonly harsh to modern ears" (*Lives*, I: 59). From Johnson's perspective, Waller is much more proprietary than Cowley in his attention to "elocution," but even Waller, in Johnson's opinion, is not exempt in his versification from a certain blind spot: "he uses the expletive *do* very frequently; and though he lived to see it almost universally ejected, was not more careful to avoid it in his last compositions than in his first. . . . His rhymes are sometimes weak words: *so* is found to make the rhyme twice in ten lines, and occurs often as a rhyme through his book" (*Lives*, I: 293–94). The blind spot, no matter how tiny, retains the essential function of disclosing a limitation in an author's mastery of his or her own activity. Johnson describes this limitation in the following terms in his essay on Pope's epitaphs:

> it will not always happen that the success of a poet is proportionate to his labour. The same observation may be extended to all works of imagination, which are often influenced by causes wholly out of the performer's power, by hints of which he perceives not the origin, by sudden elevations of mind which he cannot produce in himself, and which sometimes rise when he expects them least. (*Lives*, III: 268)

In this conception of authorship, the poet is never the spontaneous, unpremeditated subject of eighteenth-century theories of natural genius, nor is he wholly conscious, the transcendental subject of theories of the poet as artist.[10]

Clearly there is a sense in which this approach violates modern protocols about the disjunction between poet and speaker and assumes that poems can be read as if they provide information about the author. Yet this information is circumscribed in Johnson's argument: it does not enable the critic to undertake an empathic investigation of a writer's subjective experiences or detailed intentions but is largely confined to inferences about the formal characteristics of his poetry as a whole. It will be noticed that the weight of Johnson's reflections falls upon discourse, upon language. Johnson is preoccupied not so much with questions of situation, understanding, or interpretation as with matters of language and style. This is because his judgments are based on characteristics of poetry that are assumed to be common to an audience; these judgments focus on the singularity, the unperceived limitations of a writer's style. Language, to Johnson, is the medium in which poets reveal their inability to discern their own limitations during the act of composition by supplying what is missing or eliminating what is excessive. The incessant attention that Johnson attributes to Pope in the act of composition comes as close as possible to closing the gap between intention and execution. According to Johnson, Pope

> knew the mind is always enamoured of its own productions, and did not trust his first fondness. He consulted his friends, and listened with great willingness to criticism; and, what was of more importance, he consulted himself, and let nothing pass against his own judgment. (*Lives*, III: 220)

Yet even Pope was unable to repeat the success of *The Rape of the Lock* and was not without his own petty blindness:

> with those rhymes which prescription had conjoined he contented himself, without regard to Swift's remonstrances, though there was no striking consonance; nor was he very careful to vary his terminations, or to refuse admission at a small distance to the same rhymes. (*Lives*, III: 249)

Johnson's observations might strike some readers as quite paltry or even as irrelevant to the larger issues of Pope's poetry. Yet there is a more principled aspect to this particular brand of author-centered criticism, one that has to do with Johnson's views of the limitations of the human mind, his awareness of the confusions that inhabit our waking thoughts. What these views entail is the conviction that the lacunae inherent in any endeavor, the complex features of any author's conscious intentions, derive from the lacunae at the center of the human mind itself. For, unlike the theories of natural genius and imagination projected by Johnson's contemporaries, his determinedly old-fashioned theory of composition envisages a mind like those of other persons, a mind that is susceptible to the same temptations from without and within, a mind deprived of epistemological certitude, displaced, and decentered. Yet this does not mean that criticism becomes a cruel exposure of an author's delusions, or an indication of how future poets might be able to avoid them. This is because delusion, even though it is only a phantasm, is nonetheless a universal aspect of human experience, since "no human mind," properly speaking, "is in its right state" (*Rasselas*, XLIV: 150) The opposition between delusion and insight is thus only rarely an exposure or a displacement of delusion. It is rather a recovery of the deluded, the reenactment in Johnson's criticism of a drama that was systematically being overlooked or suppressed in the hagiographical writings of other critic/biographers in the eighteenth century.[11]

* * *

It is clear that this perspective, if accepted, would cast considerable doubt upon any theory that sought to transform criticism into a science. The source of that resistance is the sheer impossibility of tracing poetry back to a moment of self-possessed original invention that would serve to ground a reader's response. According to Johnson, "the task of criticism" is the separation of "those means of pleasing which depend upon known causes and rational deduction, from the nameless and inexplicable elegancies which appeal wholly to the fancy, from which we feel delight, but know not how they produce it, and which may well be termed the enchantresses of the soul" (*Rambler*, I: 122). Such a distinction, which is based on a conventional *je ne sais quoi* formula, projects an overflowing of pleasure that can never be fully comprehended, mastered, or brought under the regulation of rules and science. This qualification would seem to be important to anyone who engages in pragmatic criticism, whether with a view to ascertaining "the known causes" by which the mind has been gratified or with the aim of legislating rules for future poets.

Such reservations—including the claim that prereflective fancies and nameless elegancies are beyond the scope of rational understanding—are inevitably intertwined with an uncertainty as to whether responses are intelligible only as the product of prejudice, opinion, or interest. From a Johnsonian standpoint, this doubt is focused upon the question—crucial to present-day critical theory—as to whether an author can appeal to a contemporary audience and still create an artifact that transcends history. One of the reigning ideas in recent criticism, fostered mainly by New Historicists and cultural materialists, has been that texts as well as their authors are products of particular cultures and can only be understood in terms of these cultures. Johnson has often been seen as the exponent of a universalism that is diametrically opposed to this approach, but his actual convictions are a good deal more complicated. To begin with, Johnson takes the view that temporality can bring about profound structural changes in the response of readers to works of art. A central example—and a test case for the relation between text and a historically contingent audience—is provided by the extended treatment, in *Rambler*, number 106, of "temporary opinions." Johnson believes that it is relatively easy for the author to capture and hold the interest of his contemporaries:

> it is not difficult to obtain readers, when we discuss a question which every one is desirous to understand, which is debated in every assembly, and has divided the nation into parties; or when we display the faults or virtues of him whose public conduct has made almost every man his enemy or his friend. (*Rambler*, IV: 202)

Here Johnson attributes to controversial writings that are designed to appeal to some readers the power to reconstitute the world according to their desires and thus to dismiss other readers who don't share these desires. This simplification is not open to writers who seek to appeal to the ages and must therefore submit their work to a larger and more diverse audience. How the poet is to find a way out of this dilemma is a question that Johnson does not pretend to settle. For him, Butler's *Hudibras* is the prime example of a poem that, "however embellished with sentiments and diversified with allusions, however bright with wit, and however solid with truth," has nonetheless lost the power to please because the issues that it addressed have long since vanished. Yet Johnson is not willing to accept Joseph Warton's rather pat contention that "wit and satire are transitory and perishable, but nature and passion are eternal" (*Works*, II: 422). For an author who, in contrast to Butler, "writes upon general principles, or delivers universal truths . . . because his work will be equally useful at all times and in every country . . . cannot expect it to be received with eagerness, or to spread with rapidity," for "desire can have no particular stimulation; that which is to be loved long must be loved with reason rather than passion" (*Idler, Adventurer*, 183–84). The interest of this passage for contemporary readers lies in the fact that the contradiction at the heart of Johnson's notion of audience reception is never suppressed, that the conflict between the timely and the timeless at the "origin" of his view of the relation between the work and the reader is not resolved. Unlike many present-day cultural critics, Johnson invests the poet with agency, with the capacity to achieve a posture that transcends the worldly, situated character of human understanding. One might argue that Johnson's position implicitly recognizes the impracticality of this posture. Yet he is also convinced that there is an irremediable conflict between the demand for an art that "delivers universal truths" and one that answers to immediate socio-political concerns. If a pleasureable response demands the stimulation of desire and if the articulation of general principles requires a shift to an appeal to reason, then passion and reason are not reconciled, the temporary and the enduring remain sundered, and any theory of affects is thereby rendered incomplete. In the temporal, empirical present, an appeal to general principles and universal truths is futile, while the opinions expressed in the here and now are not general and universal.

It might appear from all this that the dilemma in question is a highly generalized affair that has no real point of contact with Johnson's practical criticism. But in fact, this conflict between the universal and the culturally mediated aspects of works of art is one that figures constantly in Johnson's specific judgments of particular works. Most often it involves—as especially in the case of the works of seventeenth-century poets—the acknowledgement of a drastically changed set of circumstances such that their enduring value—their capacity to please subsequent generations—is placed in doubt. But it is above all in Johnson's estimate of Shakespeare that one can see this clash most clearly. For, according to Johnson, it should rightfully be the case that a poet's moral vision should surmount such contingencies as the "barbarity" of his or her age. Moral truths (like the virtue of "justice") should exist in a realm that is "independant on [sic] time or place" (*Shakespeare*, VII: 71). But this argument encounters difficulties—comes against de facto problems in Johnson's estimate of Shakespeare—when it turns out that no such truths can be deduced from his plays. It may be on these grounds that Johnson identifies pleasure, not instruction, as the one essential norm for the estimate of the enduring value of literary texts. In Shakespeare's case, the relevant sources of delight would include certain broad features having to do with the representation of nature—features that are too "general" to be the subject of detailed critical exegesis but that cannot, all the same, be ignored since their very presence is what gives the plays their enduring interest.

This is not to deny that Johnson occasionally voices doubts about the ability of works to survive their initial situation. The disparity that he perceives in the differing claims of the timely and the timeless is profoundly connected to the ineradicable gap between the initial reception of a work and its transmission through the ages. The devastation of cities, the wrack of nations, and the invasion of barbarians have conspired to make it impossible to assume the durability of the text-audience relation. Even in works that have survived the "injuries of time," moreover, there is always the possibility that discontinuities may endanger the private, inwardly experienced bond between the text and reader. Thus Johnson writes in *Adventurer*, number 58:

> If in books thus made venerable by the uniform attestation of successive ages, any passages shall be unworthy of that praise which they have formerly received; let us not immediately determine, that they owed their reputation to dulness or bigotry; but suspect at least that our ancestors had some reasons for their opinions, and that our ignorance of those reasons makes us differ from them. (*Idler, Adventurer*, 372)

In other words, the discerning reader needs to be aware that time continually threatens to deform and decontextualize art, that praise, the pure natural language of undivided pleasure, can turn into indifference, that the moment of spontaneous delight may be either past or yet to come in a conjectural recovery of meaning, and that discourse may become a site of alienation, opacity, and decay.

Some critics would no doubt reject such speculations as belonging to an older humanist tradition, one that holds that meaning must somehow be wrested from the ruins of time. But in so doing they miss Johnson's point that if books are time-bound, partial, and subject to specific historical conditions, then there is a sense in which their meanings may not always be accessible to a culturally situated poetics. The question of comprehension thus persists in one's criticism as a dilemma that is ineluctable and insoluble. It is insoluble because the nature of the work of art as an empirical, not an ideal object is such that it exists in a condition of mixed independence from and dependence upon its original context. That does not prevent it from embodying its own capacity to move even when the author and original context have disappeared. Yet, by the same token, the rupture between the work and its immediate context can engender new contexts or different contexts in which a work may cease to please, its "favourite touches" losing "all their grace." It is impossible, moreover, to discern the extent to which the injuries of time have damaged works of art; indeed, "how much the mutilation of ancient history has taken away from the beauty of poetical performances" can only be "conjectured from the light which a lucky commentator sometimes effuses, by the recovery of an incident that had long been forgotten" (*Idler*, *Adventurer*, 373).

This broad theme unquestionably raises the crucial issue of the durability of a work of art, namely its capacity to survive in the face of the obstacles and difficulties that time creates. Moreover, even if the problem of the empirical context were disregarded as marginal, the text would still be subject to the irreducible temporality of the sign. The work of art has from the start in fact been threatened not only from without but also from within—through alterations in orthography, punctuation, grammar, and the meanings of words. Language, in Johnson's view, is not a simple system whereby all relationships are determined by one principle or in terms of one general grammar but a complex and continually shifting "labyrinth" of endlessly differentiating elements. This means that authors compose in a medium whose system and laws they cannot, by definition, master. Criticism must therefore aim at relations, unperceived by writers, between what they intend or command and what they cannot or fail to command in the language they use. Shakespeare is the example of a poet who "has difficulties above other writers," but this is because of the nature of his work, "which required the use of the common colloquial language, and consequently admitted many phrases allusive, elliptical, and proverbial, such as we speak and hear every hour without observing them; and of which, being now familiar, we do not suspect that they can ever grow uncouth, or that, being now obvious, they can ever seem remote" (*Shakespeare*, VII: 53). Language, as it is embodied in the texts of Shakespeare's plays, is a disorderly element, not a totalized order that only begins to disintegrate when it is interfered with by the zealous efforts of conjectural critics and editors. To read or to observe a play is to operate upon the hypothesis of an accurate text, and there is always the possibility of a gap between an ideal text and the actual, corrupted text we have before us. This gap, moreover, is an undecidable gap, one that constitutes a limit to our response to what we are reading or beholding, rendering it unavoidably tentative and incomplete.

* * *

What is evident here is perhaps not so much a retreat from a rhetorical theory of poetry as a way of affirming its irreducible limitations. Johnson's treatment of the empirical text is typical of an approach which insists that there is no certain ground of appeal, no "truth" beyond the work as we actually have it. For Johnson, the general condition by which a work gives pleasure is governed by rules but not in such a form as to yield its logic up to a criticism securely possessed of its own legitimating procedures. Thus Johnson, like a number of critics in the eighteenth century, addresses himself to the question of whether the rules of art are indeed valid in the sense of being universal, absolute, and transhistorical or whether they are what Johnson terms the "accidental prescriptions of an author," or the products of "fancy" rather than reason. Abrams, like most commentators on Johnson, is not unaware of the doubts that he displays on this issue. The status of the rules in criticism is different from that of a demonstrative science; their epistemological value is only of a probable order.[12] "The beauties of writing," Johnson notes "have been observed to be often such as cannot in the present state of human knowledge be evinced by evidence, or drawn out into demonstrations" (*Rambler*, I: 130). A state of certainty is thus envisaged, but its appearance is only a future possibility, and Johnson's argument is that deferment is intrinsic to the human experience of temporality: the gap between opinion and knowledge extends to the future as well as the past.

What is perhaps most valuable about this approach is that it works to qualify the operative concepts of a rule-bound poetics without, in the process, falling prey to total scepticism.[13] All the Johnsonian precautions concerning nameless beauties, moderation, and demonstrative reasoning are in fact an attempt to construct a satisfactory model by which the reader can work to minimize the possibility of error and ignorance. The problem is posed again in an important passage in which Johnson cites Socrates as the paradigmatic example of a critic who was reluctant

> to conclude that an author had written without meaning, because he could not immediately catch his ideas: he knew that the faults of books are often more justly imputable to the reader, who sometimes wants attention, and sometimes penetration; whose understanding is often obstructed by prejudices, and often dissipated by remissness; who comes sometimes to a new study, unfurnished with the knowledge previously necessary; and finds difficulties insuperable, for want of ardour sufficient to encounter them. (*Idler, Adventurer*, 371)

There is no question here of a rationally superior method of critical judgment; Johnson can only point to the idea that there might exist rational restraints—or forms of reflective judgment—that could act as a check upon prejudice and misunderstanding. The familiar post-Cartesian distinction between clarity and obscurity cannot be a basis for rational certainty, since the distinction presupposes what is neither absolute nor certain:

> obscurity and clearness are relative terms; to some readers scarce any book is easy, to others not many are difficult: and surely they, whom neither any exuberant praise bestowed by others, nor any eminent conquests over stubborn problems, have entitled to exalt themselves above the common orders of mankind, might condescend to imitate the candour of Socrates; and where they find incontestable proofs of superior genius be content to think that there is justness in the connexion which they cannot trace, and cogency in the reasoning which they cannot comprehend. (*Idler, Adventurer*, 371–72)

Johnson introduces only one new principle into this account of the operations of critical judgment. This is the generalized imperative to acknowledge "incontestable proofs of superior genius." It is on the basis of such proofs that the reader must assume the presence of "justness in the connexion" and "cogency in the reasonings," however unclearly these may appear to him. To read with candor is thus to read on the assumption that in every text in which there is some evidence of "genius," there may always be some gap between intention and understanding.

When the focus is shifted from the subjective individual to the *consensus gentium*, the reading subject would appear to be less overtly constrained by the possibility of error. The collective subject, freed from the idiosyncracies, interests, and prejudices of the individual reader, might be expected to rest relatively secure in the sufficiency of its own approbation. In a famous passage from the *Preface* to Shakespeare, Johnson relates how Shakespeare's works are now

> read without any other reason than the desire of pleasure, and are therefore praised only as pleasure is obtained; yet, thus unassisted by interest or passion, they have past through variations of taste and changes of manners, and, as they devolved from one generation to another, have received new honours at every transmission. (*Shakespeare*, VII: 61)

Yet it is here that Johnson comes closest to acknowledging the force of those arguments that are nowadays levelled by New Historicists and cultural materialists against any version of the argument that poetry can transcend a particular time or place. Indeed, there is always in Johnson a qualifying insistence that "approbation" is never absolutely certain, for "approbation, though long continued, may yet be only the approbation of prejudice or fashion" (*Shakespeare*, VII: 61). Indeed, the notion of the *consensus gentium* can actually mislead the reader, Johnson holds, for it can lead him to overlook

> the sentiments and opinions of those who, however neglected in the present age, had in their own times, and many of them a long time afterwards, such reputation for knowledge and acuteness, as will scarcely ever be attained by those that despise them. (*Idler, Adventurer*, 412)

Examining works that have withstood the ravages of time is not enough, therefore. The reader must do more than simply offer "reverence to writings that have long subsisted"; he must also seek to "understand the works of celebrated authors" who have been forgotten; he must seek to "comprehend their systems and retain their reasonings" (*Idler, Adventurer*, 413).[14]

Johnson's enthusiasm for the *consensus gentium* is thus not without reservation. Even in the *Preface* to Shakespeare, the acknowledgement of the poet's fame is seen as a preliminary background for a much more detailed estimate of individual plays and must not be dwelt upon too long. In such a context, the *consensus gentium* is usually referred to in general terms and does not provoke any reflection upon the problems of relativity and temporal discontinuity. Thus, when the perspective is shifted from the common reader to criticism conceived in general terms, the difficulty of resolving such questions invariably leads to the generation of a plot with characters and conflicts. In one of Johnson's earliest allegorical essays, *Rambler*, number 3, "Criticism," although personified as the eldest daughter of "Labour and Truth," and "committed to the care of Justice," is nonetheless seen as frequently unable to decide upon the merits of compositions whose "faults and beauties appeared . . . equally mingled" and is consequently forced to rely on the decisions of "Time." The absence of extratemporal criteria ruins the possibility of any simple resolution to the dilemma, and Criticism is described as withdrawing from earth, leaving "Prejudice and False-taste to ravage at large as the associates of Fraud and Mischief" (*Rambler*, III: 18). The conclusion, in which Time reasserts her authority as a surrogate for Criticism, carries a diplomatic reassurance, temporarily arresting the movement initiated by Prejudice, False-taste, and their companions, Malevolence, Flattery, Power, and Interest. But the difficulty remains unresolved, forcing the allegory to have recourse not to immediate evidence but to a secondary and delegated authority. Moreover, the workings of this authority, in spite of the reassuring tone, is not described as totally certain:

> the proceedings of Time, though very dilatory, were, some few caprices excepted, conformable to Justice: and many, who thought themselves secure by a short forbearance, have sunk under his scythe, as they were posting down with their volumes in triumph to futurity. It was observable that some were destroyed little by little, and others crushed for ever by a single blow. (*Rambler*, III: 18)

In such an allegory, Johnson points to a problem that can never be fully eliminated. The interval between contemporary claims to attention and the rectifying decisions of time means that the question of justice remains undecidable. Justice is indissolubly linked to its twin, Prejudice; it is always possible that the figure of Fame is only a burlesque simulacrum of the real thing.

It is here that Johnson's writings hold lessons for present-day critical theory. He brings out more explicitly than any other eighteenth-century critic the way in which questions about truth, justice, and reason collide with issues in the realm of history, power, and politics. It is around this kind of conflict that the alternative series of polarities—justice versus prejudice, candour versus interest, truth versus flattery, etc.—organize themselves. The impossibility of any resolution to these alternatives generates a plot in which the author is an agonistic figure, pitted against a critic whose presumption and malevolence constitute the main threat to his ill-starred quest for fame. The action of this plot engenders frustration, power struggles, and the possibility of an unmerited descent into oblivion. The ambiguity inherent in such narratives is easily perceived, as in *Rambler,* number 93, where Johnson questions whether authors who seek "to preclude all future liberty of censure" have in fact "more benevolence or modesty than the rest of mankind" (*Rambler*, IV: 133). For all practical purposes, what this means is that the human mind is always in some degree unstable, vain, deceptive, other to itself, different—and, therefore, subject to delusion. This is the place where the opposition between author and critic ceases to be relevant, and the two subjects—the subject who produces and the subject who evaluates—become submerged in a generalized model of the psyche in which "the treachery of the human heart" is seen to prevail (*Rambler*, I: 134). The antagonism between author and critic is not simply misconceived, it is a sign of the alienation of both from "reason and truth."

Given this symmetry between the author and critic, it is not surprising that Johnson provides no overarching explanation of the means by which a text can be judged. Rather, he seeks to shift the burden of judgment from Criticism to Time, understood as a highly flawed and aberrant process of canon formation. This is only to admit, as will be seen in a later chapter, that there is no certain explanation as to why one work survives and another falls into oblivion. Hence the task of the critic undergoes a shift in emphasis: it is not so much the evaluation of the works of living authors but rather the disclosure of the shifts that time and the *consensus gentium* have wrought.[15] Criticism is thus never primary but always secondary, since it draws its inspiration not from an original response but from that which is posterior to that response.

It is, of course, precisely such a discrepancy between the original estimate and the changes wrought by time that Johnson repeatedly draws attention to in the *Lives of the Poets*. In particular, when he quotes Fenton's "poetical character" of the Earl of Roscommon, he observes ironically, "from this account of the riches of his mind, who would not imagine that they had been displayed in large volumes and numerous performances" (*Lives*, I: 234–35). In a similar manner, Johnson observes the discrepancy between the praise lavished upon George Granville and James Hammond and the actual quality of their poetry. In each of these instances, the verbal deflation of an inflated contemporary estimate confirms a decline in reputation that has already taken place. When Johnson claims, in the "Life of Blackmore," to find some merit in one of the poet's epics, he is perhaps being deliberately provocative; nevertheless, his carefully measured praise takes place against the backdrop of what he obviously regards as the malicious blackening of Blackmore's reputation by a coterie of contemporary writers. Likewise, Johnson's acute sensitivity to the prejudice reflected in fashion and opinion can be seen in his resistance to efforts to rediscover the minor poems of writers whose reputations, like that of Milton or Gray, rests on one popular work. In many instances, Johnson simply allows the distance of time to do its work: the tedium that a careful examination of a body of forgotten poems would inevitably engender corresponds to the tedium that a mention of its author's name now evokes. Just as the poems have disappeared from the collective memory of a reading public, so contact with the original source of their popularity—whether personal influence or favoritism—has been irretrievably lost.[16]

Thus the conventional relation between nature and custom is actually reversed in Johnson's criticism. The initial reputation of literary texts, Johnson believes, is in part a response to contemporary situations of power and interest. What such a pattern in effect suggests is that prior to any possible natural interaction between text and reader, there is an earlier, artificial interaction among the author, work, and contemporary cultural milieu. Literary criticism becomes an act of elucidation the purpose of which is to confirm the belated, supposedly "natural" perspective of a later generation of readers against the artificially inflated or deflated estimates of contemporary critics, or to mitigate the unusually harsh judgments of a contemporary clique or coterie. The defense of the natural here turns on the ability of the critic to discern what is permanent and enduring rather than being swayed by the intial reputation. The possibilities of evaluation are thus deeply linked with an archaeological perspective; an authentic estimate has its corollary in the disappearance of artificial accretions. This process is one that the audience itself is invited to undergo. The questioning of once fashionable opinions points them to the homogeneity and permanence of nature as the place where the potential source of pleasure is located. Some readers may feel that Johnson overlooks the possible role of ideological and political factors in the supposedly universal appreciation of Shakespearean drama. Yet the persisting presence of custom and opinion is also acknowledged by Johnson. As a result of the temporal priority of the artificial to the natural, the reader's relation to the natural is always marked by an uncertainty as to its boundaries and limits.

* * *

This aspect of Johnson's criticism deserves special emphasis, since so many readers take Johnson as a pillar of critical certitude, the exponent of a powerful universalist creed that effectively consigns such factors as custom and opinion to the status of passing ephemera. Yet what one actually finds in Johnson's criticism is a discipline in which the process of judgment is divorced from a reader's initial response, which is seen as the domain of power and influence. This introduces, at the level of evaluation, an element of uncertainty that permeates all the major divisions of criticism, all judgments of specific texts, whether of major or minor poets. The oppositions between nature and art, familiarity and novelty, which constitute and give direction to Johnson's evaluations, are presented in his critical writings not as hierarchical dualities underlying the course of a text's reputation and determining its ultimate shape and form, but rather as terms that are subject to permutation, reversal, and displacement. Johnson's criticism thus tends to resist any form of reductionism by multiplying the ways a text can be judged, by contradicting with an opposing viewpoint any normative structure of values that takes itself to be definitive.

The *Preface* to Shakespeare, Johnson's most extended critical assessment, effectively brings out this pattern of affirmation and contradiction. As a text that is involved with the workings of the *consensus gentium,* it is centrally concerned with questions of nature and art as they are related to what is permanent in Shakespeare's plays and what undergoes change. Initially, Johnson appears to affirm a clear-cut distinction between the uniformity of nature and those obstacles that obscure it: namely the distortions, deflections, and fossilized prejudices endemic in the "advantages" that are derived from "personal allusions, local customs, or temporary opinions." This distinction provides a platform on which Johnson, like other eighteenth-century critics, can argue that "Shakespeare" can "now begin to assume the dignity of an ancient, and claim the privilege of established fame and prescriptive veneration" (*Shakespeare*, VII: 61). At the same time, it also appears to afford the basis for Johnson's argument that Shakespeare is "the poet of nature, the poet that holds up to his readers a faithful mirror of manners and of life." In this mirror, as Murray Krieger has pointed out, "like recognizes like, so that the universal subject reflects the universal object."[17] Indeed, if it appears that Johnson can show the means—the imitation of the characteristic features of common life—by which Shakespeare "has gained and kept the favour of his countrymen," it is because he has already attributed those characteristics to an audience that has transcended custom in the first place. Therefore, in order to affirm a mimesis grounded in common life, Johnson has already had to appeal to the common reader, to the presumption of a common reader, and, within mimesis, to the specular play of a mirror in which the other is reduced to the same. The mirror of manners and of common life is caught mirroring the images of the common reader, so that one is tempted to view the relation between the work of art, the universe, and the audience as an enclosed, self-engendered, self-reflexive system.

Yet the *Preface* to Shakespeare only appears to assert the stability of this relation because the same opposition between nature and art is subject, throughout the text, to qualifications and stresses that imperil its integrity. It reappears in a slightly different guise, for instance, in the opposition between nature and novelty, but, in Johnson's arguments, the terms are subject to permutation and reversal. By holding up the mirror to nature, Shakespeare avoids "the irregular combinations of fanciful invention of that the common satiety of life sends us all in quest" but which satisfy us only for a moment. Here the common satiety of life is an experience which is located within the horizon of the common reader, yet what it "sends us all in quest" of belongs to the realm of art (fashion, temporary opinion, etc.). Readers may look to Shakespeare for representations of nature, identifying with common life and common concerns, yet what the satiety of life impels them to seek is the strangeness that Shakespeare has excluded from his plays. Johnson seems to resolve this dilemma by assuming that, if novelty has been exiled in order to hold Shakespeare up as the poet of nature, it reappears within Shakespeare's theater in order to distinguish it "from every other stage." Shakespeare's novelty might thus be said to be the naturalness, the familiarity of his dialogue, its representation of "common conversation, and common occurrences." Novelty then is not so much excluded as situated within the natural ("Shakespeare approximates the remote and familiarizes the wonderful"), which in turn is being situated by being opposed to the novel understood as a deviation from the natural. Novelty is thus both the antithesis of the natural and a part of it—outside and inside it at the same time.

These terms are crucial to Johnson's criticism and thus deserve extended consideration in another chapter. Here it is sufficient to note that the opposition between the natural and the new is but part of a larger system in which the novel is absorbed into the conventional, the arbitrary, the fashionable. The basic instability of this system can be seen in Johnson's defense of Shakespeare's characters against the strictures of earlier neoclassical critics. What these critics objected to was the disturbing noncoincidence between behavior and rank and the corresponding failure to observe a due decorum in thought and manners. For Johnson, this objection can be met by uncovering signs of a deeper logic at work, one in which nature and art are fused, not opposed. The central image of kings who "love wine like other men" and in whom "wine exibits its natural power" as it does on other men suspends our sense of a nature that can be confined to the proprietary, the seemly, the appropriate:

> His story requires Romans or kings, but he thinks only on men. He knew that Rome, like every other city, had men of all dispositions; and wanting a buffoon, he went into the senate-house for that which the senate-house would certainly have afforded him. He was inclined to show an usurper and murderer not only odious but despicable; he therefore added drunkenness to his other qualities, knowing that kings love wine like other men, and that wine exerts its natural power upon kings. (*Shakespeare*, VII: 65–66)

In this serio-comic duality, the proprietary is the artificial, the realm of studies, habits, and professions, and the seeming incongruity between decorum and the passions is based on a hidden link between the two. Thus Johnson, as will be shown later, fully as much as Erich Auerbach or Bakhtin, embraces a notion of mimesis that encompasses different stylistic levels. Voltaire's ridicule of Johnson's position as the equivalent of the portrayal of "Alexander the Great mounted on an ass" reflects the extent to which Voltaire is still committed to the doctrine of propriety and of the strict separation of styles.[18] By insisting upon the ironic mixture of disparate elements, Johnson makes us see the unfolding of an action as the discovery of differences within a character whose conduct cannot be made to coincide with what he is saying. This serio-comic conception of character, which, as Voltaire recognizes, stems from the yoking together of high and low elements, is spatial and pictorial in conception; but when it is temporalized, it unfolds into the "successive evolutions of design" that "sometimes produces seriousness and sorrow and sometimes levity and laughter." In either its spatial and temporal manifestation, this serio-comic conception of drama shows itself capable of bridging the gap between nature and art.

To some extent the terms of this argument can be explained by Johnson's commitment to a defense of Shakespeare, his rejection of rigid compartmentalizing in whatever form. But the instability clearly goes deeper and extends well beyond specific arguments as one can see by examining his *Preface* with an eye to comparing Shakespeare's strengths with his "faults." If Shakespeare's peculiar excellence is his ability to hold the mirror up to common life, so his peculiar fault is "the quibble," a play of sounds that acts to complicate sense and produce an inversion in the hierarchy that privileges the supposedly referential nature of the drama over its linguistic nature. For Johnson, "the quibble," the pun, the low conceit is Shakespeare's "fatal Cleopatra," a purely phonic temptress "for which he will always turn aside from his career," because of the way it causes a rupture in the action or dialogue, sending it off in two directions at once. Furthermore, the figure of the temptress is itself artificial, since her allure is a painted, cosmetic allure. The implication is that Shakespeare has abandoned himself to a kind of depravity in which he has given in to the free play of the signifier, a process that complicates and undermines the established pattern of our response. The pun is the sign that the Shakespearean theater is self-reflexive as well as referential, a mirror turned inward on itself as well as outward on the world.

The "fault" in the quibble lies not so much in the way it acts as a substitute for plain sense as in the way it opposes Shakespeare's power of moving the passions: "he no sooner begins to move, than he counteracts himself; and terrour and pity, as they are rising in the mind, are checked and blasted by sudden frigidity" (*Shakespeare*, VII: 74). Shakespeare's power to move is thus never simple—the passions are never undivided but are a complex combination of referential and reflexive elements. The representation of natural passions is thus not a pure representation but is rather permeated by verbal artifice. Faults have penetrated excellences from the start and vice versa. The way in which Johnson formulates his criticism of Shakespeare's quibbles suggests that he is fully convinced of this. The attention that he devotes to the contrast between excellences and faults creates the impression of an ideal balance between the extremes of "envious malignity" and "superstitious veneration." But the metaphor of wordplay as a Cleopatra is one of many suggestions in the *Preface* that works to undo such a perfectly assured balance. The straightforward praise of the excellence of a poet whose "characters are not modified by the customs of particular places" is undermined by the criticism of one who "had no regard to distinction of time or place, but gives to one or age or nation, without scruple, the customs, institutions and opinions of another." The effect of such a turnabout is to keep us from arriving at a certainty concerning what counts as excellencies and what counts as faults (*Shakespeare*, VII: 62 and 72). Far from being opposed to one another as absolute and uncommunicating opposites, excellences and faults can also be seen as different ways of looking at the same phenomena. To praise an excellence is not necessarily to deny a fault, for Shakespeare's sacrifice of "virtue to convenience" is simply another way of appraising his exhibition of "the real state of sublunary nature," dependent on the same principle of imitation. The authenticity Johnson attributes to Shakespeare's representation of "common conversation" and the lack of "delicacy" he ascribes to Shakespeare's portrayal of ladies and gentlemen are both consequences of mimesis, positive and negative effects of Shakespeare's recreation of "common life."

To ask whether the excellencies or faults should determine a reading of Shakespeare's plays is to ask which elements of the plays should be emphasized and which should be underplayed, contextualized or even ignored—that is whether faults should be read in terms of excellences or excellences in terms of faults. In spite of the positive tone of Johnson's *Preface*, the question does not have a simple answer and may be improperly formulated. Johnson's view of the plays should be looked at as a nonfinalized mixture of beauties and flaws, open to different readings and not reducible to any fixed system of hierarchical oppositions. Johnson is not confused about a possible equilibrium between faults and excellences, and, indeed, his resort to such an equilibrium depends upon a view of the nature/art antithesis as an opposition between perception and reflection, or between the spontaneous and the calculating. A fault is an excellence reformulated in a secondary and reflexive act of negation. Yet the interaction between the two inhibits any attempt to formulate a new position that would exclude one or the other; indeed, the very strength of the opposition lies in the reversibility of its terms. Hazlitt makes this point in the following manner:

> Johnson wrote a kind of rhyming prose, in which he was much compelled to finish the different clauses of his sentences, and to balance one period against another, as the writer of heroic verse is to keep to lines of ten syllables with similar terminations. He no sooner acknowledges the merits of his author in one line than the periodical revolution of his style carries the weight of his opinion completely over to the side of objection, thus keeping up a perpetual alternation of perfections and absurdities.[19]

Hazlitt was not wrong to insist upon this aspect of Johnson's criticism. Yet rather than regarding it as an unfortunate consequence of Johnson's rhyming prose style, he should have more properly seen it as the radical outcome of a process in which a final, authoritative interpretation is indefinitely deferred. In an elegant phrase, Johnson describes the oscillation produced by this process of deferral in his discussion of Dryden's "Dialogue on Drama" as "successive representations of opposite probabilities" (*Lives*, I: 412). The successive representations of excellences and faults, nature and art, should, in this case, be taken not as the imprisonment of thought within language but as the holding together of two antithetical possibilities, without any ultimate justification for choosing between them.[20]

It is no accident that the *Preface* to Shakespeare ends by pointing to the potential reversibility of the positive and negative poles of Shakespearean evaluation. The antithesis of excellences and faults, like other aspects of Johnson's criticism, lacks the reassuring sense of certainty, the bedrock on which dogmatic judgments are raised, since both excellences and faults are articulated within the same medium. Nor can it be resolved by merely shifting from "demonstrative" to "probable" reasoning, since excellences and faults are being presented as "opposite probabilities." What complicates matters is the implication that each probability must undermine the other and that excellences and faults cannot simply be conceived to merge into a benign approximation of the *via media*. There remains an irreducible tension between the two terms, so that criticism is confronted with the limits of probabilistic reasoning. Yet Johnson is also careful to add that these are only "successive representations" of opposite probabilities. This means that the author still retains an authority as a constituting subject. It follows that what is at stake here is not a retreat into a world in which critical judgments are nothing more than the product of the concepts, categories, and oppositions that comprise a particular semantic field. Rather it is the recognition that no matter how firmly the critic's arguments may be enmeshed within a self-contained system of meaning, the critic's text is still a representation, bound to the established norms of mimetic fidelity and truth.

Yet if Johnson can be seen as raising these issues to a point of philosophical sophistication undreamed of in Hazlitt's strictures, he still allowed plenty of room for the kind of sceptical doubts about Shakespeare's achievement that Hazlitt found so unpalatable. The opposition between excellences and faults serves to delineate the extremes of popular and critical response to Shakespeare's plays in the eighteenth century and thus make evident the extent to which that response eludes the constraints of precept and is hardly reducible to a consensus. To describe what gives pleasure in Shakespeare's drama is to operate on assumptions that are subject to reversal and negation. The foundational term of pragmatic criticism takes for granted the stability and self-identity of the response, whether that of the common reader or critic, but what is described in Johnson's criticism is neither stable, nor self-identical. Indeed, in so far as Shakespeare's excellences and faults represent the views of the common reader and critic, the juxtaposition of the two within a common framework suggests that neither is pure. The response of the common reader has already become contaminated with the jargon of the schools and vice versa.

It would be a mistake, therefore, to read Johnson's criticism in terms that postulate the immediacy and continuity of the response of reader and critic. Yet it would be equally wrong to assume that Johnson repudiates pragmatic criticism in favor of a perspective that affirms one of the other categories. On the contrary, Johnson's critique of intentionality, of the limits of the writing and reading subject, relies on the notion of the subject; it never implies that one of the coordinates can be abandoned in favor of a theory that isolates and hypostasizes one of the others. To recognize the disparity between the text and the reader's response to that text, one must operate within a framework that acknowledges the audience as one part of any critical system. Johnson's argument appeals to no higher or alternative theory but rests upon the very principles it subjects to criticism. The notion of the author or an audience are not errors that criticism should have avoided but are indispensable to any informed critical judgment.

At the same time, it is also important to recognize that the relation between author and audience is intextricably linked in Johnson's criticism to Abrams's third and fourth categories, the work and the universe and is incomprehensible except as a form of mimesis. Johnson's pragmatic theory must therefore be seen in the first instance as a theory of representation: "nothing can please many and please long but just representations of general nature." Yet the aspect of "just representations of general nature" that requires elucidation appears so self-evident in Johnson's criticism as to be in danger of being left unexplained. This is the characteristic of absence that, as shall be seen in the next chapter, opens the possibility of the structure of representation in the first place, the margin of difference without which the element of representation could not originally appear.

4
Presence and Representation

In a chapter of his *Elements of Criticism* entitled "emotions caused by fiction," Lord Kames distinguishes between what he calls "real presence" and "ideal presence." Real presence arises, according to Kames, from an immediate sensuous apprehension of objects. Ideal presence occurs when an absent object is produced as if it were present. In this sense, ideal presence is also an alternative to what Kames calls "reflective rememberance," which by itself is insufficient to transform a past event into a present one. Where reflective remembrance engenders "only a faint and incomplete idea," ideal presence rouses "the attention" and turns a reader "into a spectator." Ideal presence is thus a heightened effect caused in part by a "vigorous exertion of memory" or imagination and may thus be produced by all sorts of poetry, but Kames speaks most highly of the ideal presence caused by tragedy and epic poetry. Referring to ideal presence in terms that presuppose an undivided unity of perception instantaneously present to itself, Kames describes it as "an act of intuition" in which "reflection enters not more than into an act of sight." It follows that "the distinctness of ideal presence . . . approaches sometimes the distinctness of real presence; and the consciousness of presence is the same in both." It is true that ideal presence is more fragile than real presence; like a "waking dream," it "vanishes upon the first reflection of our present situation." Yet Kames holds that "it is by means of ideal presence that our passions are excited; and till words produce that claim they avail nothing."[1]

Much of what Kames has to say in this connection confirms present-day thinking about the importance of the notion of "presence" as a normative principle, one that can act as the foundation of all thought, language, and experience. More specifically, it anticipates Martin Heidegger's definition of "presence" as whatever "brings what is present each in its own way to presence."[2] In Kames, this has to do with a theory of affects, of the means by which drama—and analogous forms of poetic narrative—can best give delight to a mind properly attuned. The drama that gives the greatest pleasure is one that refuses to acknowledge its textual status and aspires to pure self-presence independent of written signs. The consciousness of ideal presence is a consciousness that excludes any awareness of the text as existing apart from its performance as living speech. It thus leaves no room for judgment conceived as an ironic detachment from a work's action or characters. If ideal presence approaches the distinctness of real presence, then, clearly, it can make no sense to talk of the reader's freedom to suspend disbelief—hence Kames's valorization of the spectator over the reader; hence also his insistence upon tragedy and epic as the genres most likely to achieve the effect of self-present immediacy.

Kames's chapter provides a useful point of departure for considering Johnson's complex relation to eighteenth-century criticism and aesthetics. It is not by chance that Johnson's criticism includes, as one of its aspects, a number of observations that impinge on the doctrine of presence. For Kames's argument is not an isolated phenomenon but only a more theoretically coherent formulation of a basic strand in eighteenth-century critical thought. In *The Sister Arts*, Jean Hagstrum has described how the ancient rhetorical term *enargeia* and its various Latin synonyms, *descriptio*, *illustratio*, *evocatio*, and *evidentia* came to be employed in the eighteenth century as the basis for a theory of literary presence.[3] The term *enargeia* itself may be defined as the evocation of a scene as if the reader were literally present as a spectator. The figure is essentially a visual one, and thus it is not surprising that the term "vision" was frequently employed as a synonym for *enargeia*. Hugh Blair defines vision as the figure that "shall make us think we see before our eyes the scene that is observed."[4] One might assume that the purpose of employing such a figure is an artistic one such as the exact imitation of a scene, but, in this case, the artistic aim also implies a founding normativeness, the recovery of an original plenitude. That a scene is present to us means not so much that it has been portrayed accurately as that it unfolds itself directly before us as viewers. Presence is defined as what effaces representation, not merely what has been re-presented accurately. Presence is thus not merely mimetic, but a mimesis that refuses to acknowledge its own imitative status and thus aspires to the condition of pure truth.

Much of eighteenth-century critical theory, with its assimilation of the act of reading to the act of perception and its claims for a parallel between poetry and painting, reveals itself as committed to a view of *enargeia* as "ideal presence." Yet at least two critics before Johnson—Joseph Addison and Edmund Burke—display certain reservations about this principle. Adopting a Lockean distinction between primary and secondary qualities, Addison recognizes something inescapably illusory and phenomenal in the images evoked by art. Because "Light and Colours, as apprehended by the Imagination, are only Ideas in the Mind, and not Qualities that have any Existence in Matter," they necessarily entail the fictionality of whatever they purport to represent. They can only "make Scenes rise up before us and seem present to the Eye";[5] they cannot establish or guarantee the veracity of these scenes. Addison accordingly envisages aesthetic fictions as evanescent, constantly exposed to the threat of dissolution by the intrusion of reality. To forestall this threat, Addison seeks to mark off a domain that dispenses altogether with the illusion of mimetic realism. Indeed, one of his major concerns in the series of papers on "the Pleasures of the Imagination" is to defend what Dryden called "*the Fairie Way of Writing*," a realm of delusory appearances "wherein the Poet quite loses sight of Nature, and entertains his Reader's Imagination with the Characters and Actions of such Persons as have many of them no existence, but what he bestows on them" (*The Spectator*, III: 570).

In Addison, this argument is conjoined with the claim that "Words, when well chosen," have a force greater than that of painting or sculpture. Burke is not concerned with the dilemma of an art that is confined to a realm of fictive recreation without necessary bearing upon reality, but he questions the basic congruity of poetry and painting. In opposition to proponents of the doctrine of *enargeia* who, like Addison, assume that word-painting is equal, perhaps even superior, to its visual counterpart as a source of presence, Burke accepts it as self-evident that words always interpose an opacity between the reader/spectator and any conceivable representation of things seen:

> the truth is, all verbal description, merely as naked description, though never so exact, conveys so poor and insufficient an idea of the thing described, that it could scarcely have the smallest effect, if the speaker did not call in to his aid those modes of speech that mark a strong and lively feeling in himself.[6]

It seems clear enough why verbal description has been deemed "poor and insufficient" in this passage. If painting and sculpture are conceived as giving immediate access to an object, then writing can only obstruct that access by obtruding its opaque, material inscriptions in the place of an ideal transparency. It is only the speaking subject, the voice of feeling that can overcome the deficiencies of this impoverished mode of language.

These arguments of Addison and Burke exerted a deep and lasting influence on the currency of eighteenth-century critical debate. They were taken up by later theorists and were still topics of discussion among the English and German romantics. This aspect of the history of criticism has been well covered and does not need further exposition here.[7] What has not so often been noticed is the position that Johnson took on these matters. In part, this can be traced to the habit of treating Johnson as a robust empiricist and strong follower of John Locke. On this account, Johnson's practical bent, his refusal to question or to criticize the grounds of naïve sense certainty would seem to preclude the kind of theoretical engagement that characterizes the writings of critics like Kames, Addison, and Burke.

Yet what this argument fails recognize is the fact that, while Kames, Addison, and Burke were also indebted to Locke, all three developed distinctive critical positions. To understand Johnson's place in the history of criticism, we need to examine his position on the issues that preoccupied his contemporaries. And we should not be misled by the fact that he conceives of these arguments in the language of critical interpretation and evaluation. For this language was adopted partly as a matter of inclination and partly because it enables Johnson to preserve a sense of the problems involved in the passage from generalized statements of method and principle to detailed local perceptions. This point can be made by taking up Johnson's attitude to the notion of "presence." In the *Dictionary*, he defines the verb "to represent" as "to exhibit as if the thing exhibited were present." In the *Lives of the Poets*, Johnson emphatically insists upon the priority of images over thoughts or inferences, by which he means concepts. The limitations of Cowley's poetry can be traced in part to its author's inattention to this priority:

> one of the great sources of poetical delight is description, or the power of presenting pictures to the mind. Cowley gives inferences instead of images, and shews not what may be supposed to have been seen, but what thoughts the sight might have suggested. (*Lives*, I: 51)

Such "thoughts" may be supposed to appeal to what Kames termed "reflective remembrance" rather than "ideal presence." For Johnson, this means that reason has displaced the imagination in the poetic process. Cowley's fault was that "his endeavours were rather to impress sentences upon the understanding than images on the fancy"

(*Lives*, I: 59). Such images, as Johnson conceives of them, would be more authentic—closer to the nature of things—than any truth impressed upon the understanding by mere sentences.

Yet, despite these strictures, as forthright as any Kames had offered, Johnson's specific judgments about particular poets indicate that he was clearly aware of the limits of the image as a way of restoring presence to representation. In the *Dictionary*, Johnson defines images as "descriptions" that "force the image of the thing described in the mind." Yet this definition appears to be a limiting term, an ideal point of reference, for in his actual analysis of descriptive passages in the *Lives*, Johnson never claims that they reproduce all that they represent. In the "Life of Thomson," Johnson praises Thomson as a poet whose "descriptions of extended scenes and general effects bring before us the whole magnificence of Nature, whether pleasing or dreadful" (*Lives*, III, 299). But elsewhere he makes it clear that language is mediate in character and that Thomson's poetic diction, in particular, "is in the highest degree florid and luxuriant, such as may be said to be to his images and thoughts 'both their lustre and their shade'; such as invest them with splendour, through which perhaps they are not always easily discerned" (*Lives*, III: 300). Thomson's diction is by no means merely opaque and ornamental in this interpretation, as Burke might have argued. On the contrary, it is a source of both illumination and opacity, a verbal resource that can reveal as well as conceal. This is why Johnson employs the term "splendour" to refer to the paradoxical character of Thomson's style. It is precisely because Thomson's diction can blind us by its brilliance that it can never make the poet's "images and thoughts" immediately present to the reader.

Johnson's observation is made of course in the context of a particular judgment of Thomson's poetry. It is perfectly in line with the principle that elevates images over sentiments. Yet there is a very real sense in which it presupposes a point of view similar to Burke's argument that poetic language, because of its very nature—its existence as a realm of mediating signs—is far from being an ideal vehicle for description. In *Idler*, number 34, Johnson describes poetry and painting as "two arts which pursue the same end, by the operation of the same mental faculties," but "which differ only as the one represents things by marks permanent and natural, the other by signs accidental and arbitrary" (*Idler, Adventurer*, 106). Burke and Johnson agree that language is necessarily material in character—they disagree as to how much of a barrier it interposes between the reader/spectator and any conceivable experience of things seen. For Burke, verbal description is an inferior kind of painting, useful, perhaps, for evoking objects but otherwise totally unsuitable for the purposes of genuine representation. In its place, Burke emphasizes the primacy of the spoken word, the medium by which the feelings of the poet can be conveyed to a receptive reader. For Johnson, on the contrary, language, although accidental and arbitrary, is not wholly dissociated from the objects it portrays—hence the importance of Johnson's adoption of the conventional notion that "language is the dress of thought." This metaphor points to the limited but nonetheless important role of language in word-painting. Rather than interposing an absolute veil between the understanding and the thing-seen, language, like dress, turns out to have a rather different pertinence, one that requires the possibility of both disclosure and concealment.

Thus up to a point, Johnson goes along with Burke, at least in so far as he treats language as marked through and through by elements that work to prevent any immediate, self-present transcription of external objects. But Johnson is very far from believing, like Burke, that "modes of speech" can offer direct access to an author's feelings. Indeed, in his review of Joseph Warton's *An Essay on the Writings and Genius of Pope*, Johnson contends that "poetical measures have not in any language been so far refined as to provide for the subdivisions of passion. They can only be adapted to general purposes" (*Works*, II: 416–17). Thus where Burke's reversal of the relationship between clarity and obscurity, the absolute privilege given to obscurity as a characteristic of the sublime, simply replaces one norm with another, Johnson's analysis subjects the sign to a principle of difference that denies presence to language yet opens it up to critical judgment and discrimination.

It is precisely this aspect of Johnson's criticism that can easily be overlooked. His view that poetic language cannot become the unequivocal reappropriation of presence is made in the context of a local perception rather than being developed as part of a theoretical argument. The effect of such a perception is to challenge the idea that theoretical assumptions can be formulated in a way that is independent of specific critical judgments. Yet Johnson's argument can be shown to rest upon a series of principles that are neither self-evident nor obviously derivable from the texts under discussion. Perhaps the best place to begin examining these principles lies in Johnson's essays on the epitaph, a genre that, perhaps more than any other, insists upon a lacuna between presence and representation. Johnson acknowledges the existence of this gap when he notes in his early *Essay upon Epitaphs* that the "principal intention of Epitaphs is to perpetuate the examples of virtue, that the tomb of a good man may supply the want of his presence" (*Works*, II: 328). Johnson's later appendix to the "Life of Pope" is a partial reassessment of the positive answer that Johnson gave in his early *Essay* to the question of the imitative nature of the genre, its claim to overcome the interval between life and death, presence and absence. In the appendix, Johnson questions this claim in terms that are empirical and quantitative:

> the difficulty in writing epitaphs is to give a particular and appropriate praise. This, however, is not always to be performed, whatever the diligence or ability of the writer, for the greater part of mankind 'have no character at all', have little that distinguishes them from others equally good or bad, and therefore nothing can be said of them which may not be applied with equal propriety to a thousand more. (*Lives*, III: 263–64)

The difficulty that Johnson identifies here stems from an irremediable conflict between the general and the particular, between the resources of nature and the requirements of art. The characters of "the greater part of mankind" are present but unrepresentable and thus defy the dictum, asserted elsewhere, that "every piece ought to contain in itself whatever is necessary to make it intelligible" (*Lives*, I: 35–36). In this argument, the absence of distinguishing characteristics is not merely a negative awaiting imaginative transformation that will turn it into something positive. What is unrepresentable resists all representation, assimilation, and reappropriation. It poses an unavoidable limit to the writer of epitaphs and thus threatens representation with its other, the unrepresentable.

Of course if this were all that Johnson were content to say about the subject, it would be a fascinating but still essentially marginal observation. Johnson goes on in the same passage, however, to raise a much more radical query about the relation between nature and art in general:

> Nature is not the object of human judgment; for it is in vain to judge where we cannot alter. If by nature is meant, what is commonly called *nature* by the criticks, a just representation of things really existing and actions really performed, nature cannot be properly opposed to *art*; nature being, in this sense, only the best effect of *art*. (*Lives*, III: 255)

The passage constitutes a reassessment of a classical polarity in the history of criticism: the assumed priority of nature to art based on the notion of a temporal, causal order of succession. As has already been seen, this order is reversed in Johnson's account of the reception and subsequent reputation of texts. What is important here is that this order of succession itself is the subject of Johnson's critique of the naïve assumptions of a referential reading. In Johnson, this critique is linked to the claim that nature constitutes an unalterable order of things, a realm that exists beyond the reach of verbal or propositional judgments. The only proper subject for human judgments pertains to the language, conventions, and limits of artistic representation. As for what lies beyond these limits—a "beyond" that encompasses, in Johnson's view, the characters of most human beings—on these matters, one is in no position to form any judgments at all. Hence his quarrel with critics who seek to establish an unassailable ground or origin that would provide a norm by which "just representations" might be measured. Any judgment that sought to locate such a ground in the nature of "things really existing" would fail to account for the problem raised by the term "just." For if the value of a work consisted in the "justness of its representations," then there is no possibility of appealing to a concept of mimesis that would point back to a prior reality beyond the vagaries of artistic production. In this respect, nature that, from the standpoint of common sense, seems to be the origin of art may only be its effect, perhaps because the relation of an imitation to its origin cannot structurally be cut off from its relation to an originating subject. The imitation would always be the work, and, to the extent that a just imitation is natural, it would, "in this sense" at least, be the product of the poet's art.

A reading of this passage suggests just how far Johnson can at times depart from the canons of naïve sense-certainty. At the very least, the notion that nature is only "the best effect of art" draws attention to the fact that mimesis necessarily entails the absence of that which it purports to represent: the phrase "the best effect" itself implies that in art at least nature can at most become a secondary or feigned presence. Such a formulation is by no means incompatible with what Kames termed ideal presence, yet it is bound to raise doubts about the assumptions on which this ideal is founded. In eighteenth-century criticism, the theater had long been the privileged site for the contention that art can somehow reduce a preexistent nature to representation and thus liberate the spectator from disbelief. Indeed, Kames had described "theatrical representation" as the "most powerful" means for effecting "ideal presence." Theatrical representation, as a mode of imitation in which an individual is immediately present to the spectator as an actor replacing a written text, seemed in Kames's view to efface the gap between presence and representation inherent in such modes as "reading and painting" (*Elements of Criticism*, I: 116). Johnson, by contrast, in his famous discussion of the unities in the *Preface* to Shakespeare seems to renounce the more grandiose claims advanced for the theater by enthusiasts of ideal presence. Part of Johnson's argument arises from his generalized conception of the theater; part stems from his obvious reluctance to conceive of delusion as anything more than a potentially dangerous pathology. Unlike Kames and other theorists who conceived of the fusion of presence and representation under the guise of trance, reveries, and waking dream, Johnson was convinced that the waking mind must always resist this seduction into illusion. One way to do so is by denying its existence in the theater. It may be in this spirit that Johnson insists in the *Preface* to Shakespeare that dramatic performance necessarily involves a resemblance that is not an identity: "the truth is, that the spectators are always in their senses and know from the first act to the last, that the stage is always a stage, and that the players are only players" (*Shakespeare*, VII: 77).

This aspect of Johnson's argument needs stressing since two distinguished Johnsonian commentators, David Nichol Smith and Arthur Sherbo, have noted a verbal indebtedness to Kames's *Elements of Criticism* (III: 274–75) in Johnson's arguments against the unities of time and place. But this reading overlooks the possibility that Johnson may be deliberately trying to call attention to his differences with Kames. There is no doubt that Kames presupposes an alternation between ideal presence and reflection that is at odds with Johnson's view that no "dramatic fable in its materiality was ever credible." For Kames, such a perception should only occur "during an interruption of the representation," not during the representation itself. The effect of Johnson's use of Kames's language may thus be to bring about a subtle displacement of Kames's concepts and categories, a shift in which Johnson does not refer to Kames by name but nonetheless challenges certain presuppositions that would otherwise be hidden from view.[8]

This passage also shows very clearly how the emphasis of Johnson's argument had shifted in the twenty or so years since he addressed the issue in the *Rambler* essays, mainly in terms that resemble the Coleridgean notion of a voluntary suspension of disbelief. In *Rambler*, number 156, he holds that since "some delusion must be admitted," it is impossible to determine "where the limits of imagination can be fixed" (*Rambler*, V: 68). Elsewhere, he contends that "while the deception" produced by "an act of imagination, that realises the event, however fictitious . . . lasts," we experience "whatever motions would be excited by the same good or evil happening to ourselves" (*Rambler*, III: 318–19).[9] Yet these need not be regarded as anything more than preliminary formulations of an answer to a question that obviously preoccupied Johnson for many years. There is no reason to suppose that Johnson's argument in the *Preface* to Shakespeare does not represent his final thoughts on the subject.

In no way, moreover, does Johnson's argument in the *Preface* negate, or even minimize, the traditional concern of the theater with imitation. The drama is not unreal or incredible: "it is credited, whenever it moves, as a just picture of a real original" (*Shakespeare*, VII: 78). More importantly, the point at which the drama touches reality is also the point at which it becomes exposed to the knowledge of its own fictionality. The spectator is aware of this as he recognizes not that the "evils" before him are "real evils, but that they are evils to which" he "may be exposed" (*Shakespeare*, VII: 78). In this, he refuses to succumb to what the theater aspires to be: a realm of magic and pretence. Yet the effect of the drama does not reside, alternatively, in his rejection of illusion in favor of a secure, quotidian existence. This would, in effect, be synonymous with the view of critics who, like Addison, held that our delight before a tragic spectacle stems in part from "the Pleasure we receive from the Sense of our own Safety" (*The Spectator*, III: 298). The difficulty with this kind of pleasure is that it threatens to transform the pity and terror that tragedy should elicit into their opposites. To speak of the delight we receive from a sense of our own safety is to refer to an experience that appears to be antithetical to illusion and tragedy.[10] In Johnson's argument, the experience rather emerges from that ambiguous moment in a tragedy when an awareness of the difference between theatrical death and actual life also awakens an awareness of the ever-present possibility of death, as when "a mother weeps over her babe, when she remembers that death may take it from her" (*Shakespeare*, VII: 78). A certain degree of presence must, in other words, be preserved: mingling pity and fear, the spectator's experience does not achieve Kames's state of "ideal presence," yet it is considerably stronger than "reflective remembrance." Just approaching real presence, it taps the recollection that all representation presupposes, yet that constitutes for it a kind of secondary, interior representation that has never actually been present.

It is now possible to see more clearly just how Johnson differs from Kames. As Johnson's own intense response to *Othello* and *King Lear* shows, tragedy still possesses the power to "move," but the efficient source of this power is supplied by what is unrepresented and unrepresentable rather than by the representation itself. The relation between the actors and audience is thereby demystified, making it possible for the spectators to remain secure in their awareness that "the players are merely players." In contrast to Kames's theory, in which the "power of speech" is seen as central to the evocation of "ideal presence," in Johnson's argument, dramatic dialogue is never viewed as being able to confirm its representation as a living, self-present truth and is thereby thrust back into a sense of its own textuality as a performance. Thus Johnson insists that "a dramatick exhibition is a book recited with concomitants that encrease or diminish its effect" and that spectators come to hear "a certain number of lines recited with just gesture and elegant modulation" (*Shakespeare*, VII: 79 and 77). Rather than referring to itself, what is re-cited always refers back to what is being cited, thus emphasizing that it is both the same and different from what it duplicates. Perhaps the most striking aspect of this demystification of performance is the effect it has on one's estimate of the anterior text itself. Disengaged from its dependence upon the performer for its persuasive force, the text is turned back upon its own resources as imitation for its effectiveness. A substitute for something else, dialogue is unable to give the actor a foundation for what he projects except insofar as it can come as near as possible to simulating the familiar conversation that sanctions its existence as dialogue. It is probably this claim that leads Johnson to hold that "familiar comedy is often more powerful in the theater than on the page; imperial tragedy is always less" (*Shakespeare*, VII: 79). Reversing the conventional eighteenth-century emphasis on the superiority of tragedy to comedy as a stage vehicle, Johnson holds that "familiar dialogue" must take precedence over dramatic gesture: "the humour of Petruchio may be heightened by a grimace; but what voice or what gesture can hope to add dignity or force to the soliloquy of *Cato*" (*Shakespeare*, VII: 79).

This is why it seems to be highly misleading to argue, as Wellek has done, that Johnson habitually confuses art and life in his criticism.[11] Even his well-known observation that Shakespeare's dialogue "seems scarcely to claim the merit of fiction" still maintains, in the adverb "scarcely," a slender margin of difference between the two. Considered as part of his demystification of dramatic performance, Johnson's praise of Shakespeare's drama as a "just representation of general nature" takes place in a broader attempt to articulate a sense of drama that preserves rather than abolishes the distance proper to it. By way of contrast, Pope's contention, in his *Preface* to Shakespeare's *Works,* that Shakespeare "is not so much an Imitator as an Instrument of Nature" and that his "*Characters* are so much Nature her self, that 'tis a sort of injury to call them by so distant a name as Copies of her" portrays an ideal drama in which there is no distance between presence and representation.[12] Original and imitation are simultaneous, Shakespeare's characters being at the same time new creations and copies of those creations. In contrast to the extravagance of such claims, Johnson's argument that drama is credited as "a just picture of a real original," often and rightly considered to be mimetic in its implications, can also be seen as a conservative attempt to preserve a sense of the distance and difference implicit in such terms as "just" and "picture."

Johnson's polemic has considerable force when read in the context of Sir Joshua Reynolds's theory of painting. It is Johnson's distinction to have emphasized the importance of difference and distance in representation and thus to have laid the foundation for Reynolds's extension of his argument. Although never explicitly mentioned, Johnson's mode of reasoning reverberates throughout Reynolds's discussion of imitation in the *Discourses on Art.* According to Reynolds

> Painting is not only not to be considered as an imitation, operating by deception, but that it is, and ought to be, in many points of view, and strictly speaking, no imitation at all of external nature.

In a way that resembles Johnson's "just picture," Reynolds's art of painting is neither wholly representational, nor entirely nonrepresentational in the twentieth-century sense of those terms. On the contrary, there are actually two different arts of painting, arts that are guided by "two different principles, in which the one follows nature, the other varies it, and sometimes departs from it." In the latter art, painting is not to be thought of as wholly abstract or nonrepresentational in the modern sense; nor is it to be seen as governed by a principle that excludes individual particulars in an eighteenth-century sense. Such a principle guides the doctrine of *la belle nature* that Reynolds puts forth elsewhere in the *Discourses*, but here this doctrine is seen as only another, more elevated form of imitation. In place of this highly conventional notion of *la belle nature*, Reynolds envisages the second art as subject to variation, to an unpredictable, and hence pleasurable, play of difference. There is, of course, no distinction between text and performance in a painting and thus no need to insist that painting must rely on its resources as mimesis in order to guarantee its effectiveness. This is probably why Reynolds reverses Johnson's preference for comedy over tragedy. In Reynolds's view, history painting is like tragedy in the sense that it is an art that departs from imitation, while genre painting is a lower, inferior art that, like comedy, conforms closely to an anterior reality:

> the lower kind of Comedy or Farce, like the inferior style of painting, the more naturally it is represented, the better; but the higher appears to me to aim no more at imitation, so far as it belongs to any thinglike deception, or

> to expect that the spectators should think that the events there represented are really passing before them, than Raffaelle in his Cartoons, or Poussin in his Sacraments, expected it to be believed, even for a moment, that what they exhibited were real figures.[13]

Yet the basic principle behind Reynolds's argument is the same as that of Johnson: within it, the classical association of representation with *trompe l'oeil* illusionism is replaced by a theory in which the "higher sort" of painting at least is subject to a differential play of presence and absence, of representation and abstraction.

Reynolds's theory of painting, although an independent development of Johnson's ideas, is perhaps less thoroughgoing in its critique of mimetic illusionism than Johnson's conception of art. In Johnson's argument, not only comedy and tragedy but also every kind of poetry is subject to the interval that separates presence from representation: "It is false," Johnson insists, "that any representation is mistaken for reality" (*Shakespeare*, VII: 76). What Johnson here calls a representation "in its materiality" must of logical necessity be distinguished from reality, or it ceases to be a representation at all. No matter how complete the illusion, to break with the founding difference of representation is impossible, and this impossibility is what lends point to Johnson's assertion.

What is perhaps most striking in this regard, however, is Johnson's insistence that this principle applies to all works, even those in which the "representation" is "more powerful than the reality" (*Lives*, III: 247), for such works are still subject to the difference that makes representation possible. It is precisely this argument that distinguishes Johnson's position from that of David Hume. Adopting the criteria of "vivacity" as a way of distinguishing between the immediate perception of objects in the actual world and their representation in memories and fictions, Hume holds, in the *Treatise on Human Nature,* that "tho' the imagination may not, in appearance, be so much mov'd," in the case of the former, "there is always something more forcible and real in its actions than in the fervors of poetry and eloquence."[14] Poetry and rhetoric, in short, stand apart from the tacit continuities of experience and belief that we depend upon in our sense of waking reality. Most important of these continuities is the element of force or vivacity that always relates ideas back to a present impression. The difference between presence and representation is preserved in this argument but at the cost of confining presence exclusively to sense perception. Art is therefore apprehended as nothing more than an inferior, pallid replica of the living present and presence of experience. This would be the consequence of any theory that dispensed altogether with the illusion of mimetic realism while continuing to talk of the force or vivacity of sense impressions, as if they derived from some unassailable external source in the nature of things. So it is not hard to see why Johnson, by contrast, clearly allows for the possibility that a representation can, on occasion, be more vivid, more intense, more powerful than empirical reality itself. Without making a similar distinction, Hume necessarily relegates art to an epistemologically parasitic and secondary status.

* * *

To reverse Hume's principle and to assert the possibility that representation can on occasion be more powerful than reality can, of course, create a very marked shift in critical assumptions. One such line of argument, as we has been seen, was advanced by Addison who contended, in the "Pleasures of the Imagination" series, that "airy fictions," because of their charm, can come to seem more pleasing to the reader than truth. What these fictions evoke is a false presence, a chimera that functions as a supplement for a lack of reality, an absence that continually threatens their existence. Addison uses the term "pleasing Delusion" to define this false presence in terms of Locke's secondary qualities. Here the consequence is to dissociate the aesthetic sign from any claim to truth and to elevate it to an airborne and wholly enclosed realm of rococo illusion. Once the credibility of this kind of imaginative illusion is dissipated, however, it will not, like a pleasant dream, simply fade away. It will rather survive as an empty simulacrum, incurring disillusion and a recognition of its hollowness. This is essentially what Johnson argues in his critique of poetical fictions. His position is strikingly at odds with that of Addison, yet his insistence upon the referential status of poetry should not be seen merely as a pedestrian opposition to poetic mythology. Rather, it is inseparable from the view that fiction is unable to protect itself from the exposure of its own falsity. Indeed, by insisting upon the distaste attendant upon the mind's discovery of the error of its illusions, Johnson may simply be repeating, from an opposite direction, an Addisonian terminology of perception whose inadequacy Johnson is bent on exposing. Johnson's description of our response to Gray's sister odes recalls Addison's comments on poetical fictions:

> we are every where entertained with pleasing Shows and Apparitions, we discover imaginary Glories in the Heavens, and in the Earth, and see some of this Visionary Beauty poured out upon the whole Creation; but what a

> rough unsightly Sketch of Nature should we be entertained with, did all her Colouring disappear, and the several Distinctions of Light and Shade vanish? In short, our Souls are at present delightfully lost and bewildered in a pleasing Delusion, and we walk about like the Enchanted Hero in a Romance, who sees beautiful Castles, Woods and Meadows; and at the same time hears the warbling of Birds, and the purling of Streams; but upon the finishing of some secret Spell, the fantastick Scene breaks up, and the disconsolate Knight finds himself on a barren Heath, or in a solitary Desart. (*The Spectator*, III: 546–47)

Ironically, from Johnson's perspective, it is the very scene of the barren heath that would elicit delight from the knight, while the beautiful illusions would produce only revulsion. Because Johnson simply reverses the point of view of Addison's fable, the knight, in his interpretation, would no longer be disconsolate but only angry, recognizing that the images he once admired are not phantoms of delight but products of the mind's darkness rather than its dawn. Losing their origin in a plenitude of the mind present to itself, such images have become reduced to nothingness, their illusion completely dissolved, leaving in its wake only falsehood and ugliness: "Where truth is sufficient to fill the mind," Johnson writes in the "Life of Gray," "fiction is worse than useless" (*Lives*, III: 437–38).

Here as elsewhere in the *Lives*, it would be wrong to assume that Johnson is simply staking out a dogmatic position. Certainly this has been the assumption of many readers, for whom Johnson has been seen as upholding a doctrinaire commitment to commonsense reality. But this notion should not go unquestioned, for Johnson praises Pope's introduction of poetic mythology into *The Rape of the Lock*. In Johnson's opinion, Pope's invention of the sylphs is justified by its novelty and by a notion of art as play, whereby Gray is seen as defending his fictions as a "revival" of past beliefs. But because they lack the animating power of actual belief, the "revival" of such fictions not only fails to persuade but actually "disgusts with an apparent and unconquerable falsehood." The inability of these "fictions" to enchant, even when they are recognized as "fictions," means, in effect, that *le vraisemblance* now becomes indistinguishable from *la verité*. Imagination, Johnson believes, is capable of transcending the world of fact only in moments of comic inventiveness such as *The Rape of the Lock*; more often, it succeeds only so long as it is content to respect the boundary that divides fictional entities from the world of nature.

Johnson's argument is, from one point of view, a means of examining the rival claims of fiction and truth within the framework of a rhetorical theory of poetry. Thus a pastoral fiction, such as Gay's *The Shepherd's Week*, according to Johnson, is convincing (i.e., pleasurable) to the extent that it becomes "a just representation of men and manners." Such a representation can be seen as providing the continuity of interest, the basic assumptions about men and manners that sustain our response to the fictional illusion. The only virtue of such a fiction, Johnson implies, is that it functions in much the same way as an argument: it is persuasive insofar as it is truthful. The power of fiction to make beautiful what is ugly and to keep alive the ideal in a brazen world proves utterly incapable of withstanding this demand for truth.

Johnson is willing, of course, to concede a momentary, fortuitous appeal to illusion, but is reluctant to go beyond this because he, more sharply than other critics of his time, saw the need to maintain a clear-cut distinction between between pleasure arrived at through novelty and pleasure gained through a repetition of what is traditional. It was this distinction at the level of theory, quite as much as his religious views, that led Johnson to repudiate the entire Renaissance tradition of poetic mythology and pastoral. Indeed, it is his assumption that what is traditional is "easily imitated" and, when not rooted in truth, is subject to a monotony grounded in a reiteration of the same. It is thus inconceivable that Johnson would ever have been able to accept Hume's contention that "we have been so much accustom'd to the names of Mars, Jupiter, Venus, that in the same manner as education infixes any opinion, the constant repetition of these ideas makes them enter into the mind with facility, and prevail upon the fancy, without influencing the judgment."[15] For Johnson, this account would be wholly inadequate to the task of explaining how the mind acquires or retains ideas. Far from fixing opinions, constant repetition only succeeds in arousing aversion: "to shew [the classical deities] as they have already been shewn is to disgust by repetition" (*Lives*, II: 68).

Of course it might be argued that any such juxtaposition ignores the crucial difference in the roles these thinkers are performing. Thus Hume raises general epistemological questions and subscribes to a thoroughgoing empiricism, while Johnson is concerned with issues in the province of language, imagery, and poetic convention that—as he would certainly insist—must be treated quite apart from theoretical questions. But, in fact, this objection loses force if one asks what reasons he could provide for the claim that the classical deities disgust through repetition. Indeed, what Johnson finds at work in the process by which one apprehends ideas is the very reverse of a constant reiteration of the same. Our delight in poetry, as in life, stems from a process of defamiliarization, one that frustrates and baffles any desire for a recurrence of the expected. The surest way to avoid tiring the mind is to follow Johnson's cardinal principle and determine whether or not the fiction embedded in a narrative or dramatic action has as its *raison d'être* a just representation of men and manners. Thus it follows, according to Johnson, that "there is something in the poetical Arcadia so remote from known reality and speculative possibility, that we can never support its representations through a long work" (*Lives*, II: 284). Poetic mythology is not completely dispelled, but it is rather displaced into an earlier stage of existence or consciousness, where its images still possess the freshness of novelty: "such scenes please barbarians and children in the dawn of life, but will, for the most part, be thrown away, as men grow wise, and nations grow learned" (*Lives* , II: 284).

In Johnson, this position is reached only in the mature criticism of the *Lives of the Poets*. When compared to the massive pronouncements of the *Lives*, the essays in the *Rambler* seem much more equivocal and nostalgic. This strain is very marked in *Rambler*, number 151, for example, where Johnson describes our loss of confidence in poetical fictions as a progress from illusion to disillusion:

> while the judgment is yet uninformed and unable to compare the draughts of fiction with their originals, we are delighted with improbable adventures, impractible virtues, and inimitable characters: But, in proportion as we have more opportunities of acquainting ourselves with living nature, we are sooner disgusted with copies in which there appears no resemblance. We first discard absurdity and impossibility, but at last become cold and insensible to the charms of falsehood, however specious, and from the imitations of truth, which are never perfect, transfer our affection to truth itself. (*Rabler*, V: 39–40)

The problem lies in the nature of the state of mind that is seen as replacing our initial naïve delight in fiction. The mental activity that Johnson describes is not a mature marriage of fancy and judgment. On the contrary, it is presented as an impoverished process in which the mind derives pleasure exclusively from

> comparing arguments, stating propositions, disentangling perplexities, clearing ambiguities, and deducing consequences. The painted vales of imagination are deserted, and our intellectual activity is exercised in winding through the labyrinths of fallacy, and toiling with firm and cautious steps up the narrow tracks of demonstration. Whatever may lull vigilance, or mislead attention, is contemptuously rejected, and every disguise in which error may be concealed, is carefully observed, till by degrees a cer-

> tain number of incontestable or unsuspected propositions are established, and at last concatenated into arguments, or compacted into systems.
> At length weariness succeeds to labour, and the mind lies at ease in the contemplation of her own attainments, without any desire of new conquests or excursions. (*Rambler*, V: 40)

If the fancy is shown as ineffectual in comparing "the draughts of fictions with their originals," so the strenuous exertions of the judgment that replaces it make the "weariness" that "succeeds to labour" seem all but inevitable. The process of distinguishing truth from falsehood (or from fiction) is thus seen as a process of extricating the mind from a labyrinth, of climbing cautiously and laboriously up the "narrow tracks" of a ladder or path. Yet this argument is itself embedded in a narrative that provides the context and seeming rationale for its unfolding. The fact that this unfolding is not from a naïve illusion to a lucid disillusion but from a fancy recognized from the outset as a source of delight to a judgment that is defined as a tiresome and potentially oppressive mental activity makes the shift seem ambiguous.

The same ambivalence is even more evident in Johnson's allegory of truth and falsehood in *Rambler*, number 96. Here, the consequence of the descent of a personified "Truth" from "heavenly palaces" to earth is her discovery that "she obstructed her own progress by the severity of her aspect, and the solemnity of her dictates" (*Rambler*, IV: 152). This is why she subsequently dons a robe woven by the Muses in the loom of Pallas: only by wearing this robe can she attain the acceptance that her stern visage repels. Yet Truth's robe of "Fiction" suggests what is also suggested by the "loose and changeable" robe of Falsehood: namely the doubleness through which the minds and hearts of human beings must be won. It is not only Falsehood but also Truth who, with the connivance of her father Jupiter, is forced to resort to strategem and duplicity. Indeed, the allegory's complicated movement of simplicity and doubleness, concealment and disclosure, may reflect Johnson's own uncertainty about what must be surrendered to fiction in poetry.

* * *

Fiction thus defined in *Rambler*, number 96, is the determinate ground of truth, a realm of narrative or dramatic action through concepts and images that can be made comprehensible to the reader or spectator. This attitude is not hard to understand when truth is defined as referential, as an adequate matching up or correspondence between poetical fiction and reality. The precise nature of this matching up—whether of abstract general ideas, of concrete images, or of a combination of the two—gave rise to a long-running debate among eighteenth-century critics. But their versions have at least this much in common: they all assume that poems can be tested or verified by ascertaining their fit with the real world. It was the obvious limitations of this correspondence theory of poetic truth that is subject to scrutiny in Johnson's appendix to the "Life of Pope." But there is a second, less obvious concept of mimesis to which the argument of *Rambler*, number 96, might also apply. This is an expressive doctrine of truth as a poetical enthusiasm that excites "in every susceptible breast the same emotions that were felt by the Author."[16] Such emotions, as proponents conceived it, would be more authentic—closer to their origin in the originating genius of the poet—than any truth attainable by a mere copying of external reality.

A careful reading of *Rambler*, number 96, suggests that Johnson may also be concerned with this second, distinctively expressive doctrine of mimesis. And it is perhaps in the context of the claims made for the identification of the reader with the emotions of the author by advocates of this doctrine that one should view Johnson's emphasis upon the unique language of the genuine poet, the special and sometimes foreign character of his discourse. In Johnson's criticism of theories of original genius, this language occupies a status analogous to that of poetical fiction in his allegory of Truth and Falsehood in *Rambler*, number 96. Like the robe of fiction worn by Truth, the miraculously original, yet alien stylistic garments of a Milton, Spenser, or Thomson compel admiration; yet at the same time, these garments interpose something of a textual barrier between the author and reader, constitute a new language whose characters the reader can never fully master. Style, understood in this sense, becomes, at least in part, the stumbling block of expression, a textual domain in which the ineradicable originality of poetic genius asserts itself intransigently. The poet's invention, understood as a storehouse of new scenes and events that can be rendered indifferently in common language, remains useless unless it is unfolded within the privileged apparatus of style. Thomson's poetical diction performs precisely this function; it is not merely an obstacle to an appreciation of his descriptions but the medium through which they must be apprehended—or misapprehended. To convey a sense of the power of Milton's style, Johnson avers that "his call is obeyed without resistance, the reader feels himself in captivity to a higher and a nobler mind" (*Lives*, 1: 190). Such a captivity should not be confused with the sympathetic identification extolled by proponents of the doctrine of original genius. On the contrary, the word "captivity" suggests blindness as well as insight; it conveys a sense of bondage in which the weak mind is held in thrall to the power of the strong. There is nothing in this kind of bondage that entails a union between the author and reader. On the contrary, it implies a measure of distance and awe in which the reader is kept firmly in his place.

Allowing for the obvious differences in temperament, one can see why Johnson rarely adopts the Longinian accents of advocates of the doctrine of original genius. To seek the kind of immediacy in which the reader achieves an immediate or self-present access to the author's emotions is always to imply that the text points back to some kind of originary truth that transcends and effaces the language in which it is cast. When Johnson raises the issue of sympathetic identification, it is always in the context of the special problems raised by language, genre, and empirical evidence. It is significant that Johnson should be especially interested in such genres as the epitaph and portrait, for these are genres that seem to invite sympathetic identification with the subject but do so vicariously because the subject is no longer present to us. "Every man is always present to himself," Johnson argues in *Idler*, number 45, "and has, therefore, little need of his own resemblance; nor can desire it, but for the sake of those whom he loves, and by whom he hopes to be remembred" (*Idler, Adventurer*, 140). It is because he knows that the representation of character is the alternative to the confirming immediacy of self-reflective presentation that Johnson emphasizes the importance of these genres. Yet the images they embody are never meant to be taken as a means of negating absence. Indeed the very motives that propel them into existence—a desire to praise and memorialize—also testify to their surrogate status as signs that seek to take the place of the absent and recall something they can never recapture.

All the same, it is difficult (indeed, may be impossible) to avoid seeing art as a compensatory reduplication, one that renews and, therefore, blurs the line between fiction and truth. In the opening paragraphs of his essay on biography in *Rambler*, number 60, where Johnson speaks of "an act of imagination" that can place us "in the condition of him whose fortune we contemplate" (*Rambler*, III: 318–19), he reveals how easily the vocabulary of "parallel circumstances" can merge with that of identification. Here Johnson seems to affirm the "act of imagination" as a "deception" that enables the self to merge with the other as an exact reflection, a perfect double. Distinctions between inside and outside, private and public, substance and decoration, seem to claim for biography a power beyond that of history and imperial tragedy to achieve this kind of specular identification. In the early part of the essay, Johnson supports this claim, declaring that biography can transcend the separation between fiction and truth and thus bring about a union between self and other. Yet it is noteworthy that Johnson refuses to allow this argument to dominate the essay. While Johnson never overtly repudiates the oppositions that guide the opening paragraphs of *Rambler*, number 60, he devotes the latter half of the essay to an argument that undermines these oppositions and discovers in biography the very same characteristics that prevented history and tragedy from eliciting this fusion. Thus Johnson notes that biographers "rarely afford any other account than might be collected from publick papers," and "if now and then they condescend to inform the world of particular facts, they are not always so happy as to select the most important" (*Rambler*, III: 322). It might appear that these strictures are programmatic in intention, meant to reconstitute the procedures governing biographical research and thus to expand the scope of the genre. But this argument encounters further resistance—comes up against de facto problems in the nature of its endeavor—that renders any such expansion of the genre quite problematic. The author who waits until his subject is dead before writing is at a serious disadvantage, it turns out, for "the incidents which give excellence to biography are of a volatile and evanescent kind, such as soon escape the memory, and are rarely transmitted by tradition." The biographer "with personal knowledge" of his subject is, however, no better equipped than the historical biographer for

> we know how few can portray a living acquaintance, except by his most prominent and observable particularities, and the grosser features of his mind; and it may be easily imagined how much of this little knowledge may be lost in imparting it, and how soon a succession of copies will lose all resemblance of the original. (*Rambler*, III: 323)

It is precisely at the point where Johnson seeks to establish the factual foundation of biography, then, that he has to recognize the role of observation as the sole means by which such facts can be transmitted to the reader. But the inadequacy of observation and the partiality of the observer are sufficient to render this project suspect. It is here that Johnson's theory of biography—in spite of its reformist aspirations—undergoes a transformation that turns its inside into an outside, its private realm into a public one. By the very end of the essay, biography can no longer be said to possess any advantages over history and imperial tragedy.

Thus it is probably not a coincidence that in a later essay, *Idler*, number 84, Johnson makes explicit the parallel between biography and tragedy that he had initially disavowed in *Rambler*, number 60:

> he that recounts the life of another, commonly dwells most upon conspicuous events, lessens the familiarity of his tale to increase its dignity, shews his favourite at a distance decorated and magnified like the ancient actors in their tragick dress, and endeavours to hide the man that he may produce a hero. (*Idler, Adventurer*, 262)

The biographer is not sufficiently close to the "life of another," not sufficiently impartial to overcome the "distance" that characterizes such public genres as history and tragedy. The writer who "tells his own story," Johnson now goes on to argue, is in the best position to narrow the gap separating living reality from secondary duplication.[17] What needs to be emphasized in this regard is that the memoirist is not seen as encountering the same kind of obstacles as the biographer. But it is also very clear to any reader of Johnson that the autobiographer's investigations cannot, for him, be conceived in terms of a totalizing model, an access to a mode of immediate, self-present self-knowledge that will transcend the limits of human understanding. In fact, Johnson is unwilling to go beyond the declaration that "impartiality may be expected with equal confidence from him that relates the passages of his own life, as from him that delivers the transactions of another" (*Idler, Adventurer*, 263). Moreover, this impartiality is always threatened with contamination by "self-love," and, even though Johnson holds that "all are on the watch against its artifices," he also concedes that "he that writes an apology for a single action, to confute an accusation, or recommend himself to favour, is indeed always to be suspected of favouring his own cause" (*Idler, Adventurer*, 264).

This essay on the literary possibilities of autobiography, although lukewarm in its endorsements, is perhaps the closest Johnson ever came to affirming the possibility of transcending the limits of a faulty or partial understanding. The memoirist who withstands the temptation to "partiality" and "self-love" is immediately present to him-/herself in a way that is denied to the historian and biographer. Yet the arguments that Johnson advances in favor of autobiography are cast in such a way as to suggest that not even he was fully convinced of their validity. To recount the events of one's own life is the result of an endeavor that is made after the events occurred, not simultaneously as they unfold. In other words, the memoirist's narrative of the events of his or her own life is never immediate. In

Idler, number 84, Johnson implicitly recognizes this but locates the nonimmediacy of autobiography in our "partiality" toward our own thoughts and actions. The *amour propre* of the memoirist is a measure of the distance that discourse interposes between itself and the imaginative sympathy of the reader.

* * *

We are now, perhaps, in a better position to grasp the nature of Johnson's rugged independence, his opposition to some of the major themes of eighteenth-century criticism. But to leave it at that—having registered Johnson's disagreements with proponents of the doctrine of *enargeia*, poetical fiction, or original genius—would still be to miss one of the most revealing aspects of his place in eighteenth-century critical thought. For it is not just a question of demonstrating Johnson's resistance to the prevailing aesthetic fashions of his day. It is important to notice also that some of the crucial issues in eighteenth-century epistemology are given a distinctive interpretation in Johnson's writings, even where there is no evidence of influence, direct or indirect. In general, this has to do with the powers and limits of the human mind. In Johnson's observations on human consciousness in the *Rambler*, *Idler*, and *Adventurer* essays, perception and reflection play roles that would effectively prevent "representation" from ever becoming "mistaken for reality."

Clearly there is a sense in which this subject precedes and subsumes all the others discussed in this chapter. For Johnson has a good deal to say about the human mind, and what he says must affect our reading of his work at every level of analysis. In fact, there is evidence that Johnson conceives of perception and reflection in a manner that is different from the way they are defined in the writings of theorists who embraced an aesthetics of presence. Thus Addison's distinction between the primary pleasures of the imagination derived from perceived objects and secondary pleasures arising from remembered and absent objects is reminiscent, as noted, of Locke's distinction between sensation and reflection. In Addison's theory, the secondary pleasures of the imagination seem to transcend their nominal secondariness in becoming a separate realm of pure illusion. Kames goes even further, claiming, as we seen, that, in tragedy and epic, memory can transcend "reflective remembrance" in approximating a state of ideal presence. The logic of these arguments presupposes the unity of an experience immediately present to itself. Ideal presence must be produced in the undivided unity of perception or its reduplication in imagination or memory, so as to be exempted from intrusion by the agency of reflection. Thus David Hume argues that "every distinct perception which enters into the composition of the mind, is a distinct existence, and is different, and distinguishable from every other perception, either contemporary or successive."[18] Johnson, by way of contrast, is careful never to claim this naïve unity of perception or its imaginative reduplication. In fact, the act of perception is never immediate or distinct in Johnson's view, but is inseparable from the act of reflection. Thus in *Rambler*, number 80, he argues that our sense of delight is in a great measure comparative and arises at once from the sensations that we feel, and those which we remember:

> Thus ease after torment is pleasure for a time, and we are very agreeably recreated, when the body, chilled with the weather, is gradually recovering its natural tepidity; but the joy ceases when we have forgot the cold, we must fall below ease again, if we desire to rise above it, and purchase new felicity by voluntary pain. It is therefore not unlikely that however the fancy may be amused with the description of regions in which no wind is heard but the gentle zephir, and no scenes are displayed but vallies enammelled with unfading flowers, and woods waving their perennial verdure, we should soon grow weary of uniformity, find our thoughts languish for want of other subjects, call on heaven for our wonted round of seasons, and think ourselves liberally recompensed for the inconveniences of summer and winter, by new perceptions of the calmness and mildness of the intermediate variations. (*Rambler*, IV: 56–57)

Such is the entropic impulse, which permeates every aspect of existence and which threatens to reduce distinct and successive perceptions to a wearying repetition of the same idea. The only effective means of resistance is a mode of comparison that insists upon the unity of perception and reflection and consequently aligns itself with an integrated rather than an atomistic model of human understanding.

Of course, it might be argued that what is involved here is just a more sophisticated version of Imlac's claim concerning "that hunger of the imagination which preys incessantly upon life" in *Rasselas*. But this line of argument ignores the fact that comparison, as a mode of apprehension in which past and present are combined, seems to deny the power claimed for perception by eighteenth-century empiricsts when they describe it as a source of authenticating presence. We experience pleasure in our apprehension of the external world, but this pleasure, like its opposite, pain, is a compound of presence and absence rather than a pure plenitude that unites perception to its object. Curiously enough, one can find what looks like a strong statement of exactly this position in Locke's *An Essay Concerning*

Human Understanding, in which he contended that "the removal or lessening of a pain is considered and operates, as a pleasure: and the loss or diminish of a pleasure as a pain." By contrast, it is Edmund Burke who denied Locke's contention, maintaining that one can "discern clearly that there are positive pains and pleasures, which do not at all depend on each other." Hume, needless to say, agreed with Burke, holding that "pain and pleasure, grief and joy, passions and sensations, succeed each other, and never all exist at the same time."[19]

So Johnson's position is clearly a part of an ongoing debate in eighteenth-century philosophy. More specifically, Johnson repudiates the notion—so vital to Hume and followers of his radical empiricism—that the present moment is an undivided unity of perception. This, at least, seems the most obvious interpretation of a passage from *Rambler*, number 41, in which Johnson holds that the present moment is not a present at all, but a process of reinscriptions of the effects of the past combined with anticipations of the future: "almost all that we can be said to enjoy is past or future; the present is in perpetual motion, leaves us as soon as it arrives, ceases to be present before its presence is well perceived, and is only known to have existed by the effects which it leaves behind" (*Rambler*, III: 223–24). One could read this as a statement in Johnson's best moralizing mode, that is to say, as having to do with the importance of acknowledging the swift passing of time. Such a reading would be consistent with everything Johnson has to say on this commonplace topic. But it is also in such passages as this one that Johnson recasts the argument in epistemological terms. What is significant, indeed, is that the comparitive activity evoked here can be construed in terms that are spatial as well as temporal. The mind that reflects at the same time that it perceives is a mind that can be aware that the stage is merely a stage even as it observes the dramatic action within.

When Johnson turns from the present to the past or the future, he invariably uses the verb "represent" to refer to whatever the mind holds up to inspection. I place the word in quotation marks because this aspect of consciousness acquires a distinctive meaning in Johnson's lexicon as opposed to what might simply be "present" to the mind. When Johnson writes that "we represent to ourselves the pleasures of some future possession, and suffer our thoughts to dwell attentively upon it, till it has wholly ingrossed the imagination" (*Rambler*, III: 93), he is referring to a possession that is defined as much by its absence as by its presence. Neither anticipation, nor recollection, nor temporal immediacy in the here and now ever ultimately constitutes a real simultaneity in Johnson's moral psychology. The closing off of the moment, whether past, present, or future, can only be accomplished at the expense of its multiplicity, in the name of false presence and delusion. Johnson's alternative to the complexity of experience is not a real alternative, therefore, because it is posed in terms of a pathological suppression of difference.

Yet even as Johnson conceives of delusion as an aberration, he also envisages it as constituting an ever-present threat to the conscious mind. To the extent that "imagination" predominates over "reason," the mind is capable of sundering perception from reflection, thus erasing the difference between image and object. Johnson is far from alone in this view; his analysis of delusion participates in a common cultural perception that Michel Foucault saw exemplified in the character of Don Quixote. In the eighteenth century, according to Foucault, the quixotic madman "is Different only in so far as he is unaware of Difference."[20] Thus Dennis explains that "the warmer the Imagination is, the more present the Things are to us of which we draw the Images; and, therefore, when once the Imagination is so inflam'd, as to get the better of the Understanding, there is no Difference between the Images and the Things themselves; as we see, for Example, in Fevers and Madmen."[21] Unlike Kames's benign "ideal presence," this mode of delusion is not confined to the merging of representation and presence but can also engender fictions that, like those of Addison, may have no objects or only unreal objects. The thrust of Johnson's version of this argument is apparent in the recurrent imagery of elevation in his moral writings: "airy delusions," like the airy fictions Johnson condemns, produce as well as reproduce and thus lay bare the element of deception implicit in all eighteenth-century theories of *enargeia*. What the deluded spectator actually experiences is never the presence of an object but only an airy image, a simulacrum that substitutes for the former in its absence. What the spectator envisions is never the "reality" behind the representation, but its illusory repetition or a substitute in the distorted mirror of his mind. "The state of elevation" above reason and truth deceives the eye by engendering an image that may, or may not, conform to the object it putatively imitates. Through the imagery of elevation, Johnson thematizes the predicament of a fancy that has severed itself from the very reality it has supposedly reduplicated.

Yet to see through the phantasms of the mind is not necessarily to renounce them. Where Kames and other eighteenth-century critics see the visions, reveries, and waking dreams of the spectator/enthusiast as pleasing delusions that will vanish once the curtain has fallen or the book has closed, Johnson sees these delusions as aberrations that to some extent are inextricably mingled with all our waking thoughts.

It is clear that this contention, if accepted, would cast considerable doubt upon a certain strain of early modern philosophy: the idea that consciousness can attain knowledge through an effort of self-mastery that somehow frees the mind from merely contingent illusions. What is wrong with this idea is that it rests upon a confusion between logic and philosophy, such that truths are presented as being arrived at through a species of inward cerebration rather than following one from another in a chain of inductive or deductive arguments. It is worth emphasizing that Johnson eventually came to reject a version of the Coleridgean contention that there can be a "voluntary lending of the Will" to the "suspension of one of its own operations (i.e., that of comparison and consequent decision concerning the reality of any sensuous Impressions)."[22] According to Johnson, we would never be in a position to exercise such an operation, since it presupposes the availability of a high ground from which we could establish an absolute power over our minds. Of course the distinction between logic and psychology doesn't figure expressly in Johnson's argument, belonging as it does to a later (twentieth-century) framework of inquiry. Instead, Johnson gives an implicitly pessimistic answer to the question of the psychological grounds of certain knowledge. But perhaps he was bound to do this. For, as is known from the *Prayers and Meditations*, Johnson wants desperately to regulate the imagination by reason, but he also admits that "there is no man . . . who can regulate his attention wholly by his will, and whose ideas will come and go at his command" (*Rasselas*, XLIV: 150). Thus, if Johnson sees perception and reflection as unified in a single act of apprehension, he also finds reason and imagination as blended in an unstable, perpetually shifting and virtually undetectable amalgam of illusion and reality. Agostino Lombardo has described "the narrative method" of *Rasselas* as "inevitably ironic, centering on a constant process of construction and destruction, affirmation and negation."[23] Lombardo's account has a significance that extends beyond *Rasselas*, for it points to Johnson's acute sensitivity to the unfortunate tendency of the mind to relapse into what it has exposed and thus to regenerate what it seems to undermine. The "luscious" falsehoods of the fancy are too pleasurable to be confined easily within "the limits of sober plausibility." Or to put it somewhat differently, absolute clarity, the ironic exposure of "fictions as fictions" through their unending deflation, proves impossible to achieve. Thus there is always the possibility within Johnson's theater of the mind that the condition of consciousness, in which one is always aware that a stage is a stage and the actors merely actors, may give way to its opposite, the deluded belief that the setting and the characters are real.

Johnson thus finds it not only possible, but necessary, to accord to delusion a power to engender a false presence that is at odds with the complexity of the conscious moment and that persists alongside it, although generally subordinated to it. Even though Johnson flatly asserts in the *Preface* to Shakespeare that "representation is never mistaken for reality," there is an argument implicit everywhere in his writings, that the suspension of disbelief is involuntary, that it arises from a present incapacity—determined most often by the pressure of personal circumstances—to reach a clear distinction between illusion and reality. What is needed in Johnson's view is no more—and of greater importance, no less—than an awareness that delusion gains in power and in mastery of the mind to the extent that it conceals itself. The sense of this false presence is never completely present, for it effaces itself in the measure that it dominates the mind.

I have pursued this point at some length because it helps one to grasp what is at stake not only in Johnson's theory of poetic representation but also in his more explicitly ethical writings. The one overarching purpose of both strands of his thought is to vindicate the claims of rationality in all matters touching on human thought and practice. And he believes it basic to any such endeavor that reason should fulfill its implicit potentiality and not be subject to the distorting mirrors of illusion and false presence. Hence, it is the main premise of his moral writing that truth can only be arrived at through a rigorous and unrelenting scrutiny of delusory ideas, and following from this, that there is nothing in the order of experience—including the experience of poetry—that doesn't conform to this inherent structure of rational necessity. Anyone who denies the latter thesis would be placed in the untenable position of claiming to have grounds for asserting that illusion is, in some aspect or form, preferable to reality. All of which can be derived from Imlac's conclusion that "all power of fancy over reason is a degree of insanity." This is why Johnson takes it as axiomatic that there must exist something in human consciousness that enables the mind to distinguish representation from reality. In this respect, his argument finds a parallel in the writings of certain twentieth-century theorists, especially those who (like Bertolt Brecht) have challenged any form of illusionistic doctrine as regards questions of dramatic representation.

5
Recollection, Curiosity, and the Theory of Affects

I have been arguing that present-day critical theory still needs to work out the full implications of Johnson's thinking, even in areas where his ideas seem most conventional and unproblematic. Take the case of Johnson's understanding of the way we respond to poetry and painting. For Abrams—and for many other commentators—there is a limit point of argument in all of Johnson's critical writings at which critical judgment has to recognize its prior commitment to a certain kind of pragmatic, rhetorical enterprise, a commitment that cannot be subject to further scrutiny since it provides the unreflective, commonsense basis for Johnson's own expert judgments of particular authors and texts. Most often one finds this argument put forward by those who regard Johnson's critical assumptions as little more than an orthodox restatement of the Horatian doctrine that poetry should delight and instruct. The most obvious modern heirs of Horatian thinking are those commonsense reader-response critics who see little virtue in producing ever more sophisticated interpretations of individual poems but rather believe that one should follow Johnson's example in concentrating on the way readers actually respond to literary texts.

In fact, as has already been implied, there is a different way of reading Johnson's criticism, one that takes in account the full implications of his epistemology. It is on the basis of his argument that perception is temporalized—that our ideas are a compound of sensation and reflection—that Johnson effectively disqualifies any immediate sensuous response to works of art. In this aspect of his thinking, Johnson provides a needful corrective to the widespread notion that poetry provides access to a simple form of delight. Indeed, Johnson's major premise—that "the present is gone as soon as it arrives, ceases to to be present before its presence is well perceived"—compels rejection of the kind of pleasure of imagination that Addison described as arising "originally from Sight." Instead, the pleasure of the text has become temporalized, carrying within itself traces of the past and anticipations of the future: it is "necessary to fix attention," Johnson writes, "and the mind can be captivated only by recollection, or by curiosity; by reviving natural sentiments or impressing new appearances of things" (*Lives*, I: 458–59). This opposition between the natural and the new necessarily takes place for Johnson within the temporalized structure of recollection and curiosity and not as a matter of straightforward empirical perception. This is why the reader's response is always divided; it can only be riveted to the text by a mode of remembrance or anticipation. It is also why simple presence—the immediate response to what is immediately presented to the reader—is related to the mental "wandering" that Johnson, as has already been shown, associates with "airy delusion" in the *Preface* to Shakespeare. For at the point at which the mind becomes exempt from the activity of comparative judgment, which is central to both recollection and curiosity, it also becomes ungrounded, incapable of rising to a point where it can address itself to the matter at hand.

So Johnson is far from espousing any simple reformulation of the venerable Horatian dictum that poetry should delight and instruct. Indeed, at the center of his distinction between what fixes the attention and what allows the mind to wander is a clash between two views of what constitutes pleasure in general. One view is consistent with Hume's contention that the mind acquires beliefs through a constant repetition of ideas. According to this view, the characteristic feature of delight is that it is repeatable, that its renewal, as a renewal of the same ad infinitum and is thus inscribed within present pleasure itself. The second view is in keeping with the pronounced emphasis that Johnson gives to the importance of novelty in phenomenal cognition. Thus he suggests, in contesting a popular misconception about the sources of poetic delight in the "Life of Milton," that in poetry a repetition of the same is a virtual impossibility; "it is no more to be required that wit should always be blazing than that the sun should always stand at noon. In a great work there is a vicissitude of luminous and opaque parts, as there is in the world a succession of day and night" (*Lives*, I: 187).

Recalling and extending Pope's dictum that "as Shades more sweetly recommend the Light, / So modest Plainness sets off more sprightly Wit,"[1] this argument insists that opacity, dullness, or nonsignification is an integral part of what is experienced as illumination, wit, or meaning. Behind the "vicissitude of luminous and opaque parts" lies an epistemological system that maintains that pleasure can only be experienced when it is compared with pain. Just as the mind can never experience the warmth of the spring without invoking the cold of the winter, so it can never admire the splendors of *Paradise Lost* without also opposing these splendors to its flat passages. Interpreting this opposition as an alternation within a succession, rather than as a division within what is experienced as a simultaneity, allows Johnson to emphasize the irreducible temporality of literary discourse. To read or to observe is to respond to a text as a series of moments within a temporal sequence that has a beginning, middle, and end rather than as a repeated moment of present experience.

There is no question, of course, that this is an elegant reformulation of a conventional neoclassical doctrine. But it is placed within a context that derives its terms of analysis from the realm of human understanding. Within this context, the temporalization that divides our experience of works of art into modes of recollection and curiosity also introduces a further division between pleasure and instruction. Even though "the end of poetry is to instruct by pleasing," pleasure is an experience that arises from our apprehension of the novelty of what we perceive. Since what is new is also what gives surprise, pleasure must occur within a single instant: "what professes to benefit by pleasing must please at once. The pleasures of the mind imply something sudden and unexpected: that which elevates must always surprise." Instruction, which is linked to the recollection of what was once known but has been forgotten, is precisely the opposite: "what is perceived by slow degrees may gratify us with the consciousness of improvement, but will never strike us with pleasure" (*Lives*, I: 59). Pleasure thus appears simultaneous, while instruction is a successive mode forever unable to participate in the immediacy of the self-present moment. For Johnson, therefore, pleasure cannot be seen in any simple way as the means by which poetry conveys its moral teachings. His way of putting this is to note that instruction is "perceived by slow degrees." But what is "perceived by slow degrees" is what occurs over a period of time, and this means that what we learn is always the product of a long-term purview, a specific mode of understanding that cannot attain to the status of self-present pleasure. This would make it hard to avoid the conclusion that Johnson's theory of affects—those ideas which, according to Abrams, constitute the heart of his criticism—cannot be assimilated to any conventional exposition of Horatian ideas.

One should notice, of course, that Johnson occasionally refers to "pleasing instruction" in a way which suggests that he accepts the customary view of the two terms as a single combination of interrelated elements. Undoubtedly, this is the guise in which Johnson's interpretation of the Horatian *utile-dolce* formula has made its greatest impact. Its attractions are evident enough—and nowhere to be seen to more beguiling effect than in Johnson's occasional speculations on the instructive value of such poems as *The Rape of the Lock* and the *Elegy in a Country Churchyard*. What these speculations implied—in stark opposition to the newly emerging philosophy of aesthetics—was that poetry could and should be made accountable to moral norms, that its delights were continuous with our practical, everyday understanding of human conduct. Nonetheless, the more sophisticated epistemological formulation of the Horatian doctrine also deserves attention, not the least because it takes several forms in Johnson's criticism. This opposition, for example, is central to Johnson's account in *Idler*, number 45, of the difference between poetry and painting. Thus Johnson, in a manner that anticipates Lessing's *Laocoon*, distinguishes between history painting and narrative poetry by holding that the history painter "must have an action not successive but instantaneous; for the time of a picture is a single moment" (*Idler, Adventurer*, 141). Johnson's model for history painting is spatial, a simultaneity limited to the present, bordered not only by what-is-not-shown visually but also by what-has-just-occurred and what-is-soon-to be. Representation in history painting, enclosed in a space constituted by the present moment, is not modeled upon phenomenal experience, which, as we have already seen, is a compound of perception and reflection. It is for this reason that the experiential origin of history painting is actually never original and unitary but derived and incomplete, for what is original is always the product of succession, of the temporality inscribed in our commonplace, prosaic habits of perception. It would thus be nothing more than a species of wishful thinking—a perverse disregard for the limitations of the genre—to imagine that a history painting could offer grounds for a comprehensive reading of narrative.

The comparable difficulty in poetry occurs in the genres of loco-descriptive and didactic poetry, genres in which the writer is compelled to compose successively what is apprehended simultaneously. Thus, as Johnson writes of loco-descriptive poetry:

> as the scenes, which they must exhibit successively, are all subsisting at the same time, the order in which they are shewn must by necessity be arbitrary, and more is not to be expected from the last part than from the first. (*Lives*, III: 225)

The unity of a poem, which is imposed upon it by its linearity, is a formal temporal unity. Like the unity of experience, it must have a beginning, middle, and end, which necessitates that a poem be evaluated as a temporal progression rather than as a spatial form. In *Windsor Forest*, Pope has excelled his masters, Denham and Waller, "in variety and elegance," but the underlying spatial organization imposed by the poem's focus on verbal description must inevitably seem "arbitrary" from the temporal perspective of poetry. This is not to say that Johnson condemns Pope for failing to respect the boundaries of his elected genre. In fact, he makes a point of praising Pope's efforts to overcome the limitations of his chosen form, and yet he also insists that any notion of overlooking these limitations is another form of delusive special pleading, one that can only revert to the most naïve of uncritical assumptions.

What Johnson emphasizes in *Windsor Forest*, thus, is the strain produced by Pope's attempt to impose a spatial model upon a temporal form. This distinction is crucial to Johnson's theory of affects. It is the basis of an implicit argument that what must be represented as simultaneous rather than successive must also be portrayed as general rather than particular. The issue of the relation between the general and the particular has of course been one of the most perplexing issues in modern commentaries on Johnson. It was possible for older exegetes to present Johnson—largely on the basis of a reading of certain passages in the *Preface* to Shakespeare and *Rasselas*—as an out-and-out exponent of generality in poetry. But it has seemed evident to most recent commentators that this reading is unable to account for all the ramifications of Johnson's argument in these texts. This impression was reinforced by the recognition that there are a number of other passages—mostly in the *Lives*—where Johnson criticizes poems for their lack of particularity. It would be hardly too much to say that Johnson finds room for particularity as a proper—and indeed indispensable—component of any theory of affects.

Yet there is another aspect of Johnson's thinking on this issue that deserves further attention: this is his conviction that words are rigorously circumscribed in their ability to portray the spatial and temporal aspects of physical entities. His friend, John Hoole, recalls Johnson as amplifying this conviction in the following manner:

> on the great defect of words to discriminate material objects, Dr. Johnson once observed to me, that no description, however accurately given, could impress any determinate idea of the different shapes of animals on the mind of one, who had never seen those animals. Hence it must be concluded, that the appearance of nature at large may be the province of poetry; but that the form of particular objects must belong to the painter.[2]

Johnson's demand for generality in word-painting is the logical corollary of this limitation: that verbal transcription cannot be visually particular because it contains, along with that graphic indeterminancy, a further, necessary mode of arrangement that exists only in temporal succession. This is why his criticism of Shakespeare's description of Dover Beach in *King Lear* for its "enumeration" of particulars is not necessarily in conflict with Johnson's praise of particularity in other contexts. For it is clearly aimed at the insertion of objects that must be apprehended temporally as well as spatially; in the *Dictionary*, Johnson defines the noun "particular" as "a single instance, a single point," giving as one of his examples, "the particulars of a story." The question is no longer to describe things successively that occur successively in a duration, but to portray "one great and dreadful image of irresistible destruction." It is possible that the implied model for Johnson's criticism of the Dover Beach passage is Milton's famous description of Mulciber's expulsion by Jove from heaven (*Paradise Lost* I. ll. 740–46), a spatial model in which a successive action is compressed as far as possible into a single image. One can, of course, never experience the representation of a fall from a precipice as a single event, but the sense that it is the representation of a free fall through an empty space, an abyss, should justify the exclusion of particulars. This is undoubtedly why Johnson believes that "the enumeration of the choughs and crows, the samphire-man and the fishers counteracts the great effect of the prospect"; in his words, "it peoples the desert of intermediate vacuity, and then stops the mind in the rapidity of its descent through emptiness and horrour" (*Shakespeare*, VIII: 695). Such an image, when properly composed, is not a just representation of the particularities of a scene but a new, constructed simultaneity, a new spatial order.

It is precisely this commitment to generality in certain contexts that has divided Johnson's recent critics into two radically opposed interpretive traditions, one regarding Johnson as a Platonist in the grand neoclassical tradition, the other (more recent) treating him as a thoroughgoing empiricist and exponent of Locke's doctrine of abstract general ideas.[3] Yet if one thing is clear, it is that we cannot grasp the relevance of either conceptual model without raising a series of theoretical questions concerning, for instance, the specific conditions that require the presence of general images. There is no doubt, for example, that this side of Johnson's thinking—his provision of a norm of generality as part of his account of verbal description—is what seems to align him most closely with Edmund Burke. But in striking contrast to Burke's line of reasoning, Johnson does not identify the sublime with the obscure nor the general and the beautiful with the clear and the particular, but rather subsumes both categories within the framework of what is general (i.e., visually indeterminate). In so doing, Johnson frees himself from need to subscribe to a Burkean hierarchy in which the sublime is seen as obviously superior to the beautiful. Details must be excluded from both categories, for to include particulars is to divide and temporalize the mind's attention, a weakness Johnson most famously finds in the metaphysical poets:

> their attempts were always analytick: they broke every image into fragments, and could not more represent by their slender conceits and laboured particularities the prospects of nature or the scenes of life, than he who dissects a sunbeam with a prism can exhibit the wide effulgence of a summer noon. (*Lives*, I: 21)

Now Johnson's point—to put it very simply—is that the labored particularities of the metaphysical conceit cannot sustain an ideal of verbal description. The question is not the description of things successively that occur successively, but the exhibition of an image that—like "the wide effulgence of a summer noon"—must be apprehended in terms of an undifferentiated unity if it is to be experienced at all. If a sublime or a beautiful description is fundamentally an enclosed entity, a single moment, then a description must become insofar as possible like landscape or history painting. Something is lost, on the other hand, when a temporal action is interpreted spatially, that is to say, as a series of pictorial tableaux. Johnson's model for drama is temporal, a successive action in which "each Change of many-coloured Life" must be registered, "in which characters must be carefully discriminated and every passion nicely displayed "in its progress" (*Lives*, II: 76). The example of Nicholas Rowe's tragedies, in which "all is general and undefined," supports the idea of the drama as a linear sequence that stands at the opposite extreme from a history or landscape painting. "A just representation of general nature," which functions within this temporal conception of drama as the opposite of what is customary, local, or transient, becomes compatible with the careful discrimination of differences. The spatiality of drama, by contrast, can only be accomplished at the expense of its particularity, in the name of scenic propriety. The "elegance" of Rowe's "diction and the suavity of his verse" are not adequate to the task at hand, for, like the broad brush strokes of the history painter, they gloss over detail and create scenes rather than actions (*Lives*, II: 76).

It is thus certainly true that particularity plays an essential role in Johnson's theory of affects. If the need for particularity is what distinguishes tragedy from history painting, it also provides a norm by which at least one spatial form—the portrait—can be judged. This is probably because Johnson implicitly defines the portrait as the representation of "character" (*Idler,* number 45), and he derived the English word "character" from a Greek instrument for marking or incising. Among the meanings of "character" in the *Dictionary* is "stamp" or "mark." In a similar fashion, Johnson gives as one of the definitions of "discrimination," "marks of distinction" and defines "impression" as "an act of impressing one body upon another" and "a mark made by pressure," a "stamp." It is probably in the spirit of these etymological meanings that Johnson conceives of the portrait of an individual, whether in a poem or painting, as a graphic or material process of discriminating or marking those "peculiarities" which distinguish one character from another. There is thus a significant difference between Johnson's view of portraiture and that of Reynolds. According to Reynolds, "the excellence of Portrait-Painting" depends "more on the general effect produced by the painter, than on the exact expression of the pecularities or minute discrimination of the parts." Johnson, on the other hand, obviously viewed the portrait as something akin to an inscription—a way of marking or incising those distinctive features that distinguish one individual from another, features that time will otherwise obliterate. Thus he writes, as has already been seen, that "the difficulty in writing epitaphs is to give a particular and appropriate praise" (*Lives*, III: 263). By contrast, he reproaches Dryden because, in the elegy to *Eleonora*, "the praise being inevitably general fixes no impression on the reader" (*Lives*, I: 441–42). The "graphic" and material implication of such terms as "character" and "impression" seems apparent.[4]

This distinction between generality and particularity is at the heart of Johnson's account of the requirements of differing spatial and temporal forms. What consequences follow from the attempt to derive a coherent theory of affects from the application of this distinction in a variety of contexts? Clearly, there is no need to account for this theory in terms of what some commentators have described as a blind groping toward nineteenth-century categories like "the reconciliation of opposites" or "the concrete universal."[5] Far from anticipating later developments in romantic criticism, Johnson's argument is at once plausible and internally consistent. When Johnson criticizes *Macbeth* because it has "no nice discriminations of character," he is making his case in terms of a "graphic" conception of "character" and a temporal norm in which "succession is not perceived but by variation." By contrast, when he condemns Edward Young's *The Last Day* because "a succession of images divides and weakens the general conception," he is advancing his argument on behalf of a spatial model in which the *dies irae*, if it can be apprehended at all, can only be apprehended as a single, sublime image (*Lives*, III: 393).

* * *

It might seem perverse to press so hard on a series of lines and passages that are scattered throughout Johnson's criticism. But his readiness to let drop statements of an offhand nature on such large questions as the difference between poetry and painting, the limits of verbal description, or the nature of poetic imagery occurs, in a great variety of contexts, on almost every page of his critical writings. The effect is to situate his specific judgments of poems and passages on a broad terrain of tacit but nonetheless reasoned understandings of the way poets achieve (or fail to achieve) that union of the natural and the new that Johnson prized in *The Rape of the Lock*. This method is perfectly consistent with Johnson's general critical outlook. It derives quite plainly from his deep-rooted scepticism concerning the value of abstract philosophical systems. Practical criticism, Johnson believes, can get on with the business of formulating its specific judgments, while the argument advances its larger claims without having to involve the reader in abstruse theoretical speculations.

These points might still seem less than pertinent when set against the splendidly manifold scenery of Johnson's major critical statements—the *Preface* to Shakespeare and the *Lives of the Poets*. Indeed they would be were it not for passages of felt misgiving in which Johnson questions the deeper implications of his own most cherished interpretive norms. These doubts have to do with the conflict, as Johnson perceives it, between the values enshrined in the terms natural and new. The two terms are often seen as twin aspects of an interlocking process in Johnson's criticism; one aspect of this process makes the new familiar, the other makes the familiar seem new. Yet there are many points in Johnson's writings where they appear to be placed in an unresolvable conflict, thereby making the task of establishing the excellences and faults of any poem enormously more difficult. This is because one term derives its value from its opposition to the other: familiarity is opposed to novelty as uniformity is opposed to singularity. Such a conflict, as Johnson clearly recognized, cannot be resolved simply by privileging one norm over the other, for this would immediately expose it to criticism by the other—the criticism of the strange and the perverse in the name of the natural is a part of the very definition of the natural in the much same way that the criticism of the familiar and commonplace is central to what is perceived as new.

This tug of commitments is nowhere more evident than in passages in which Johnson appears to recognize something simulated and therefore factitious about what might initially have impressed the reader as a union of "the natural and the new." When this happens, the mind, which was at first satisfied by "that which, though not obvious, is acknowledged to be just," subsequently becomes subject to the kind of disillusion that Johnson describes in *Adventurer*, number 138:

> novelty always captivates the mind; as our thoughts rise fresh upon us, we readily believe them just and original, which, when the pleasure of production is over, we find to be mean and common, or borrowed from the works of others, and supplied by memory rather than invention. (*Idler, Adventurer*, 495–96)

The very word "captivates" suggests an element of illusion: when the illusion is dispelled, the duplicity of wit, its tendency to conceal its action as an emptying out of the memory rather than the filling up of invention, is disclosed. Since "our thoughts" are always open to revision and reflection, they leave us unavoidably uncertain as to their ultimate worth. Inevitably, moreover, this process of disillusion, directed at the thoughts that "rise fresh upon us," also exposes our blindness to those seductive factors in language which cannot be accounted for by any theory that derives its terms of value solely from the order of human thought. For Johnson, the source of our uncertainty as to whether an idea has been newly minted or copied, reawakened or overlooked, stems from our habit of overlooking the difference between the natural referent and its artificial sign. It is precisely this habit that Johnson warns against when he draws attention in the "Life of Pope" to the "seductive powers of eloquence" that Pope lavishes upon the ideas embodied in *An Essay on Man*. The danger, Johnson believes, lies in a mode of wit that, through its "blaze of embellishments" and "sweetness of melody," possesses the power to efface itself as sign and discourse. If Pope's verse could be "disrobed of its ornaments" and "left to the powers of its naked eloquence," it would lose its aura of novelty and disclose its ideas as nothing more than the commonplaces that "all have heard before."

This is not to say that the sources of seductive mystification are confined in Johnson's criticism to matters of language with no bearing on cognitive or ethical issues. Indeed, what links literary texts to other orders of experience is Johnson's tendency to treat them as analogous to entities in the natural world, as engendering delight or aversion in the same way that objects acquire resonance in the field of perception. But this analogy is curtailed by Johnson's conviction that the mind is quite limited in its capacities: in both its breadth of experience and in its power to find ways of making strange, of defamiliarizing our commonplace, prosaic habits of perception. As a result, Johnson tends to view the natural in two interdependent ways: one invoking the fundamental unity of experience necessary to conceive and excite "the pains and pleasures of other minds," the other calling forth a sense of negativity attendant upon the repetition of what "all have heard before." Repeatedly, in the course of the famous section on wit in the "Life of Cowley," Johnson draws attention to the failure of the metaphysical poets to represent or move "the passions." Yet he implicitly reverts near the end of this section to a contrasting point of view, one which insists that it is not so easy to determine whether any poetic representation is an "imitation" that reveals sentiments hidden in the heart or a copy of a prior original:

> no man could be born a metaphysical poet, nor assume the dignity of a writer by descriptions copied from descriptions, by imitations borrowed from imitations, by traditional imagery and hereditary similes, by readiness of rhyme, and volubility of syllables. (*Lives*, I: 21).

This passage explicitly alludes, of course, to a tradition of derivative eighteenth-century poetry for which Johnson held only the highest contempt. But it also raises a large question about the "originality" of what imitates the uniform and permanent in nature, whether it represents a universal nature or merely an anterior text. Indeed, as has been shown, in the use of the term "born," Johnson calls into question the existence of an innate source of invention, a spontaneous genius that transcends memory and judgment. In the absence of the exercise of the "powers of reflection and comparison," what we have are not originals but only copies, that is to say, only fictions that have lost the power to move, imitations that do not imitate, without truth or falsity and hence without any real interest for the reader.

The problem of textual imitation, as is shown in the next chapter, is one that preoccupied Johnson in the *Rambler*, *Idler*, and *Adventurer* essays. Like Siamese twins, the representation of what is uniform in human experience and the imitation of an anterior text are envisaged in all respects as congruent. The imitation duplicates the representation and confirms the difficulty of achieving difference in a context in which mimesis is confined to a repetition of the same. Johnson is reluctant to admit that a text may not be a representation of the external world and that words may be unable to break outside the enclosed circle of intertextuality. Several of his early essays—especially *Rambler*, number 143 and *Adventurer*, number 95—are born of a desire to prove that "the mutability of mankind will always furnish writers with new images, and the luxuriance of fancy will always embellish them with new decorations."[6] Inevitably—like the analysis of wit in the "Life of Cowley"—these essays thematize the problems of a text that cannot establish itself as the source of its own imitations and is constantly thrust back into a sense of its own belatedness. Thus when Johnson seeks to show how writers can become the origin of their own discourses, he can only draw attention to a realm of the marginal and adventitious, which is implicitly opposed to what is universal and hence is not exempt from the temporal erosions of custom and fashion:

> they are to observe the alterations which time is always making in the modes of life, that they may gratify every generation with a picture of themselves. Thus love is uniform, but courtship is perpetually varying; the different arts of gallantry, which beauty has inspired, would of themselves be sufficient to fill a volume; sometimes balls and serenades, sometimes tournaments and adventures have been employed to melt the hearts of ladies, who in another country have been sensible of scarce any other merit than that of riches, and listened only to jointures and pin money. (*Idler, Adventurer*, 427–28)

Johnson's contention here that originality and imitation are related not as interior and exterior but as a play of differences and resemblances on the surfaces of things requires a Newtonian optics of the imagination. But this Newtonian optics, which distinguishes, in Lockean terms, between "distinct and primogeneal colours" and an "infinite diversification of tints," cannot attain the reintegration of interior and exterior achieved by Shakespeare and indeed reverses the distinction Johnson advances in the *Preface* to Shakespeare. There he opposes "the adventitious peculiarities of personal habits" to "the discriminations of true passion." Where the former are "only superficial dies, bright and pleasing for a little while, yet soon fading to a dim tinct, without any remains of former lustre," the latter are "the colours of nature; they pervade the whole mass, and can only perish with the body that exhibits them" (*Shakespeare*, VII: 70). But the fact that both passages depend upon a metaphor drawn from visual perception works to undermine the assumption that underlies both arguments.

What seems to be advanced in the *Rambler*, *Idler*, and *Adventurer* essays, then, is a definition of originality that necessarily places the modern writer outside the realm of nature, in a time-ridden world of fashion. His contributions will of necessity be marginal; his "conceptions" will be those "in which all men will agree, though each derives them from his own observation" (*Idler, Adventurer*, 427). Hence the lack of any radically "new" subject matter must be supplemented or compensated for by an attention to style and genre. This preoccupation dominates *Adventurer*, number 95, where Johnson develops at considerable length the different modes of composition by "which a moralist may deserve the name of an original writer":

> he may familiarise his system by dialogues after the manner of the ancients, or subtilize it into a series of syllogistic arguments; he may enforce his doctrine by seriousness and solemnity, or enliven it by sprightliness and gayety; he may deliver his sentiments in naked precepts, or illustrate them by historical examples; he may detain the studious by the artful concatenation of a continued discourse, or relieve the busy by short strictures and unconnected essays. (*Idler, Adventurer*, 426)

The fact that these modes are organized into the kind of opposition that Wimsatt termed complete rather than illustrative only serves to demonstrate how thoroughly the writer is confined within the circle of repetitive closure. Here "modes of discourse" are akin to "the modes of life" described in *Rambler*, number 143, and thus are opposed to nature. Even more open forms of discourse—dialogues, essays, exempla—are no more able than their rigid counterparts to move beyond duplication and claim an authentic origin.

The rather consistent relegation of learning and letters to a realm of repetition and diversification in the *Rambler*, *Adventurer*, and *Idler* essays deserves special attention in a separate chapter, since Johnson is clearly not engaged in a purely speculative activity, but rather in an attempt to justify a definition of the essay as the rewriting of a given set of topoi. The familiar opposition between original and copy is displaced by an originality that is itself an imitation that manages to avoid the charge of counterfeiting and plagiarism only by the narrowest of margins. Johnson's observation to Boswell that the dominant and guiding ideas of Edward Young's *Conjectures on Original Composition* are themselves "mere common maxims" illustrates the depth of the problem. Johnson's insistence to Boswell that the proposition that genius imitates nothing is itself only an imitation functions as a metonymy for Johnson's assumptions about discourse in general. This assumption and the reduction it implies are characteristic of Johnson and could be biographically grounded as the rationalization not only for his Juvenalian imitations but also for the remarkable amount of ghostwriting he produced for others.[7] Hence also his decision to compose a dictionary that preserves a durable subject matter in the form of definitions and illustrations while ignoring the form of the original source texts. Things are uniform and unchanging; words, by contrast, arise from the differentiated and ever-changing "caprice" of men and are thus subject to articulation and definition. The identity of the various senses must be preserved, thus asserting the necessity of difference, at least within the realm of discourse.

* * *

There is of course another side to the opposition between the natural and the new, one that is provided by the term "novelty." Set within the space of difference, novelty seems to offer the surprise necessary to make familiar things new. This solution, however, does not prove to be a real solution in Johnson's criticism, for the novelty of the metaphysicals, at least as Johnson envisages it in the "Life of Cowley," is not a renewal of the familiar but a learned and lexical activity of reflection and recombination, analysis and amplification. It is vastly superior to mere rote imitation but is, nonetheless, a form of composition in the mode of memory. Hence there is no question of resolving the problem thus posed: the activities of combination and imitation are mutually exclusive, so that it would be misleading to argue that Johnson, in the last analysis, was contending for a union of opposites. There is, thus, a crucial difference between Johnson's cautious and pessimistic assessment and Addison's conviction that the new exists alongside the great and the beautiful as an independent aesthetic category. It is true that Addison seems to anticipate Johnson's point of view when he declares that novelty is that which "improves what is great or beautiful and makes it afford the Mind a double Entertainment" (*Spectator*, III: 541–42). But Addison's "double Entertainment" is totally subservient to an ideal of unified perception and thus effectively denies any tension between or within the different categories. Johnson's opposition is better understood as an elaboration of the traditional Aristotelian antinomy between the probable and the marvellous (*Poetics*, 1452a). The characteristic feature of the Aristotelian argument is that it is only able to join the two norms through a paradoxical conjunction of opposites. Johnson's elaboration of this antinomy assimilates the beautiful to the natural and the sublime to the novel and both in turn to the tension between the two. But the development of this tension appears as the unfolding, within the section on wit, of an oscillation between two poles: the possibility of a union of opposites thus gives way to a sense of the fundamental cleavage between the natural and the new. Clearly Johnson is not arguing for the noncoincidence of the two categories. But the rhetoric of this section carries with it this suggestion—if only by way of contesting the simplistic, holistic assumptions of critics like Addison.

This shuttling movement between the natural and the new is what helps to account for a fundamental instability within the experience designated by the term "novel." The source of that instability, for Johnson, is the difficulty of tracing novelty back to an original moment of perception that would serve to ground it. Johnson assumes that what is surprising and unexpected is subject to the same leveling reduction as the natural. Or to put it in epistemological terms, the perceptual delight that is implied in the word "surprise" is subject to the same erosion as time itself. The disappearance of the present into the past is paralleled in the perceptual world by the swift transformation of the new into the familiar; all objects, from this vantage point, are self-consuming. Moreover, "the effect of all external objects however great or splendid," Johnson writes in *Adventurer*, number 67, "ceases with their novelty":

> the courtier stands without emotion in the royal presence; the rustic tramples under his foot the beauties of the spring, with little attention to their colour or their fragrance; and the inhabitant of the coast darts his eye upon the immense diffusion of waters, without awe, wonder, or terror. (*Idler, Adventurer*, 383–84)

Of course, there are undoubtedly plenty of precedents for the notion that familiarity breeds indifference. The idea is a commonplace. But Johnson's version of this commonplace requires that it be placed it in a broader epistemological framework. Within this framework, as we saw in the last chapter, novelty is associated with the dream of a world in which nature or art is experienced as an immediate sensuous plenitude, undisturbed by reflection. It is important to note, moreover, that the ideal of unmediated perception embodied in this dream is never denied. Rather, it is displaced by being located, like the delight in poetical fictions, in an earlier stage of consciousness. In *Idler*, number 44, Johnson in effect argues that the only time we perceive natural objects in their full presence is in childhood. In an almost Wordsworthian passage, he writes

> we are naturally delighted with novelty, and there is a time when all that we see is new. When first we enter into the world, whither we turn our eyes, they meet knowledge with pleasure at her side; every diversity of nature pours ideas in upon the soul; neither search nor labour are necessary; we have nothing more to do than to open our eyes and curiosity is gratified. (*Idler, Adventurer*, 137)

Yet even as Johnson affirms the glory of this state of perceptual innocence, he takes care to preserve it from an illusory nostalgia by making it virtually irrecoverable or even unimaginable. For Johnson, there is an unbridgeable gap between the awakening of perception in childhood and the awakening of consciousness and reflection that is characteristic of maturity:

> much of the pleasure which the first survey of the world affords, is exhausted before we are conscious of our own felicity, or able to compare our condition with some other possible state. We have therefore few traces of the joy of our earliest discoveries; yet we all remember a time when nature had so many untasted gratifications, that every excursion gave delight, which can now be found no longer, when the noise of a torrent, the rustle of a wood, the song of birds, or the play of lambs, had power to fill the attention, and suspend all perception of the course of time. (*Idler, Adventurer*, 137–38)

There is no doubt that this early state is meant to be seen as a time of total presence: our "attention" was wholly filled, and "the course of time"—that is to say, the invasion of the present moment by the past and the future—was suspended. But the gulf between perception and reflection in effect prevents us from ever recovering this past or even being certain that it actually existed. We can remember it but can never reproduce it in the sense of restoring it to immediate self-present consciousness through an act of recollection or representation. What we are left with are a "few traces," and, inasmuch as these "traces" are meant to be understood as only the vestigial glimmerings of a time of full presence, they are clearly incompatible with any kind of Wordsworthian drama of recovered plenitude.

It is precisely this argument that may distinguish Johnson's thinking most sharply from that of the romantics. When Johnson invokes "the noise of a torrent, the rustle of a wood, the song of birds, or the play of lambs" in order to recapture a sense of childhood wonder, he is resorting to the standard props of an emergent eighteenth-century poetry of natural description. It is probably not a coincidence that sound rather than sight serves as the focal point for this evocation of childhood joys. For sound is perhaps the single most effective sense in conveying the illusion of a direct access to the sources of immediate self-present pleasure. In which case it would seem—if we follow the logic of Johnson's argument—that the sense with the greatest potentiality for perceptual delight is also, inseparably, the sense that is most susceptible to the deadening play of repetition. Underlying this argument is a language that refuses to descend below the level of the general and the commonplace. As compared with the discourse it invokes, Johnson's language offers none of the satisifactions to be had from poems that offer a vividness of perception, a "defamiliarization" in which the poetic image somehow incorporates and makes present what is in the outer scene. In this sense, it answers to Johnson's need for a principled scepticism, an attitude that refuses to accept the claims of nature poetry at anything like its face value.

This might seem to lend support to an argument that Johnson belongs squarely in that eighteenth-century tradition of thought that identifies the transition from childhood to maturity with a loss of perceptual innocence. Thus, according to Kames

> during infancy, every new object is probably the occasion of wonder, in some degree; because, during infancy, every object at first is strange as well as new. But as objects are rendered familiar by custom, we cease by degrees to wonder at new appearances that have any resemblance to what we are acquainted with. A thing must be singular as well as new, to excite our curiosity and raise our wonder. (*Elements of Criticism*, I: 320)

Burke, in a similar fashion, argues that "in the morning of our days, when the senses are unworn and tender, when the whole man is awake in every part, and the gloss of novelty fresh upon all the objects that surround us, how lively at that time are our sensations, but how false and inaccurate the judgments we form of things" (*A Philosophical Enquiry*, 25). The theories of Burke and Kames are perhaps best understood as a persistent attempt to discover the means by which the adverse consequences of this perceptual fall can be mitigated. This project is most clearly visible in their attempt to demonstrate that poetry is a uniquely privileged mode of understanding, a language that can somehow transcend the limitations of our commonplace, prosaic habits of adult perception and that does so by virtue of its power to restore the mind to a state of self-present consciousness. But it is precisely this possibility that Johnson excludes when he treats this state of total presence as little more than an illusion aimed at sustaining our adult awareness of perceptual satiety. For Johnson, on the contrary, adult existence is what ultimately resists all such seductive illusions, all attempts to treat art as a kind of emancipating promise, a domain wherein the natural and new might at last be fully reconciled, thus offering a glimpse of that childhood condition from which we, as adults, have been permanently exiled.

So the critique of romantic illusion in Johnson has implications that extend far beyond the realm of poetry as commonly understood. It has to do with the way degeneration as satiety, as the fall from novelty into familiarity, has always already begun. This is also the burden of

Rasselas, a tale in which the individual is seen as losing the capacity to apprehend variety as difference. In *Rasselas*, quality is shown as decomposing itself into quantity. The unmediated vision of eighteenth-century aesthetic aspiration is perceived as reducing itself to a matter of discrete and piecemeal observations in which the mind becomes absorbed in an empty and endless Borgesian cataloging of the streaks of the tulip and the shades of the verdure in the forest. Foucault aptly describes this kind of activity as a "resurgence of repetition," in which we are "reduced to counting sheep."[8] Thus the hermit in *Rasselas* becomes condemned in his solitude to the empty nominalistic enterprise of "examining the plants which grow in the valley" and "the minerals" which he "collected from the rocks" (*Rasselas*, XXI: 82). In a similar manner, the Arabian ladies are described as passing part of their time "in watching the progress of light bodies that floated on the river, and in part in marking the various forms into which clouds broke in the sky" (*Rasselas*, XXXIX: 139). In both instances, satiety is synonymous with *in-difference*, with the reduction of variety to uniformity, the other to the same. In part, *Rasselas* can be understood as a persistent—even obsessive—attempt to show why the experience of variety or diversity can never attain the sense of wonder in which every entity is experienced in all its empirical singularity. The effect is most clearly visible in the emphasis it places on the element of repetition in our perception of things, a repetition in which each object bears a resemblance to other objects. This necessary repetition is even at work in our apprehension of what is new. Perception, being temporal in nature, as has already been seen, is never simply present and thus can never fully relieve us "from that Satiety we are apt to complain of in our usual and ordinary Entertainments."

* * *

I can anticipate at least one objection that might be raised to this emphasis on repetition as a central factor in Johnson's critical thinking. This is the indisputable fact that there are several passages in Johnson's Shakespearean criticism and *Lives of the Poets* in which he seems to acknowledge the power of poetry to renew our commonplace habits of perception, habits that afflict us with the lethargy of custom and habit. But this argument overlooks one important aspect of these passages: whenever they do affirm a reconcilation of opposites, the union of the natural and the new, they do so vicariously, through an appeal to the *consensus gentium*. Thus Johnson's contention, to cite only one instance, that "new things are made familiar, and familiar things are made new" in *The Rape of the Lock* takes place against the backdrop of his reference to "the praises which have been accumulated" on the poem "by readers of every class, from the critick to the waiting maid" (*Lives*, III: 232). This perspective seeks to convey a sense of ideal presence by describing how the reader "immediately mingles" with Pope's aerial beings, "adopts their interests, and attends their pursuits, loves a sylph and detests a gnome" (*Lives*, III: 233–34). What it lacks, however, is the ability to account for this union outside the relation of text and reader—hence the pronounced emphasis on engagement, mingling, and partiality. Even though Johnson makes clear that he rejoices to "concur" with the general applause of a particular poem, the secondary nature of that applause as a reflective activity which is not quite the same as the critic's primary response to the poem seems apparent.[9] It is as though the experience is not possessed spontaneously and as though there is a latent recognition that poetry cannot achieve the unequivocal reappropriation of presence. Indeed the union of the common reader (the representative of the natural) and the critic (the representative of the novel) almost seems to supervene, so to speak, as the looked-for resolution promised by the great poem.

The point is that Johnson's criticism not only invites this kind of reservation but also invites it in a sharply insistent form that finds no room for an escape in poetry from our common predicament. This is nowhere more apparent than in Johnson's habit of dealing with a large number of late seventeenth- and eighteenth-century poems in terms of a canon that subjects them to limitations imposed by the attention span of the ordinary mind. It is this aspect of Johnson's thinking that led critics from Walpole to Hazlitt to propose a different point of departure for the evaluation of English poetry, one that would show greater respect for poetic values and thus would avoid the reductionist error that treated individual poems as so many variations on a limited stock of themes and images. What is crucial here—and what distinguishes their project from Johnson's critique of poetic illusion—is his insistence on a deep continuity between questions of literary value and questions of presently acceptable consensus belief. Thus, for Johnson, it is an item of critical faith—as well as a touchstone of value for distinguishing those few poems that have survived the test of time—that the expert judgment of the critic is joined to the applause of the common reader, both by their shared agreement and by their seamless continuity of perceptual experience.

6
The Dialectic of Original and Copy

An important tradition in modern critical theory stresses the extent to which mimesis is substitutive rather than originary: a text imitates other texts rather than the external world. This predicament, as has been shown, is explicitly recognized by Johnson, both in his assessments of other writers and in the visible intertextuality of his own writings. But it is important to remember that Johnson was also a man of his age, a critic who accepted it as axiomatic that there is an author behind the text and that no author "was ever great by imitation." One could scarcely envisage a principle more completely at odds with the current understanding—at least among literary theorists who have considered intertextuality—that texts can only be interpreted through a knowledge of the cultural codes and literary contexts that first gave rise to them. In this respect, Johnson's convictions place him at the farthest remove not only from thinkers like Barthes and Michael Riffaterre, but also from just about every theorist who would deny Johnson's belief that the poet lays claim to a domain of genius and invention that cannot be accounted for in any such reductionist terms. Nothing that this chapter argues should be taken to suggest that this distance is illusory or merely the result of not having assimilated Johnson to the point where such distinctions lose their force.

Nevertheless, it would seem that grounds do exist for comparison, especially if one acknowledges Johnson's conviction that most of the writing produced in any age is likely to be derivative. It was this belief, more than anything else, that gives his criticism a tension absent from the writings of recent theorists of interextuality. Indeed, there is always, in Johnson, an acute awareness of the obstacles confronting the author who aspired to produce a wholly "new" text. What makes Johnson's thought so instructive in this regard is the fact that he gives full weight to both sides of the argument, acknowledging the force of the intertextualist claim while insisting that the poet must strive for an invention that will liberate the mind from a passive enslavement to prior texts. Such is the justification for the eighteenth-century genre of imitation, a form that functions as the recreation and modernization of an earlier poetical text and thus provides a kind of middle ground between the servile copy and the ultimate goal of originality. Johnson's Juvenalian imitations are, of course, exemplary instances of this genre. Yet there are also passages in the *Lives of the Poets* that appear to cast doubt on the worth of the imitation as a literary kind. They have to do with the conviction that poetry should speak clearly to the common reader and thus should not be constrained by the reader's ability to compare a paraphrase with its original.[1] One could argue, therefore, that there is an ambivalence—perhaps, at the limit, an ultimate conflict of beliefs—between Johnson's belief in the power of invention and his view that most poetry is imitative. Indeed, Johnson was convinced that the affiliations of the derivative poet are more likely to be with his peers than with a common precursor. Rather than seeking to rival and vie with his model, such a poet is often likely to produce imitations that are nothing more than copies of copies. It is precisely this kind of substitutive secondariness to which Johnson may be drawing attention when he condemns "the law and lawless versification" of the Pindaric ode, a practice that so much concealed the

> deficiencies of the barren, and flattered the laziness of the idle, that it immediately overspread our books of poetry; all the boys and girls caught the pleasing fashion, and they that could do nothing else could write like Pindar. . . . Pindarism prevailed about half a century; but at last died gradually away, and other imitations supply its place. (*Lives*, I: 48)

If this problem remains unresolved in Johnson's criticism, however, one can see how its negative aspect persists in the historical paradigm he constructed to account for the prominence of derivative poetry in every age. Johnson regards the disappearance of an origin and the emergence of an illusory substitute ("Pindarism") for that origin as the conditions of a textuality that is exiled from the spirit it is supposed to emulate. But he also claims that this textuality and the play of repetition and substitution that for him constitutes "fashion" was ironically established by the precedent of Virgil:

> if Virgil could be thus seduced by imitation, there will be little hope, that common wits should escape; and accordingly we find, that besides the universal and acknowledged practice of copying the ancients, there has prevailed in every age a particular species of fiction. At one time all truth was

conveyed in allegory; at another, nothing was seen but in a vision; at one period, all the poets followed sheep, and every event produced a pastoral; at another they busied themselves wholly in giving directions to a painter. (*Rambler*, IV: 284)

Here Johnson defines the history of poetry in terms of a traditional neoclassical distinction between nature and art, or between the invention of Homer as opposed to those virtues attained by the Virgilian practice of strict imitation. Once the Virgilian convention of "copying the ancients" was "acknowledged," however, its structure implied that copying could be duplicated, the original text replaced by its double, and this double multiplied, so that every age could witness the emergence of a prevailing "species of fiction."

What this historical schema works to promote is an awareness of the undeniable existence in every age of a large body of derivative poetry. In his writings, Johnson offers two possible explanations for this phenomenon. One is that artistic imitation is—in some paradoxical way—natural to man, perhaps more natural even than referential imitation: thus "new arts," Johnson holds, will be "long in the world before poets describe them; for they borrow everything from their predecessors; and commonly derive very little from nature or from life" (*Lives*, I: 430). But this common-sensical account of the origin of imitative writing is matched by a less obvious one of temporal priority and precedence. Rhetorical imitation only came into existence when unlimited access to "nature" and "life" was no longer thought to prevail; the same content, previously represented by the earliest poets, would henceforth be transmitted by imitations of imitations. Imlac describes this process of borrowing in terms of power, displacement, and dispossession, but it seems fair to suggest that the precedence of the imitated over the imitation is a condition of this dispossession: "the first writers took possession of the most striking objects for description and the most probable occurrences for fiction, and left nothing to those that followed them, but transcriptions of the same events and new combinations of the same images" (*Rasselas*, X: 40). The priority of original to copy thus becomes derivative of the classical priority of nature to art, of content to reproduction.

So there is clearly a strain in Johnson's critical writings that might appear to go against the aspects of his thought that have been emphasized so far: those aspects that align him with modern theorists of intertextuality. These include Johnson's criticism, in the appendix on Pope's epitaphs, of the confusion that arises when a critic typically mistakes the "justness" of a representation for the knowledge it gives of a nature that somehow preexists its elaboration in narrative or dramatic form. The "justness" in question is then identified with an order of actual objects and passions that would stand as an index of the work's value. Yet there is one sense in which Johnson's emphasis on the priority of nature to art, of original to copy, can be said to support his criticism of the kind of critical approach that would seek out the "truth" of a literary text as if that truth were revealed at the point where all consideration of the characteristic features of the text disappeared. This is because Johnson's emphasis on the priority of nature to art goes along with a pronounced insistence on the homogeneity and permanence of nature, such that the topoi of art are quickly impoverished or exhausted. All the arts can offer, it sometimes appears in Johnson's criticism, are replicas or surrogates.

This introduces a strain into Johnson's mimetic creed. How can judgment be confined to nature when the most striking objects of description have been so quickly exhausted? How can criticism arrive at any kind of settled estimate of the relative merits of different authors when the passions are so few and so uniform? Given this predicament, it is hardly surprising that Johnson seeks to shift our attention from the realm of natural truth to the modes and priorities of textual production that characterize literary genres. Johnson's desire for the stability and permanence of truth requires that he uphold faith in the authority of origins, in the text, as providing some clear guidance as to its value. For Johnson, it is self-evident that every text must belong to a genre and within any genre there is the ever-present possibility that a belated poet can supplant the original author. This comes about because a generic original contains within itself the possibility that it can be duplicated, replaced by a text that could then assume a posture more originary than the original. Any such claim, however, would run up against the imperative of determining just where the text in question belongs in the temporal chain of succession. To make sure that justice is served, Johnson believes that it is necessary to view every genre as an intertextual construct, comprehensible in terms of a single great predecessor to whom all credit for originality should be given. Thus he writes of John Denham, for example, that *Cooper's Hill* is the work

> which confers upon him the rank and dignity of an original author. He seems to have been, at least among us, the author of a species of composition that may be denominated *local poetry*, of which the fundamental subject is some particular landscape to be poetically described, with the addition of such embellishments as may be supplied by historical retrospection or incidental meditation. (*Lives*, I: 77)

Where the genre is slighter in substance than "local poetry," the value of successive imitations may of course be quite limited, as in the case of Miltonic travesties. Johnson avers that

> the merit of such performances begins and ends with the first author. He that should again adapt Milton's phrase to the gross incidents of common life, and even adopt it with more art, which would not be difficult, must yet expect but a small part of the praise which Philips has obtained; he can only hope to be considered as the repeater of a jest. (*Lives*, I: 317)

This distinction between original and copy is crucial to Johnson's criticism. It is the basis of his insistence that a primary guage of the worth of a poem is an assessment of its place in a generic tradition. Yet this activity is complicated for Johnson by the possibility that an original can be duplicated, and this possibility in turn is inseparable from the chance that this copy can be passed off as an original. Such is the possibility that Johnson considers in his *Notes* to Shakespeare's *Two Gentlemen of Verona* in which he challenges the contention of the Shakespearean commentator, John Upton, that copies can always be distinguished from originals by an author's "peculiar style and manner." Johnson holds that Upton "confounds the copy of a picture with the imitation of a painter's manner." What one must instead recognize, Johnson argues, is that "copies are easily known, but good imitations are not detected with equal certainty and are, by the best judges, often mistaken" (*Shakespeare*, VII: 161). It is impossible to be certain what Johnson means by the distinction between "copies" and "good imitations," but one can hazard a guess that it depends upon the difference between a literal transcription and an imaginative adaptation. This is because Johnson appears to assume that the identity presupposed by a literal copy is of necessity a breached or divided identity. It is a reduplication in which the copy is necessarily separated from itself, doubled in itself. Ironically, it is the failure of an imitative author to take this divided identity into account that prevents him from ever passing his copy off as a successful forgery. Without this nonidentity, there would in fact be no copy, only a second (and hence impossible) original, yet the possibility of a good imitation, including the imitation of an author's "peculiar style and manner," depends upon the recognition by the copyist of this minimal difference. Only a counterfeit that already inscribes within itself the possibility of its difference, as a difference between original and copy, can become a good imitation, that is to say, one that might in fact be mistaken by "the best judges" for an original.

What Johnson seems to be objecting to here is Upton's failure to distinguish between two closely related but distinct concepts of imitation. On the one hand, imitation may be conceived in the traditional sense, as a strict matching up, a one-for-one correspondence between original and copy. On the other hand, it may be envisaged in a more modern sense, as an adaptation that is constituted by a margin of difference from its prototype. It is Johnson's main argument against the first concept that it tends to promote a mystified version of artistic originality, since a literal copy is rarely—if ever—able to pass itself off as the real article. This is why Johnson perceives a close relation between a "good imitation"—an imitation that incorporates this margin of difference—and an imitation that is more original than its precursor. Such is the case of *Paradise Lost* which, Johnson insists, "is not the greatest of heroick poems, only because it is not the first" (*Lives*, I: 194). The originality of *Paradise Lost* is thus the originality of a poem that has departed so far from its generic model as to lose the status of an imitation. This ruptured generic identity is also what makes *Paradise Lost* to some extent *sui generis* and thus not subject to imitation by other poets. As a result, its originality is different from the originality of *The Iliad*. Indeed, if the latter could have not been imitated, it would not be what it is. As a consequence of its capacity to encourage imitations, *The Iliad* must have already been inhabited by the possibility of their appearance. Hence it must not only be an original but also originary, a poem that possesses the characteristics of what Johnson means when he uses the terms "species of composition" or "mode." These are the characteristics that make a poem susceptible to imitation, to reduplication. Perhaps because the word "mode" retains its affiliation with "fashion," Isaac Watts, in a passage that Johnson quotes in *The Dictionary*, declares that "few would allow" it "to be called a being in the same perfect sense as a substance." It is in this less than "perfect sense," Johnson believes, that *The Beggar's Opera* has acquired value as an original:

> we owe to Gay the Ballad Opera; a mode of comedy which at first was supposed to delight only by its novelty, but has now by the experience of half a century been so well accommodated to the disposition of a popular audience, that it is likely to keep long possession of the stage. (*Lives*, II: 282–83)[2]

Johnson's point is to argue that the novelty of the ballad opera is not to be confused with the originality of *Paradise Lost*. For this is to confuse the two distinct orders of mode (where the original establishes a pattern that successive poets can easily copy or adapt) and the unique text (where the singular greatness of the work distinguishes it sharply both from precursors and later imitations).

What Johnson has to say about generic originality and imitation would also apply to Shakespeare, a poet who is viewed as both an original and an originating figure. For, as the "father of our drama," Shakespeare occupies the role of first poet and great precursor in eighteenth-century literary mythology. Perhaps more than any other poet, Shakespeare thus seems to fulfill Johnson's definition of an author in the *Dictionary* as the "first beginner of anything, he to whom anything owes its original." Yet even this inaugural position is subject to strains and contradictions that arise when critics attempt to assess literary works in accordance with precept or principle. Thus, even though Johnson speaks—in the conventional encomiastic language of eighteenth-century Shakespearean criticism—of Shakespeare as having "all the world before him," he still finds it necessary to reassess the norm that accords a priority to nature over art in Shakespearean drama. This is because he deems it essential to contest the hypothesis, advanced by Nicholas Rowe, concerning the relative merits of Shakespeare's plays. Rowe envisages Shakespeare as the preeminent "poet of nature" and thus concludes that "the performances of his youth, as they were the most vigorous," must have been "the best" (*Shakespeare*, VII: 87). The theoretical—as opposed to the practical—contribution of this argument does not lie in the empirical validity of Rowe's claim, which is the logical upshot of any interpretation that would seek to apply this priority rigorously to a poet's career. But, in so doing, it ignores the point that Johnson subsequently affirmed in his appendix on Pope's epitaphs, namely that "the power of nature is only the power of using to any certain purpose the materials which diligence procures, or opportunity supplies. Nature gives no man knowledge, and when images are collected by study and experience, can only assist in combining or applying them" (*Shakespeare*, VII: 87). From this, it follows that the direct observation of nature is only the effect of art, in the sense that it requires the same kind of diligent "study" and "experience" as books and precepts. Thus, when Johnson concludes that Shakespeare's career displayed a pattern of development, he means that Shakespeare matured in his capacity for observation at the same time that he was perfecting his craft as a dramatist.

Yet one could argue that Johnson belongs just as much within the tradition that sees Shakespeare as the poet of nature as Rowe. For it is apparent that Johnson assigns Shakespeare first place in a temporal chain of successive imitations. Of course, Johnson assumes, as has already been seen, that every "good imitation" contains within itself a difference that severs it from its original. In the *Preface* to Shakespeare, he contends that this margin of difference multiplies itself in successive imitations until the "books of one age gain in such authority, as to stand in the place of nature to another" and "imitation, always deviating a little, becomes at last capricious and casual." Shakespeare's advantage as an inaugural poet is thus that "he has seen with his own eyes; he gives the image which he receives, not weakened or distorted by the intervention of any other mind" (*Shakespeare*, VII: 89–90). This power of immediate, self-present observation does not apear to have been disrupted, moreover, by the obvious fact that Shakespeare "borrowed" all of his plots from others. Such borrowings are evidently not of the same order as the transcription of specific lines and passages. Of the latter sort of imitations, Shakespeare has a few instances, Johnson observes, "but so few, that the exception only proves the rule" (*Shakespeare*, VII: 85).

What in fact is it, then, that distinguishes Shakespeare's borrowed plots from such passages? Johnson's answer is not entirely explicit, but one can speculate that it depends on the fact that these borrowed plots were based not upon what Shakesepeare "knew himself, but what was known to his audience" (*Shakespeare*, VII: 86). This is precisely the opposite of that wrongheaded, secretive copying of others that Johnson later detected in derivative minor poets. Johnson may be implying that Shakespeare, in adapting stories that he shared with his audience, was somehow able to accommodate them to what he observed in the fields and shops. Or, to put it rather differently, Johnson may be arguing that Shakespeare rendered these adaptations original by his power of observation, since observation, by implication, might be said to produce the same margin of difference in an imitation that successive imitations produce in an initial observation. It is this margin of difference that results in the coincidence of the beginning of English drama with the forgetting of the condition of its origin in once popular but now "forgotten" novels and histories.

This is the kind of speculative analysis that probably needs to be undertaken when interpreting Johnson's various statements on Shakespeare's originality. He is not, any more than Rowe, denying that Shakespeare borrowed a great deal from others. What he is denying is the notion of art that imposes a certain reified concept of indebtedness and so closes off the dimension of productive exchange between observation and imitation, the world and the text. Unlike more doctrinaire eighteenth-century critics, Johnson sees how easily these classical oppositions can become misleading, to the point where they actually obscure as much as they reveal about a poet's achievements. Yet there is no suggestion that criticism can dispense with these oppositions, on account of their partiality, or of the distortions that go along with their claim to provide an interpretive framework. On the contrary, Johnson is likely to insist that criticism must maintain an awareness of its dependence upon theoretical principles, even as it subjects these principles to an unremitting scrutiny. Only through a scrupulous attention to the problems involved in evaluating poetry through our categorical representations of it can the confusions that are endemic to criticism be minimized.

* * *

It might appear—from all of Johnson's talk about imitation—that he simply denies the possibility of originality and thus of transcendence to the modern author. In the *Rambler*, *Idler*, and *Adventurer* essays, as has already been seen, contemporary writing is frequently reproved as a secondary, parasitic activity in relation to the original texts that preceded and inspired it. Thus, "of the innumerable books and pamphlets that have overflowed the nation," Johnson writes, "scarce one has made any addition to real knowledge, or contained more than a transposition of common sentiments and a repetition of common phrases" (*Idler, Adventurer*, 460). In another context, Johnson repeats the common charge "that with all their pretensions to genius and discoveries" writers "do little more than copy one another; and that compositions obtruded upon the world with pomp and novelty, contain only tedious repetitions of common sentiments, or at best exhibit a transposition of known images, and give a new appearance to truth only by some slight difference of dress and decoration" (*Idler, Adventurer*, 424–25).

In the assertion that "we are come into the world too late to produce anything new," Johnson's essays seem to call into question the possibility of an original modern writing. Yet this is to ignore one main point about the structure and implications of his thinking. This is the fact that Johnson refuses to foreclose altogether the possibility of a poetics of intertextuality. Indeed, even as he acknowledges the temporality of writing, he also seeks to develop an argument in which the anxiety of influence is at least partially displaced by the more manageable anxiety of literal transcription. Thus he insists that "the author who imitates his predecessors only, by furnishing himself with thoughts and elegancies out of the same general magazine of literature, can with little . . . propriety be reproached as a plagiary" (*Rambler*, I: 395). Parallel lines, passages, and parts of preexisting texts can assume this role because they are derived from a "general magazine of literature" that is itself only a compilation and an imitation. The freedom of the imitative author arises from the multiplicity of his sources, which are the *disjecta membra* of a pre-existing corpus.

Implicitly challenging Swift's conception of an originality that is totally emancipated from a dependence on prior texts, Johnson insists that, inasmuch as a repeatable line or passage is one that must be conceived as detachable from its original context, it can compensate for an original lack of invention by its insertion into a new context:

> the adoption of a noble sentiment, or the insertion of a borrowed ornament may sometimes display so much judgment as will almost compensate for invention; and an inferior genius may without any imputation of servility pursue the path of the antients, provided he declines to tread in their footsteps. (*Rambler*, IV: 401)

Rather than depict such borrowings weakly, as a mechanical repetition of the same, Johnson views them strongly, as the repetition of identical and at the same time different entities. His instances are mainly drawn from poets of "inferior genius," poets like Horace, Waller, and Prior, and they provide him with a generalized theory of imitation as the origin of alteration, a creative imitation that makes possible the legitimate adapting of, alluding to, or borrowing from an earlier line or passage.

This distinction between servile copying and repetition as alteration is crucial to an understanding of Johnson's anxiety about the belatedness of his own texts. It is the basis of his awareness that his constant references to the proliferation of books and exhaustion of themes could easily give rise to a potential allegory of reading or misreading of his own *Rambler*, *Idler*, and *Adventurer* essays. Hazlitt clearly acknowledged the possibility of this misreading when he observed that "after closing the volumes of the Rambler, there is nothing that we remember as a new truth gained to the mind, nothing indelibly stamped on the memory," yet he went on to insist that it would be wrong, therefore, to suppose that Johnson's essays are merely commonplace. Indeed, "there is a wide difference," Hazlitt argued, "between perfect originality and perfect common-place; neither ideas nor expressions are trite or vulgar because they are not quite new. They are valuable, and ought to be repeated, if they have not become quite common."[3] In effect, this passage restates Johnson's own arguments on behalf of the existence of a class of ideas that are neither wholly original, nor absolutely derivative. In Johnson's understanding, such ideas are derivative in the sense of being a modification of originality, a derivative originality that can never be characterized as merely commonplace.

By itself, however, this poetics of citationality and grafting is unable to allay completely the anxiety of influence. For while it may enable a latecomer to find a marginal space for his own originality, it cannot really be expected to overcome his sense of belatedness. As a consequence Johnson, fully as much as Harold Bloom, conceives of the relation of the latecomer to his precursor in terms, not of continuity but of an agonistic posture of conflict and dispossession. This is the "psychological naturalism" that Paul De Man describes so vividly in his review of Bloom's *Anxiety of Influence*.[4] But where Bloom's version of this naturalism is cast in the Freudian vocabulary of a clash between father and son, Johnson's is couched in the language of the classical moralist. For Johnson, the poet clearly shares "that natural jealousy which makes every man unwilling to allow much excellence in another" (*Lives*, I: 290). The most visible manifestation of this jealousy is the kind of carping criticism in which a poet seeks to denigrate the achievements of earlier poets. In "the epilogue to the second part of the *Conquest of Grenada*," Johnson complains, "Dryden indulges his favourite pleasure of discrediting his predecessors" (*Lives*, I: 349), and it is possible that Johnson's adverse treatment of his own great precursor, Swift, reflects a similar indulgence. For Johnson, this jealousy is so intense that it extends to contemporaries as well as predecessors and accounts for the numerous quarrels and controversies that he describes in the *Lives*.[5] Thus Addison, for example,

> sought to be the first name in modern wit: and, with Steele to echo him, used to depreciate Dryden, whom Pope and Congreve defended against them. There is no reason to doubt that he suffered too much pain from the prevalence of Pope's poetical reputation; nor is it without strong reason suspected that by some disingenuous acts he endeavoured to obstruct it. Pope was not the only man whom he insidiously injured; though the only man of whom he could be afraid. (*Lives*, II: 120)

It is in such passages as this one that Johnson deserves to be recognized as a precursor of current debates about the politics of theory. On the one hand, he perceives, fully as much as Nietzsche or Foucault, that critical disputes are never resolved in some serene heaven of disinterested discussion, that they are demonstrably an effect of certain self-constituted interests rather than a self-caused activity of the human mind. On the other hand, for Johnson, it is no argument against the ultimate value of critical reputations that they take their rise in the climate of such quarrels. What provides an ultimate test of their durability is precisely the fact that they are shown as enmeshed in a larger world beyond their own particular, self-interested claims. For inasmuch as this world is absorbed in its own rivalries, it is ultimately indifferent to the seductions and partiality of these claims.

This argument can be restated in Foucauldian and New Historicist terms without too much in the way of revisionist license. The struggle for dominion gives rise in Johnson's criticism to a clear-cut division between heroic and servile consciousnesses. Domination, subjection, and strife are present everywhere Johnson looks. He may have been the first critic, for example, to draw attention to the servile posture of seventeenth-century poets like Waller and Dryden toward persons in positions of power and influence. One important difference between the New Historicists and Johnson is that, whereas the former appear to subordinate issues of morality and honor to the dynamics of the political context, Johnson subjects the conduct of poets to clearly discernible ethical standards. Instead of simply seeking to discover how power relations work themselves out in particular contexts, Johnson criticizes the conduct of individual poets in terms of consensus values or communal ideas of what should count as right in every possible situation. "It is not possible to read, without some contempt and indignation," Johnson writes of Waller, "poems of the same author, ascribing the highest degree of 'power and piety' to Charles the First, then transferring the same 'power and piety' to Oliver Cromwell; now inviting Oliver to take the Crown, and then congratulating Charles the Second on his recovered right" (*Lives*, I: 270–71).

This is not to suggest that Johnson sees himself as somehow exempt from the issues raised in his censure of Waller and Dryden. On the contrary, the force of his judgment cannot be grasped unless one recognizes that it takes place against the backdrop of his own highly public encounter with Lord Chesterfield. Even though Johnson never refers to himself in his observations on earlier poets, his own experience is what gives such massive weight of authority to these pronouncements. It also shows very clearly just what is involved in Johnson's propensity for stating unpleasant truths about poets and their shortcomings. These truths take their rise from the root conviction that all men are subject to the same basic assumptions about human behavior—assumptions that it is the task of the moralist to articulate and apply. To this extent Johnson would be fully in agreement with any critic who sought to draw attention to the limitations of his own conduct and poetry. In this respect, Johnson, far from viewing himself as having reached some unassailable high ground of moral certititude, implicitly sees himself as subject to the same principles that guide his criticisms of other poets.

This is why, in the specific fields of biography and criticism, Johnson's version of the politics of theory deserves to be viewed an extension of "the perpetual struggle for emulation" that as a moralist he sees as endemic to human existence. What is important is that this perspective amounts to an undoing of the more high-minded notion that the great poet must always be a good man. At the same time, the struggle for emulation is not always a hopelessly one-sided contest in which the late poet is forever overshadowed by his precursor. When attention is shifted from the mythic struggle of ancients and moderns to the more diminished historical rivalries of recent times, the competition becomes more equalized. It becomes possible, for example, to suppose that a major but belated poet like Pope can occasionally be expected to surpass his models. Thus, "the design of *Windsor Forest* is evidently derived from *Cooper's Hill*, with some attention to Waller's poem on *The Park*, but Pope cannot be denied to excel his masters in variety and elegance, and the art of interchanging description, narrative, and morality" (*Lives*, III: 225). In a similar manner, Johnson holds that "the hint" of *The Dunciad* "is confessedly taken from Dryden's *Mac Flecknoe*; but the plan is so enlarged and diversified as justly to claim the praise of an original, and affords perhaps the best specimen that has yet appeared of personal satire ludicrously pompous" (*Lives*, III: 241). It is here that Johnson comes closest to acknowledging the force of those objections that were leveled by critics like Joseph Warton against the view that Pope was a major poet on the order of Milton or Shakespeare. For there is always, in Johnson, a countervailing stress on the degree to which Pope compensates through "artifice" for whatever disadvantages he may suffer from his belatedness. It is true that Johnson praises Pope for the "Invention, by which new trains of events are formed, and new scenes of imagery displayed, as in *The Rape of the Lock*; and by which extrinsick and adventitious embellishments and illustrations are connected with a known subject, as in the *Essay on Criticism*" (*Lives*, III: 247), but, even in the latter instance, Pope's invention is confined to the "extrinsic and adventitious" rather than the intrinsic and essential. The fundamental disparity between the early and late poet is never really overcome—Pope, with certain qualifications, remains the great poet of elegance and refinement, not strength and invention—but is partially displaced by the emergence of a much less harrowing inequality between major and minor poets.[6]

So it would be wrong—a determinate misreading—to represent Johnson as simply perpetuating an eighteenth-century tradition in which the late, belated poet is seen as being forever overshadowed by his great precursor. Too many passages in his criticism refuse to rejoin that tradition on its own dogmatic terms. But it would be equally misguided to see Johnson as undertaking a simple inversion of this schema in his "Life of Pope"—an insistence, for example, on the value of refinement as opposed to invention. Readers who are familiar with the *Preface* to Shakespeare and the "Life of Milton" might regard this as an interpretive strategy that seeks to adjust its conceptual categories so that they fit whatever poet happens to be under consideration. But this explanation bears little resemblance to what Johnson actually performs in his carefully balanced and nuanced estimate of Pope. Here it is a matter of giving weight to both sides of an ongoing debate, acknowledging the force of Warton's argument, while holding nevertheless that the belated poet can attain an order of elegance and refinement that liberates him from a secondary position in relation to his predecessors. And this requires a scrupulous attention to the value of the received categories, an attention which is at the opposite extreme from a reading that would attach no importance to questions of validity, since these would be seen as produced within the context of an implicit critical debate and thus as lacking all claim to a determination of what should count as an adequate critical judgment of Pope.

* * *

So we won't understand what Johnson is doing unless we take full stock of the problems created by the opposition between original and copy, early and late poets. In the *Lives*, that opposition is couched in epic terms, as an outcome of a struggle for emulation in which heroic endeavor triumphs over slavish imitation. The imperative of going beyond the conventional and the derivative encourages—indeed requires—the kind of restless dissatisfaction and heroic aspiration that one associates with a Hector or an Achilles. Thus, in different ways and to a different extent, Milton, Pope, Swift, and, to a lesser extent, Dryden and Addison are seen to embody this kind of aspiration, while Cowley, Waller, Prior, Gray, and a host of lesser poets exemplify the servile consciousness.[7] Cowley in particular is a signal instance of the servile aspiration of a latecomer who seeks yet fails, in his translations and adaptations of Pindar, to emulate the spirit of a great and heroic predecessor. Great poetry, Johnson believes, must be properly great: the "force" of metaphor and "grandeur of generality" are signs of its power. Rather than manifesting such signs, however, Cowley's metaphors are "little," and "what is little can be but pretty, and by claiming dignity [it] becomes ridiculous" (*Lives*, I: 45). So striking is the incongruity between Cowley's plebeian mind and the mind of his heroic predecessor that it encourages Johnson to undertake a kind of mock-heroic inventory of Cowley's lapses in epic propriety. These lapses stand revealed in Johnson's inventory not as sublime poetry, in Pindar's terms, but as bathetic eloquence, an inverted rhetoric whereby—to adapt the perspective of Pope's *Art of Sinking in Poetry*—the minor poet deceives himself as to what he is actually accomplishing.

Johnson thus differs from Bloom in reinscribing the dialectic between heroic and plebeian in such a way that it ceases to be solely a relation between subjects and becomes something that also inhabits the poetry itself. It is here that Johnson approach converges with that of De Man. Both emphasize that the anxiety of influence should be examined in terms of linguistic and rhetorical models. But Johnson is also insistent—as against De Man—that criticism cannot make a start in examining these models unless it also acknowledges the broader moral and psychological context within which they arise. Pope may have been the first to articulate this dual understanding of criticism as a discourse that is obligated both to take account of the difference between strong and weak poets and to subject that difference to a rhetorical critique. In the *Lives*, this critique takes the form of a detailed attention to local effects. Thus, when Johnson turns to Milton's poetry, the values that governed his critique of Cowley's Pindarism are simply reversed. In which case, the opposition between the general and the particular ceases to function, in purely aesthetic terms, as part of a contrast between spatial and temporal modes and becomes part of a broader opposition between the great and the diminutive, the sublime and the pretty, one that provides a focus for the positive aspects of Johnson's estimate of *Paradise Lost*. "The subject of an epic poem is naturally an event of great importance," Johnson writes, and Milton's subject is "the fate of worlds." Indeed, "great events can be hastened or retarded only by persons of elevated dignity. Before the greatness displayed in Milton's poem all other greatness shrinks away"(*Lives*, I: 172). The opposition here is stark and simple, and the fundamental structure of values it rests upon and assumes to be shared by the reader could hardly be clearer.[8] Positive values are defined as generality, greatness, originality, universality, and unity; negative values include particularity, pettiness, imitativeness, topicality, episodic diversity, and incongruity. Although this system of oppositions has a negative as well as positive side, the negative side—which is apparent in the enumeration of the "faults" of *Paradise Lost*—is not allowed to displace the basic opposition. Throughout the *Lives*, the contrast between the heroic and the servile, derivative poet remains a central organizing principle of critical evaluation.

In this elision of the poet and the man, the opposition between the good and the bad writer, the genius and the dunce becomes a displaced version of the gap between desire and its object. Johnson's exploration of the ironies engendered by this gap is particularly evident in the *Rambler* essays in which his discussion of the contemporary and belated poet is frequently subsumed within a broader commentary on the vanity of human wishes. In *Rambler*, numbers 106, 146, and 176, Johnson is engaged in the kind of moralizing discourse that locates the poet in a world where reality is no longer the materialization of desire and has become the scene of the poet's estrangement from his aspiration. Unable to actualize his or her conscious intentions, the poet in these essays has become a prime instance of the kind of deception that fails to recognize its own illusions and thus confuses the servile gestures of vanity for the master strokes of original genius:

> to raise "monuments more durable than brass, and more conspicuous than pyramids," has been long the common boast of literature; but among the innumerable architects that erect columns to themselves, far the greater part, either for want of durable materials, or of art to dispose them, see their edifices perish as they are towering to completion, and those few that for a while attract the eye of mankind, are generally weak in the foundation, and soon sink by the saps of time. (*Rambler*, IV: 200)

This post-Swiftian moralizing irony is not particularly original or controversial, but Johnson goes a step further in the *Lives of the Poets*. In contrast to the purely fictive situations of the moral essays, the *Lives* incorporate an ironic contrast between original and copy, sublimity and elegance, heroic genius and plebeian servility, and desire and attainment within the framework of an evaluation and revaluation of specific poets and poems. One of the least attractive aspects of any poet—and a sign for Johnson of the poet's lack of genius—occurs when one of his or her poems can be traced back to an original. The transcription of a line, passage, or poem seldom has a positive value in this context. It is always attributed to a servile willingness to copy rather than invent. This kind of copying, moreover, is not to be understood as the origin of an alteration. It is not the repetition of an identical and, at the same time, different entity. It is thus not to be confused with the highly self-conscious poetics of grafting and intertextuality that Johnson endorses in his earlier essays. Rather, it is an empty repetition regardless of whether it is an empirically effective translation of an absent original, indeed precisely because of the fact that its effectiveness hinges on the absence of the original. If the original were immediately present to the reader in the same way as its copy, the copy would not survive. This judgment almost certainly guides Johnson's observation that William Broome

> had such power of words and numbers as fitted him for translation, but, in his original works, recollection seems to have been his business more than invention. His imitations are so apparent that it is part of the reader's employment to recall the verses of some former poet. Sometimes he copies the most popular writers, for he seems scarcely to endeavour at concealment: and sometimes he picks up fragments in obscure corners. (*Lives*, III: 80)

Such imitations should not be confused with the kind of imitation that, inasmuch as it openly establishes a relation to the natural world, subjects that relation to a play of difference. Thus, in Shenstone's *The Schoolmistress*, "we are entertained at once with two imitations, of nature in the sentiments, of the original author in the style, and between them the mind is kept in perpetual employment" (*Lives*, III: 359). Even though we may wonder why we are not entertained in the same way by Pope's *Imitations of Horace*, "which"—perhaps because they are derived from a Latin rather than a vernacular original—"cannot give pleasure to common readers," we can understand why Johnson refuses to attach any such value to duplicitous imitations. In their servile dissimulation, these imitations seem to recognize and bear witness to the discontinuity between genius and judgment that Johnson acknowledges in *Rambler*, number 106. "What" Prior "has valuable he owes to his diligence and his judgment," writes Johnson, for "his greater pieces are only tissues of common thoughts; and his smaller, which consist of light images or single conceits, are not always his own. I have traced him among the French epigrammatists, and have been informed that he poached for prey among obscure authors" (*Lives*, II: 208 and 207). Great poetry, for Johnson, is the product not only of "diligence and judgment," but also of genius and imagination, diligence without genius being the recourse of pedantry, deceit, impotence, and servility.

It is not too much to say, therefore, that a subject of Johnson's irony in the *Lives* is the disparity between the weak poet's pretensions and his achievment. His identity is an identity of ruptured identification, a broken identity that accounts for the intertextuality of his poems. Sometimes Johnson's irony is reflected in his reluctance to trace poems back to their originals. At other times, it is shown in his deflation of the presumption of originality. In publishing a passage from Wolverus's *De Umbra* and a complete poem, the *Nihil* of an obscure sixteenth-century Latin poet, Passerat, Johnson is, in effect, troping Rochester's *Upon Nothing*, revealing a supposed original to be nothing more than a copy. Rather than challenge the poetic values of the poem, he exposes those qualities that link it to Rochester's *Satyr against Man,* where, Johnson argues, Rochester "can only claim what remains when all Boileau's part is taken away" (*Lives*, I: 226).

Tradition at this point is manifested in the erudition—the vast system of poetic antecedents—that enables Johnson to exercise a godlike function, revealing hidden analogues and exposing poetic mendacities. The referent of Rochester's *Upon Nothing* turns out, in this analysis, to be not a primal vacuity but other poems, a plurality of texts, a material, self-existent something.

Lack of originality is thus exposed as the hidden characteristic of the weak poet; equally important, mere elegance, beauty, or prettiness are the visible aspects of his or her style. Waller's poems, though original in subject, are "pretty," and "compositions merely pretty have the fate of other pretty things, and are quitted in time for something useful: they are flowers fragrant and fair, but of short duration; or they are blossoms to be valued only as they foretell fruits" (*Lives*, I: 284).

The pretty is akin to the petty, and of Waller's "petty compositions," Johnson remarks that neither "the beauties nor the faults deserve much attention" (*Lives*, I: 287). Here pettiness is not to be confused with the particularity that Johnson sees as essential to dramatic character; whereas the latter belongs to the realm of nature and invention, the former is the product of artistic elegance and refinement. Johnson often associates beauty with elegance and refinement, though he believes that beauty can be redeemed, as in the case of Pope, when it is so finely wrought that it becomes "exquisite." Thus the conventional Longinian distinction between cold correctness and flawed genius lies behind Johnson's assessment of the earl of Roscommon's poetry as "elegant but not great" and the description of it as never laboring "after exquisite beauties," nor falling "into gross faults" (*Lives*, I: 239).

The presence of an element of credulity in these endeavors carries with it a corrosive irony, for the weak poet, as has been seen, is frequently misguided about his own powers. Cowley becomes ridiculous by his ill-considered attempt to don the Pindaric mantle, while Waller devotes himself to subjects that "are often unworthy of his care":

> it is not easy to think without some contempt on an author who is growing illustrious in his own opinion by verses at one time, *To a Lady, who can do anything, but sleep, when she pleases.* At another, *To a Lady, who can sleep, when she pleases.* Now, *To a Lady, on her passing through a crowd of people.* Then, *On a braid of divers colours woven by four fair Ladies; On a tree cut in paper*; or, *To a Lady, from whom he received the copy of verses on the paper-tree, which for many years had been missing.* (*Lives*, I: 283–84)

The invariable feature of this aspect of Johnson's irony is the incongruity between subject and expression. What is imitated is either superior or inferior, higher or lower than what imitates it. One should bear in mind that this kind of irony, which delights in exposing pretension, extends to the critic as well as the poet. Thus Dryden's blatant flattery of Dorset is followed by a pointed question: "Would it be imagined that, of this rival to antiquity, all the satires were little personal invectives, and that his longest composition was a song of eleven stanzas?" (*Lives*, I: 307). In undertaking this kind of ironizing commentary, Johnson frequently has recourse to a kind of frame device in which he inserts extracts, sometimes rather lengthy ones, along with his own reflections. The frame serves the function of a protective mirror that allows Johnson to comment at a distance either verbally or silently on these extracts. By its repetition of the original in a different context, this mirror breaches the monologic intentions of the author of the extract, dividing it and opening it up to the dialogic response of irony or amazement. For the most part, the introduction of these extracts into the text is intended to deflate, but it can also be used to correct an earlier, unfavorable estimate, as, for example, when Johnson appends Luke Milbourne's strictures on Dryden's translation of *The Aeneid* with the comment that "his outrages seem to be the ebullitions of a mind agitated by a stronger resentment than bad poetry can excite, and previously resolved not to be pleased" (*Lives*, I: 449).

The critical question about these extracts from Milbourne is why Johnson inserts them at all. It is by no means self-evident that Dryden's *Virgil* needed to be rescued from Milbourne's strictures. The extracts are presented specifically to expose the vanity and resentment concealed beneath the illusory facade of rationality, so that Milbourne's original tract now contains its own double or shadow. The placing of these extracts beside a later, more affirmative estimate of Dryden's translation reduces Milbourne's diatribe from its initial Brobdingnagian pretensions to nothing more than one of the "perpetual shower of arrows" to which every great writer is subject. In so doing, it exposes his "resentment" as the dark underside of the plebeian desire to copy, the characteristic feature of the weak author in all ages.

One can therefore see why Johnson's later critical writings (notably the *Lives*) show a marked preoccupation with topics that arise in the discourse of originality and influence. He brings out more clearly than any other critic the way in which questions of a broadly moral and political nature—questions about originality, power, rivalry, anxiety, and influence—may nonetheless connect with strictly literary questions of subject and style. But, at the same time, he shows that one cannot just sidestep those ethical questions by adopting a purely rhetorical approach or assuming (like De Man) that they will simply drop out of the picture once one recognizes just how central is the figural and tropological dimension to an understanding of poetry. This is why the best commentators on Johnson's criticism—Hagstrum, Bate, Damrosch—have always felt obliged to give some account of his life history and moral and political commitments even when their primary concern is to elucidate matters of a purely critical nature. They have implicitly recognized that it is only by giving full weight to the continuity between the political and the rhetorical that one can do justice to the scope of Johnson's criticism.

* * *

The generally positive tone that characterizes Johnson's exploration of the difference between the strong and the weak poet in the *Lives* needs to be placed beside the much more pessimistic theory of influence set forth in *Rasselas*. Indeed, it is possible to argue that Johnson's thinking in *Rasselas* has much in common with the conventional topics of eighteenth-century criticism in the sense that it adheres to a point of view that would relegate the modern poet to a secondary, marginalized position in relation to his illustrious predecessors. In *Rasselas*, the twin contexts of the "remains of ancient magnificence" and a renounced poetic ambition serve as the backdrop for Imlac's bemused reflections upon the immense gulf that exists between the "first manifestations of original genius" and its pallid, derivative imitations. In Imlac's account, the triumph of these initial "manifestations" is so complete that it condemns late poets to a parasitic status as masters of art and elegance. What is imitated is always more real than what imitates. The elegance and refinement of the latecomer is a dilution, inferior in much the same way the the beauty of Pope's *Iliad* and *Odyssey* is ultimately inferior to the sublimity of the Homeric originals.[9]

In fact Imlac couches this opposition in terms that are so extreme that the notion of imitation virtually seems to recoil upon itself:

> And yet it fills me with wonder, that, in almost all countries, the most ancient poets are considered as the best: whether it be that every other kind of knowledge is an acquisition gradually attained, and poetry is a gift conferred at once; or that the first poetry of every nation surprised them as a novelty, and retained the credit by consent, which it received by accident at first; or whether, as the province of poetry is to describe nature and passion,

> which are always the same, the first writers took possession of the most striking objects for description, and the most probable occurrences for fiction, and left nothing to those that followed them, but transcriptions of the same events, and new combinations of the same images. (*Rasselas,* X: 61)

Inasmuch as the priority of original to copy is only a function of the priority of nature to art, the derivative copy appears in this passage to be an impoverished imitation of what itself is already impoverished. The belated poet can never invent out of whole cloth but can only choose combinations from a repertory of images and events already prefabricated for this purpose. But this combinatory activity may not be essentially different from the invention of the first poets, for the images of the early poet turn out to be copies of "a nature and passion which are always the same" and are thus subject to virtually the same possibility of repetition as the imitations of later writers. This is because the contrast is not between simple imitation and simple originality but between a secondary repetition that is spurious and compensatory and an originality that itself must select "the most striking objects . . . and probable occurrences" if it is to avoid repetition. Moreover, because of the fact that the initial possession occurred by an "accident" of history, as it were, the "most ancient poets" are themselves divided from within by the possibility that they are no different than their followers. A second, purely historical division between early and late poets thus breaches the hierarchical relation between strong and weak poets. The apparent simplicity of Imlac's argument may temporarily protect from view the unstated metaphysical implications of the text. But the very fact that the dualism between ancient and modern authors exists only as a matter of common "observation," of common "consent," that there may be more in it than is apparent, invites one to excavate beneath its surface. We are certainly made aware that Imlac, while he accepts this division, circles around the question of whether any poet can escape this temporal predicament, leaving the issue ultimately unresolved.

Modern critical theory is also concerned with the choices involved in Imlac's argument. The very opposition between precursors and latecomers is analogous to Coleridge's distinction between imagination and fancy or to Claude Lévi-Strauss's distinction between the engineer and *bricoleur.* The problem facing theorists who alternatively propose and deny the originality of the poet is one that reflects on the possibility of an unmediated transition from a "naïve" art to one that is genuinely creative in the modern sense. Where Coleridge affirms the primacy of the creative imagination, Imlac, like Lévi-Strauss, envisions an activity that is essentially combinatory.[10] Later poets can do nothing more than endlessly arrange and rearrange "common sentiments" and "common phrases" into different patterns, reconstitute and decorate variant expressions of preestablished ideational patterns. Such sentiments and phrases are inevitably embodied in larger structures—in plays, poems, and fictions—for, as in a kaleidoscope, one sees the chips arranged in some pattern, however regular or irregular. But, as in a kaleidoscope, they are detachable from these structures and arrangeable into "new combinations," combinations that differ from those of their more illustrious predecessors only by virtue of their greater "elegance and refinement." The published text, composed of disjunctive elements that can be brought together only by a conscious effort is seen by Johnson as a product of the kind of systematic grafting he describes in evaluating Pope's Homer. This grafting characteristically occurs when invention is subordinated to translation:

> It is remarked by Watts that there is scarcely a happy combination of words or a phrase poetically elegant in the English language which Pope has not inserted into his version of Homer. How he obtained possession of so many beauties of speech it were desireable to know. That he gleaned from authors, obscure as well as eminent, what he thought brilliant or useful, and preserved it all in a regular collection is not unlikely. (*Lives*, III: 251)

Johnson obviously believes that Pope's grafting of earlier lines and passages was not random and possessed an importance that bore little relation to their original contexts. It is the recontextualization of "beauties of speech" that matters, not their putative origin.

Imlac's argument has to do with the question whether all poetry is creative or merely combinatory. Because *Rasselas* enacts a movement from illusion to reality, it is initially the creative aspiration that predominates: thus Imlac's ambition to become a poet prompts him to describe how his first attempt to overcome his belatedness was through an encyclopedic act of mnemonic retrieval: "I was desirous to add my name to this illustrious fraternity. I read all the poets of Persia and Arabia, and was able to repeat by memory the volumes that are suspended in the mosque of Mecca." Behind this prodigious feat lies an effort to escape history and the anxiety of influence, to achieve a "transcendental" vantage point comparable to that of the earliest poets. Yet this project is soon recognized to be only a more grandiose form of *bricolage*, one that Imlac's aspiration leads him to repudiate: "But I soon found that no man was ever great by imitation. My desire of excellence impelled me to transfer my attention to nature and life." The transfer shows, however, that Imlac now seeks to overcome history by achieving a privileged point of observation of the natural world, by shifting, that is, from diachrony to synchrony. In place of a Miltonic program that encompasses a multitude of languages and books, Imlac substitutes a Shakespearean prospectus that would encompass a multitude of nations and natural vistas. The strong poet is a traveler, seeking to escape intertextuality by wandering through unknown climes. But temporality is not wholly banished, for Imlac also seeks to overcome the burden of the past by focusing on the future. The strong poet also "must write as an intepreter of nature, and the legislator of mankind, and consider himself as presiding over the thoughts and manners of future generations: as a being superior to time and place" *(Rasselas*, X: 63).

Of greater significance in Imlac's reformulated conception of his task as a poet is the way objects and events are to be described—namely in a manner that engenders novelty rather than the obsessive repetition he seeks to overcome. Here, however, novelty is not to be confounded with nominalistic individualization; the perspective under consideration is a perspective that allows individual entities, whether texts or natural objects, to be organized into a potent network of formal similarites and differences. In the same way that rhetorical imitation is generic—i.e., is concerned with the heroic poem or pastoral, not with the individual poem—so natural imitation is concerned with the differences between species, not individuals. Its characterizing mark would thus be the will to transcend such limiting perspectives and to attain—or at any rate to aspire—to become a poetry beyond all mere particularities of time and place.

But we have already seen what difficulties commentators have encountered when they attempt to do justice to this aspect of Johnson's thought by taking him at his word or by offering interpretive guidelines that would somehow make sense of this seemingly abstract conception of poetry. Typical of these difficulties is the claim that Imlac's argument consititutes a rejection of "all concrete specificity in the rendering of experience." Yet it is possible to maintain that this claim appears to be a relatively late development in the popular tradition of Johnsonian commentary; it does not appear (insofar as I have been able to tell) in the earliest criticisms of Johnson. One can thus argue that Imlac's reasoning may well possess the lost intelligibility of an argument that was once viewed quite differently from the way it has been seen in the recent past. In this regard, it is surely striking that the great landscape painter, John Constable, inscribed Imlac's passage on "the business of the poet" in his copy of Reynolds's *Works*, after Reynolds's *Idler* letter of 10 November 1759.[11] Constable's attitude toward this passage must have been founded on an interpretation of the way it relates the general to the particular that is wholly different from the conventional one. It is true that Constable's understanding will never be fully recovered, yet it can be argued that Imlac's contention that the "business of the poet" is to examine "not the individual but the species" does not necessarily indicate that he wants to stress the value of generality per se. To understand what Imlac might have in mind, one needs to examine the imaging activity described in an earlier paragraph:

> I ranged mountains and deserts for images and resemblances, and pictured upon my mind every tree of the forest and flower of the valley. I observed with equal care the crags of the rock and the pinnacles of the palace. Sometimes I wandered along the mazes of the rivulet, and sometimes watched the changes of the summer clouds. To a poet nothing can be useless. Whatever is beautiful, and whatever is dreadful, must be familiar to his imagination: he must be conversant with all that is awfully vast or elegantly little. The plants of the garden, the minerals of the earth, and meteors of the sky, must all concur to store his mind with inexhaustible variety. (*Rasselas*, X: 62)

The operation described here exists prior to the process of selection and combination described in Imlac's paragraph on the streaks of the tulip and consists in a series of successive dichotomies—mountains and deserts, trees of the forest and flowers of the valley; mazes of the rivulet and changes of the summer clouds; crags of the rock and pinnacles of the palace. These dichotomies are further refined in terms of even more fundamental oppositions—nature and art, high and low, large and small, the sublime and the beautiful, space and time—all of which are meant to be viewed as the elementary components of any possible system of observation and signification.

There is no denying the elegance and generality of Imlac's argument when measured against some of the more dense and richly concrete examples of natural description in the poetry of later generations. But Rasselas's subsequent observation that Imlac "must surely have left much unobserved" naïvely assumes a perspective that would leave the poet, like the titular hero of Borges's *Funus the Memorius,* marooned in a prison-house of nominalistic particulars. While these particulars would provide an inexhaustible source of materials for the poet, they would still be useless since they could never be organized into a meaningful system of differences. In place of this nominalistic ontology, Imlac describes an approach to the natural world that makes observation its methodological base, yet imposes severe restrictions on its scope. Although Imlac initially "pictured . . . every tree of the forest and flower of the valley," he eventually discarded much of what he perceived. In this respect, his approach resembles the broader formulation of Alexander Gerard, published in the same year as *Rasselas*. According to Gerard, "the main excellence of poetical or eloquent descriptions . . . arises from the author's judiciously selecting the most essential and striking qualities of his subject, and combining them into such a picture as quickly revives in the reader, and strongly impresses on his mind a lively idea of the original."[12]

To better understand what Imlac and Gerard are proposing, one needs to recognize that it approximates one side of a division within eighteenth-century natural history. That is, it resembles the so-called "artificial system" of Linnaeus rather than the more inductive procedures of Buffon, Adanson, and other eighteenth-century naturalists.[13] Central to the Linnean system is a method that repudiates the illusion of full mimetic realism. It selects a relatively finite number of similarities and differences rather than seeking to encompass all the features of the object under consideration. To Buffon's charge that this procedure is arbitrary, it replies that a total description that includes all the possible empirical particulars is an impossible task. It is here—in their similar treatment of particulars—that Imlac and Linnaeus can be compared. Thus the artificial system of Linnaeus finds a parallel in Imlac's emphasis upon "general properties" and "large appearances." Where both differ from the inductive method of Buffon is not over the issue of generality versus particularity, but over the limits of what we can know (the number of "characteristics" any description can handle), and the most effective means of portraying nature (by "such prominent and striking features, as recall the original to every mind" or by an accumulation of details according to number, size, shape, etc.). At once general and particular, their approach is thus consistent with Johnson's conviction, stated elsewhere, that "poetry cannot dwell upon the minuter distinctions, by which one species differs from another, without departing from that simplicity of grandeur which fills the imagination; nor dissect the latent qualities of things, without losing its general power of gratifying every mind by recalling its conceptions" (*Rambler*, III: 197).

Described in this manner, Imlac's approach appears to conform to what Foucault has described as the epistemological constraints of "the Classical Age." According to Foucault, this age assumed that "if everything were absolute diversity, thought would be doomed to singularity, and . . . also to absolute dispersion and absolute monotony." As a consequence, it sought to restrict observation to a homogeneous "table of identities and differences."[14] The logical procedures by which this table is organized are encompassed by the two principles Alan T. McKenzie recently described as central to Johnson's thought.[15] These are the principle of distribution, which governs the "general properties of things," and the principle of extension, which encompasses their "large appearances." These two principles allow the poet to distinguish the salient properties of a species from random enumeration (the number of the streaks of the tulip, which may differ for each tulip), and to distinguish the portrayal of large appearances by which an object can be made comprehensible from the comprehensive description of an object (the description of the different shades in the verdure of the forest). What can be described or represented is further divided horizontally into an outside ("Nature") and an inside ("the Passions" or "Life"). But where the former gives certain knowledge, the latter yields only probable knowledge; for the poet can only be "acquainted" with "all the modes of life" and thus must "estimate the happiness and misery of every condition." This second realm submits itself in turn to a vertical division into moral (upper) and psychological (lower) spheres. Where the poet traces "the changes of the human mind" as they are "modified," in terms that Montesquieu would have understood, "by various institutions, and accidental influences of climate and custom, from the spriteliness of infancy to the dependence of decrepitude," he must distinguish those "general and transcendental truths" that exist by themselves from those "prejudices, modifications and accidents" that one can never find in an independent state.

A significant feature of these oppositions is clearly the opportunity they afford the poet for establishing meaningful, analogical relations between "nature" and "life," illustration and instruction. This hypothetical storehouse of natural knowledge is not only structured, but structuring: its wealth of images and ideas permits the poet to move easily from one conceptual realm to another, in ways that can be natural yet surprising:

> for every idea is useful for the enforcement or decoration of moral or religious truth; and he who knows most, will have most power of diversifying his scenes, and of gratifying his reader with remote allusions and unexpected instruction. (*Rasselas*, X: 62)

Imlac defines the relation between nature and life in terms of ornamental decoration, in which images drawn from the outer world are seen as illustrating a preexisting content taken from the inner world. But this external relation must not make one neglect the same relation, this time internal, which exists in a very much more comprehensive fashion between nature and human life. What is involved is a reciprocity of perspectives in which the two worlds mirror each other by means of classificatory systems that operate as systems of meaning. Analogical thought works by generating a series of structural similarities and differences that are readily comprehensible to the reader and yet can provide the framework for a distinctive moral vision. What should be noted here is that this analogical perspective is consonant with an eighteenth-century outlook in which the natural and moral realms are seen as essentially homologous, the product of the same divine wisdom.

Yet it is precisely at this point that Imlac's argument involves a "resistance to theory" that is also a resistance to its own fulfillment. For Imlac's program will only seem convincing—only carry the suasive force it is intended to have—if one accepts his implicit confinement of rhetoric to its logical, cognitive, or strictly nonperformative aspects. It is true that Imlac never actually repudiates the program he enunciates, yet the problem it poses may, in the most general terms, be ascribed to its proliferation of tasks. It opens up the possibility of a restoration of the "transcendental" vantage point of the earliest poets; but the enumeration of successive imperatives postpones completion, inviting the poet to contemplate instead the prospect of fragmentation and deferral:

> he must divest himself of the prejudices of his age or country; he must consider right and wrong in their abstracted and invariable state; he must disregard present laws and opinions, and rise to general and transcendental truths, which will always be the same: he must therefore content himself with the slow progress of his name; contemn the applause of his own time, and commit his claims to the justice of posterity. He must write as the interpreter of nature, and the legislator of mankind, and consider himself as presiding over the thoughts of future generations; as a being superior to time and place. His labor is not yet at an end: he must know many languages and many sciences; and, that his style may be worthy of his thoughts, must, by incessant practice, familiarize to himself every delicacy of speech and grace of harmony. (*Rasselas*, X: 63)

From a critical point of view, the difficulties inherent in any comprehensive overview of the poet are here presented in their most acute form. The seemingly inexorable expansion of the poet's role, which is intended to insure the overcoming of belatedness, also operates as disruption and subversion. The multiplication of responsibilities, which demand an ever-increasing expenditure of labor, is implicitly subject to deflation and perpetual deferment. Its presence as an agenda denotes the absence of what it aspires to become.

Indeed, the demand that the poet "must know many languages and many sciences" appears as a regression: a reversion from nature and life to books that is only another form of the immense labor of mnemonic retrieval that Imlac had earlier repudiated. Moreover, in his requirement that the poet must "by incessant practice, familiarize to himself every delicacy of speech and grace of harmony," Imlac seems to return to the ideal of rhetorical imitation that his program had initially been designed to replace. The conjunction of nature and art in this section is significant. The discourse on the "modes of life" reaches toward a perspective that is emancipated from involvement in time and history, yet in the final discourse on art this emancipation appears to be undercut by an immersion in what it cannot possibly hope to transcend.

Whether the ambitious ending of Imlac's discourse permits one to read it ironically as a relapse into what it repudiates has been the subject of scholarly dispute.[16] But one thing appears certain: even if the tasks that Imlac prescribes are meant to be taken seriously, they are presented in the narrative as little more than a dream of consummation. As for the argument that the observation of nature is meant to offer an alternative to the imitation of books, it is important to remember that for Johnson the natural world cannot offer itself as an autonomous subject to the poet whose "proper study" is man. At most, it can supply materials for the moralized landscape or loco-descriptive poem whose subject, as Johnson succinctly puts it in the "Life of Denham," "is some particular landscape, to be poetically described, with the addition of such embellishments as may be supplied by historical retrospection or incidental meditation" (*Lives*, I: 77). In most instances, moreover, the natural world can only furnish the poet with the kind of ornaments that would be expected of one who is in "possession of art," not of nature, and who excels in elegance and refinement rather than strength and invention. The fact that the exhaustive search envisaged by Imlac only leads to the discovery of such "ornaments" is what may prevent its fulfillment. As secondary and adventitious elements, ornaments stand in much the same relation to strength and invention as copies stand in relation to preexisting originals.

Imlac's discourse on poetry is thus pervaded by the feeling that his quest is doomed from the start to failure and that as a belated poet he is condemned to secondary status in relation to his predecessors. A sense that poetic invention is either located in a distant past or deferred to an indefinite future may not be the only sense that emerges from a reading of his discourse, but it is the final one. *Rasselas* is organized around a conception of temporality in which the past and future are not merely modifications of the present but represent an absolute past that, once having been, can never be again and an absolute future that, because it has not yet occurred, may never be. One may thus consider Imlac's discourse as an argument in which the latent and secondary theme is the temporalization of poetic ambition itself. It is, in other words, an argument involved in reflecting whether the gap between ancient and moderns is not, in fact, a reflection of the gap between desire and its object. In this sense, Imlac's discourse expresses a wish to overcome not only the dichotomy between original and copy but also between nature and art, inside and outside, presence and absence. The conclusion, in which Rasselas cries out, "Enough! Thou hast convinced me that no human being can ever be a poet" constitutes an ironic inversion of the romance convention whereby the hero pledges to fulfill the enormous tasks set for him by the sage. In its comprehensiveness, Rasselas's exclamation supports the view that these tasks are not only too vast for human comprehension but also that they would fail to surmount the obstacles they were initially designed to overcome. It thus makes explicit what is perhaps not quite as apparent in Imlac's argument: namely, that Imlac's renunciation of his poetic ambition is, in effect, a renunciation of this aspiration.

Imlac's discourse thus adopts a position much more debilitating than what is found in the *Rambler*, *Idler*, and *Adventurer* essays or in the *Lives of the Poets*. It is true that the latter does not envisage any progress that could lead beyond its declared boundaries. The so-called evolution from Denham and Waller to Dryden and Pope is never presented, as has been shown, as anything other than a purely artificial development in versification within a much broader opposition between nature and art, precursors and latecomers. Yet the *Lives* discover a productive originality in the careers of Milton, Dryden, Pope, Swift, Thomson, and Gray that, while seen as inferior to Homeric or Shakespearean productivity, is still viewed as immensely significant. The failure of minor poets and poems is also being vigorously asserted but in terms that are moral and psychological as well as historical. Poems are judged from the standpoint of reading as the discovery of difference. Johnson reformulates the historical split between early and late poets as a tension between the new and the familiar, the natural and the perverse. Thus the failure of the metaphysicals to achieve a union of the natural and the new becomes a generic predicament to which all imitative poets are subject. In order to come to terms with that predicament, Johnson undertakes a preliminary and partial reformulation of the traditional theory of genres, a reformulation that occupies a position of prominence equal to that of a theory of influence in his writings. It is to this reconstructed theory of genres that we must now turn.

7
Redefining Genre

There are several objections that might be raised to any treatment of Johnson as a signal precursor of one of the various strands that make up twentieth-century genre studies. One of the most obvious is that Johnson apparently had little that was new to say about the traditional neoclassical or neo-Aristotelian hierarchy of literary kinds, that he was writing, after all, at a time well after that hierarchy had ceased to exert a significant influence on critical thought. In fact, there is no evidence that he took the least interest in different systems of generic classification as a theoretical issue or in the epic (apart from the question of *Paradise Lost*) as a dominant literary form. But this objection is beside the point, since, as this chapter hopes to show, Johnson's role is to raise problematical issues in the realm of genre theory, issues that go well beyond traditional considerations of literary classification. On the one hand, it can be shown that there is a deep continuity between Johnson's thinking about literary forms and the kinds of questions he raises as a moralist. On the other, these questions lead to a shift in emphasis in Johnson's conceptualization of the question of genres, a shift that clearly anticipates major developments in present-day genre evaluation.

The problematic status of the traditional literary kinds in Johnson's criticism may, in the broadest sense, be related to his obvious dissatisfaction with specific genres. Keast has demonstrated the extent of that dissatisfaction, showing how Johnson undermines the neoclassical hierarchy of genres by subjecting such received forms as pastoral and devotional poetry to a rigorous critique.[1] In addition, Johnson's contentions that there is "scarcely any species of writing, of which we can tell what is its essence" and that "every new genius produces some innovation, which . . . subverts the rules which the practice of foregoing authors had established" (*Rambler*, IV: 300) are central, not only as an argument that militates against any conception of genres as fixed and prescriptive categories by which literary works may be classified, but also as the enunciator of a fundamental principle which is prior to generic redefinition and, as it were, "grounds" it. This is the fact that, once generic innovation is admitted to be possible, it follows that this possibility becomes an essential part of a genre theory, that the latter must be such that "innovation" is always possible, and hence that it must be taken into account in describing such a theory in terms of rules or definitions of essences. The consequences of this kind of structural possibility may appear to be purely hypothetical, yet its effect on Johnson's criticism is easily seen: the success of an innovation can only be measured by its capacity to endure the test of time, so that in effect genre theory becomes an extension of a theory of the reading process.

Admittedly, Johnson's observations about literary kinds are scattered widely throughout the essays in the *Rambler*, *Idler*, and *Adventurer*, the *Preface* and *Notes* to his edition of Shakespeare, and the *Lives of the Poets*, but when they are considered together, they can be seen as forming a distinctive pattern. In emphasizing the importance of the reader's response in the evaluation of genres, Johnson is affirming a particular kind of theory, one found in a conception of genres not as principles of classification, nor as codes or instruments of communication, but rather as sources of pleasure. They can only serve in this capacity to the extent that a reader's response is founded not in a repetition of the same but in the reiterated renewal of the experience of change. This renewal, grounded in the "variety" that is the "great source of pleasure" in poetry, is rooted in human nature. As Keast puts it, "the demands which readers make on literature are," in Johnson's analysis, "not confined to literature but are, indeed, the general causes of pleasure, operative in the affairs of life as well."[2] Thus the tedium to which Johnson sees the reader as being acutely susceptible turns out to be a special case of the satiety to which man—because of the "insufficiency of human enjoyments"—is generally prone. This satiety, as we have already seen, is an ever-present possibility and, for that reason, can never be ignored in any account of literary forms. Any projection of literary expectation as a manifestation of "that hunger of imagination which preys incessantly on life" is also the necessary reconstitution of the genres in order to meet that expectation. Genre becomes less the codification of specific rules for classification or communication than a larger epistemological system, a way of offering the pleasure that we as human beings and as readers have a right to expect.

This conception of the relation of literary form to human experience may seem perfectly obvious, yet it acts to prevent generic evaluation from becoming purely conventional, making it contingent upon a normative response to the text rather than an imposition upon that response. When subject matter is made the basis of generic identification, the tedium of which Johnson complains is produced by those genres whose subjects offer few "topics" for amplification and ornamentation. This kind of monotony can be found in just those kinds of poetry that were most highly esteemed during the eighteenth century—i.e., descriptive, didactic, pastoral, and religious verse. Yet it is not inherent in a number of nonfictional prose genres that had not received a great deal of attention in genre theory before Johnson—biography and autobiography, the periodical essay, history, travel, and the vernacular prose letter.[3] Hence the attention that Johnson gives to these kinds in various *Rambler*, *Idler*, and *Adventurer* essays may be regarded as quietly revisionist in the sense that it points to their worth at the same time that other essays are devoted to the devaluation of more conventionally-admired literary kinds. Johnson examines autobiography in *Idler*, number 84; biography in *Rambler*, number 60; the periodical essay in *Ramblers*, numbers 1, 23, and 201; travel in *Idler*, number 97; history in *Rambler*, number 112, and *Idler*, number 65; and the prose letter in *Rambler*, number 152. There may be some readers who feel that these scattered essays do not amount to a coherent program of generic revision, yet it can be argued that the emphasis they give to nonfictional, mimetic prose genres points toward the actual attention devoted to these genres in the cultural life of the nineteenth and twentieth centuries. The documents in which this attention can be found are not modern-day genre systems but weekly reviews, best-seller lists, and the inventories of bookstores. To this one might add the strong interest that Johnson evinced in pamphlets and controversial writings in *An Essay on the Origin and Importance of Small Tracts and Fugitive Pieces* (1744). The relative neglect of this aspect of Johnson's generic criticsm can be explained in part by the tendency of modern genre theorists to neglect nonfictional prose. If genre classification is defined in narrowly "literary" terms, nonfictional prose—almost by definition nonliterary in the modern sense—will fall outside the net of generic criticism.

Johnson's subordination of genre to the reading process is evidenced not only in his demand for a multiplicity of "topics" but also in his insistence on the general necessity of poets to avoid "uniformity," even though it be "uniformity of excellence" (*Lives*, I: 212). Indeed the variety that serves as the horizon and limiting condition of every work can never be constituted, as we have already seen, by a succession of brilliant self-present moments of intense pleasure, no matter how delightful or astonishing they may be. For Johnson, the repetitive nature of such moments contains within itself the origin of a difference that renders the ideal of "perpetual pleasure" illusory. He insists that a "poem must have transitions," implying not so much a continuum of dazzling, identical moments as an alternation between presence and absence: "the skillful writer *irritat*, *mulcet*; makes a due distribution of the still and animated parts. It is for want of this artful intertexture and those necessary changes that the whole of a book may be tedious, though all the parts are praised" (*Lives*, I: 212). Thus even though the "inexhaustible wit" of Butler's *Hudibras* seems to promise the endless repetition of pure plenitude through the continual "association of images . . . never found before," it is ultimately monotonous and monologic, the assertion of a single voice successively repeated. Each paragraph of *Hudibras* affords amusement, and the accumulation of striking images becomes a source of "astonishment," but "astonishment is a toilsome pleasure," and the reader "is soon weary of wondering, and longs to be diverted" (*Lives*, I: 212).

Given the importance that Johnson attaches to novelty, it is not surprising to discover that he finds a similar tedium in sublimity; like wit, sublimity possesses the capacity to evoke wonder without moving the passions. The monologic nature of sublimity is something to which Johnson draws attention, as already noted, in the "Life of Milton." Although Milton does not fail to provide an artful intertexture of still and animated parts, his "sublimity" transports the imagination to a state "which no other man or woman can ever know," and thus fails to arouse the "natural curiosity or sympathy" of the reader. A Johnsonian theory of genre thus sees an exclusive focus on the qualities of wit or sublimity as creating a wholly self-enclosed monologic world, a world that is grounded in repetition and is thus wanting in "human interest." By contrast, "dramatic writing," which celebrates the difference between self and other, is always already within a world of human experience, of dialogue rather than monologue.

Of course this demand is by no means unique to Johnson's way of stating the issue. In fact it is a version of a dialogic conception of genre, as described by Bakhtin: the argument that texts are distinguished according to whether they are the product of a single perspective, or, instead, the bringing together, in tension and dialogue, of not only opposing viewpoints but also differing cultural and historical contexts. Johnson's dialogism is prescriptive, in the sense that he does not assume, as Bakhtin sometimes does, that it is a necessary aspect of all language; rather, it serves as a regulative ideal that holds out the prospect of novelty and variety in conversation and discourse. For Johnson, novelty or variety is generated out of a response to alterity. Unlike Bakhtin, moreover, Johnson extends this dialogic conception of genre to include lyric as well as narrative and dramatic poetry. Thus Cowley's *The Mistress* fails, in Johnson's opinion, because it is only an exercise and, therefore, does not relate itself to an other who might be the object of its passions. Or to put it another way, Cowley's *The Mistress* is incapable of reaching "the heart" because it doesn't point to a real surrogate beyond the conventional figure who exists only in the poet's mind:

> the compositions are such as might have been written for penance by a hermit, or for hire by a philosophical rhymer who had only heard of another sex for they turn the mind only on the writer whom, without thinking on a woman but as the subject for his task, we sometimes esteem as learned, and sometimes despise as trifling, always admire as ingenious, and always condemn as unnatural. (*Lives*, I: 42)

Johnson has been reproached for applying a naïve canon of "sincerity" to the elegies of Hammond, Prior's amatory verse, and *The Mistress*, yet his strictures in the "Life of Pope" on the commonplace that "the true characters of men may be found in their letters and that he who writes to his friend lays his heart open before him" (*Lives*, III: 206) makes that charge seem implausible.[4] Johnson locates that ideal in a naïve and purely fictive state of childhood. Moreover, his criticism in the passage on Cowley's amatory compositions is not so much that they are insincere, for insincerity, fully as much as sincerity, may imply the existence of an other. Rather it is that they "turn only on the writer." To the extent that the lyric is dialogic, it implies a strategy of response to another's discourse. Yet the monologic structure of Cowley's compositions comments on something lacking in the very nature of the passion they purport to represent, a lack that transforms their putative object into a fictional "subject" that it becomes the task of the writer to amplify. Johnson never questions Cowley's "sincerity" in undertaking this task; indeed, it is the fact that Cowley conceives of himself as a lyricist rather than a lover that appears to repress the emergent dialogism of the genre. In so doing, Cowley fails to recognize that the auditor of this kind of poetry is its constituting alterity, the constituting non-presence that allows its passion to emerge by providing the poet with another subject from whom he differs. This dialogic conception of amatory poetry prevents generic identification from becoming purely fictional, thus making it the projection of an imaginary speaker who is not the poet. However one may wish to approach it, Johnson appears to assume that certain genres are not so much individual and fictive as social and performative, establishing a real connection between sender and recipient, and that love poetry, much like the personal letter and elegy, conforms to this requirement, because it expresses a passion that displays "no tendency but to the person loved," and wishes "only for a correspondent kindness" (*Lives*, I: 458). In terms of such a requirement, the person loved becomes the object of an I-Thou predication which then must be inscribed in the discourse of the poet.

One might argue, then, that what Johnson fails to consider in "the Life of Cowley" is the possibility that the situation he describes might be reversed: that a poem addressed to an actual woman might seem stiff or pretentious, artificial or vapid, while a literary exercise might contrive to appear genuinely spontaneous, intimate, or passionate. For Johnson, it was Cowley's failure to project the "person loved" as a genuine alter ego to the poet that rendered *The Mistress* a failure. It was Prior's failure to project a similar alter ego in his didactic poem, *Solomon*, that is also the subject of Johnson's criticism, inasmuch as "the tediousness" of *Solomon* stems, he believes,

> not from the uniformity of the subject, for it is sufficiently diversified, but from the continued tenour of the narration, in which Solomon relates the successive vicissitudes of his own mind, without the intervention of any other speaker, or the mention of any other agent, unless it be Abra: the reader is only to learn what he thought, and to be told that he thought wrong. (*Lives*, II: 207)

Prior's failure to expose his monologic effusion to the dissent of another voice renders his discourse similar to that of the astronomer in *Rasselas*. Like the astronomer, Prior gives credence to the "dictates" of his own mind without finding it necessary to submit these dictates to the external circuit of debate with another. Despite the fact that *Solomon* seeks to establish a link between the writer and his audience, the utter predictability of what circulates within this internal circuit of hearing oneself speak is what renders it tiresome to the reader. Genuine variety only arises when this closed cycle is ruptured in order to allow the discourse of difference. Such a disclosure is intrinsic to dialogic narratives and dramatic compositions that, at their purest, stand at the opposite extreme from the monological autonomy characteristic of Cowley's *The Mistress* or Prior's *Solomon*.

This is not to suggest that Johnson believes that actual dialogues in poetry or prose represent a norm against which other forms constitute a deviation. This error takes hold through a widespread habit of thinking of a dialogue as a friendly and polite discussion in which a difference of opinion is acknowledged as unresolvable but is nonetheless reconciled to the extent that each speaker "takes into account" the opinions of the other. Yet a philosophical or literary dialogue may actually be constituted by a series of monologues that remain unfractured because they are not animated by any geniune conflict and thus demand to be read in isolation from one another. For Johnson, this is the reason why the "dialogue" of Butler's *Hudibras* is less than "perfect." Johnson is convinced that

> some power of engaging the attention might have been added to it, by quicker reciprocation, by seasonable interruptions, by sudden questions, and by a nearer approach to dramatick spriteliness; without which fictitious speeches will always tire, however sparkling with sentences, however variegated with allusions. (*Lives*, I: 211–12)

The sort of "fictitious speeches" referred to here are a parasitic organism that threatens continually, in Johnson's view, to invade and devour dramatic writing from within. Indeed, they have virtually taken over English tragedy since *Cato*, replacing the give-and-take of sprightly exchanges with a "dialogue too declamatory, of unaffecting elegance, and chill philosophy" (*Lives*, II: 133).

Thus the literary dialogue, because of its proximity to philosophical discourse, is associated, paradoxically, with a monologic style that can only convey a single mood or dissolve difference into an underlying consensus. By contrast, genuine drama makes explicit the dialogic nature of speech, because the exchanges are not only significant in themselves but also occur within the context of an action in which what ultimately matters is the power to impose some particular reading of events against other competing accounts. Or to put it rather differently, dialogue is duplicated within action because the latter is structured as a similar force field of nonverbal conflicts. Viewed in the context of these two criteria, Butler's *Hudibras* fails not only because of the monologic character of its speeches, but also because of the "paucity" of its "events." As Johnson puts it, "every reader . . . complains that in the poem of *Hudibras*, as in the history of Thucydides, there is more said than done" (*Lives*, I: 211). But if dialogue and action are interrelated, the former is much easier to invent than the latter:

> it is indeed much more easy to form dialogues than to contrive adventures. Every position makes way for an argument, and every objection dictates an answer. When two disputants are engaged upon a complicated and extensive question, the difficulty is not to continue, but to end the controversy. But whether it be that we comprehend but few of the possibilities of life, or that life itself affords little variety, every man who has tried knows how

> much labour it will cost to form such a combination of circumstances, as shall have at once the grace of novelty and credibility, and delight fancy without violence to reason. (*Lives*, I: 211)

Rasselas might well be understood as a persistent—even obsessive—attempt to uncover the sources of this inequality between dialogue and adventure and show how difficult it is to overcome. The effect is most clearly visible in the difference between a "dialogue without action" and what Johnson calls a "union of narrative and dramatic powers." Addison's *Cato* is "rather a poem in dialogue than a drama," a poem that mutes the difference between characters inasmuch as it "refers us only to the writer; we pronounce the name of *Cato*, but we think on Addison" (*Shakespeare*, VII: 84). An awareness of the author behind the characters transforms a dialogic into a monologic form; of its characters "we have no care; we consider not what they are doing, or what they are suffering: we seek only to know what they have to say" (*Lives*, II: 132). The phrase "what they are doing" suggests not only "the necessity of doing something" but also "the difficulty of finding something to do" (*Lives*, I: 216). In this way, the task of inventing incidents recreates what Johnson sees as the essential challenge of existence, the challenge of finding "a sufficiency of employments necessary to fill the hours of life." The difficulty of the former is coterminous with the difficulty of the latter. A dramatic or narrative event is thus something invented in a peculiar double sense of the term. Contrivance, adventure, and action are events that not only imitate what is imitated. They can also reverse the priority of what is imitated to its imitation. When invention is conceived as making present what has been forgotten, then imitation is the representation necessary to this process, the doubling that enables something familiar, something that has already occurred to reappear. But when invention is intended to appeal not to "sympathy" but to "curiosity," then "contrivance" and not "representation" is the source of what is narrated or dramatized, the unitary production of something novel. Different values may be associated with this dual process: an event may be condemned as overly familiar or obviously incredible or praised insofar as it appears natural or new. But, as we have already seen, there is an implicit conflict within this dual system of evaluation, for the quality of one is precisely the error denounced by the other and is undone by it. Nor can the reader decide which of the two should be given priority over the other; there can be no recognition without imitation, no surprise without contrivance.

The unresolvable nature of this opposition is what helps to make the invention of events so difficult. But in either case, dramatic action for Johnson is not merely the change from one state or condition to another. In drama or narrative as in life, variety emerges most clearly in conflict, when the way in which things are said becomes visible as an object of contention or as the subject of dispute. Johnson frequently calls this interpenetration of mimesis (action) and diegesis (dialogue) a "transaction" and clearly regards it as the norm for effective drama and narrative. The explicit conditions for every "transaction" are spatial as well as temporal. In spatial terms, a trans-action requires the presence in every scene of at least two parties, a presence that makes one aware that all meaningful drama involves conflict: a conflict between self and other that forces us to go outside of ourselves and be decentered. In temporal terms, a trans-action implies a sense of movement that compels the viewer to apprehend each event not in isolation but in relation to what precedes and follows it. Given the Aristotelian injunction that a "regular composition" must have a beginning and an end, this means that the middle must be transitive, "must join the last effect to the first cause by a regular and unbroken concatenation" (*Rambler*, II: 370). The limitation of Milton's *Samson Agonistes*, in Johnson's opinion, is not that its central events are not dialogic in the spatial sense. The encounters between Samson and Manoa, Dalila, Harapha, and the chorus are described in terms of confrontations between self and other. Rather it is that these confrontations do not lead beyond themselves. Once Dalila leaves, Johnson argues, she is "no more seen or heard of; nor has her visit any effect but that of raising the character of Samson" (*Rambler*, IV: 374). One might be tempted to dismiss such strictures as a form of rigid neo-Aristotelianism. Yet it is important to remember that they correspond to Johnson's view of the temporal nature of perception. Just as our consciousness of time present is only a compound of past, present, and future, so a dramatic action, if it is to satisfy our sense of time, must also incorporate within each scene a similar sense of why it should precede or follow another scene. If a dramatic composition lacks this sense of sequentiality, the conflicts it seeks to represent will also suffer. If it fails to project a transitive movement, it will fail to project any final difference among its characters. The absence of a "middle" in *Samson Agonistes* reduces all the characters except the protagonist, Johnson implies, to playing a single role—the role of foil to Samson. The static sense of a succession of isolated scenes leaves no room for character development or for an extended interaction among the principle characters. Although Johnson believes that *Samson Agonistes* is obviously superior to a dramatic dialogue like *Cato*, it still falls below the normative ideal that Johnson discovers in the Aristotelian definition of tragedy.

Of course it might be argued that *Samson Agonistes* is the point at which Johnson finally does give way to a particularly limited form of neoclassicism. But there is, as has been suggested, a stronger case for regarding his use of such terms as "transaction" as a means of asserting a prescriptive theory of genre based on the claims of dialogue and action as the final test of dramatic or narrative value. In this respect, Johnson goes well beyond the Aristotelian canon of mimesis. He obviously agrees with Aristotle that a tragedy "should have a beginning, middle and end," but he also finds the Aristotelian object of imitation too narrow and extends it to include not only fictional texts but also other kinds of discourse as well. If this notion of "regular composition" is broadened to include certain nonfictional prose forms, then the practice of those forms will preserve and extend the characteristics of mimesis and transaction that are a part of an Aristotelian theory of tragedy. The most obvious instances of this extension are to be found in Johnson's essays on history, biography, autobiography, and works of travel. These mimetic prose genres exploit dialogic means—the creation of characters, for example—for purposes that, though nonefictional, are in no way essentially different from what is found in tragedy. According to Johnson, even historical writings in which the characters are somewhat remote from common experience can achieve the eminence typical of "other species of literary excellence." Richard Knolles's *Generall Historie of the Turkes* (1604) shares in that literary eminence. This "mimetic" prose text exploits literary means—the preparation of a character's actions—for nonfictional purposes, to the effect that "a wonderful multiplicity of events is so artfully arranged, and so distinctly explained, that each facilitates the knowledge of the next" (*Rambler*, IV: 290). Among English examples that fail to match the standard set by Knolles, Johnson cites Sir Walter Raleigh and Edward Hyde, the Earl of Clarendon. According to Johnson, Raleigh "has produced an historical dissertation, but seldom risen to the majesty of history," while Clarendon's diction "is neither exact in itself, nor suited to the purpose of history" (*Rambler*, IV: 289).

One might quarrel with Johnson's judgments of particular historians—especially his decision to elevate the rather obscure Knolles over the more prominent Raleigh and Clarendon. Yet the impulse behind his estimates seems clear: to establish a shared understanding on basic assumptions about plot, character, diction, and so forth. This is not to say that Johnson's concerns are confined to matters of literary excellence with no bearing on other (referential) dimensions. Indeed, there is no suggestion that Johnson's aim—like that of such contemporary critics as Hayden White—is to make history into a more naïve, unselfconscious form of fiction.[5] As has been seen, difficulties arise for Johnson as to the status of empirical truth claims vis-à-vis the biographer's reliance on limited sources of information. But this is not to say—far from it—that biography is thereby discredited or shown up as an intellectual fraud. On the contrary, Johnson seems to have regarded the materials of biography, history, or travel, subject to certain characteristically stringent precautions, as an unquestioned empirical given. Yet he also viewed the principles of "regular composition" as a literary a priori—as something akin to the precondition by which those materials can be made intelligible and pleasing to the reader. Nature is still nature, even if it is only the best "effect" of art. Yet even there, Johnson is likely to insist, often the only evidence we have of the supposedly factual situation and subject of a nonfictional prose text is the narrative itself.

This Johnsonian extension of Aristotelian canons about what constitutes poetry allows the same dialogic conception of genre to be applied to the novel as well as to nonfictional prose forms, despite the polarity of their positions in terms of reference. Indeed, the novel differs from such factual genres as history, biography, and autobiography in that it can provide role models, "examples" for the reader to imitate. In emphasizing the importance of the imitation of heroes and heroines found in books, Johnson constructs a theory of fiction that enacts the generic theme of what he calls "comic romances": just as Don Quixote, the paradigmatic hero of the comic romance, imitates the famous knight of romance, Amadis de Gaul, so we, as readers, imitate characters whom we admire. But the idea of choosing an imitative model contains a clear and present moral danger for Johnson. The notion of the example as a projection of the reader's desire allows "hope" to externalize itself without ceasing to be present to itself. In this friendly guise, the exemplum becomes the basis for an illusory dream of spontaneity, immediacy, and undivided self-presence, the dream of a mode of being that might be able to master all exteriority by overcoming it through force or fraud. But the introduction of the model as "other" effectively transforms the comic romance from a monologic into a dialogic form. In this particular mutation, the example is no longer necessarily a projection of the reader's desire but comes, through its inflexible exteriority, to be experienced as a negative model, a threat or a danger to the self. Johnson formulates the difference between the two alternatives in the following way:

> the purpose of these writings is not only to show mankind, but to provide that they may be seen hereafter with less hazard; to teach the means of avoiding the snares which are laid by Treachery for Innocence, without

> infusing any wish for that superiority with which the flatterer betrays his vanity; to give the power of counteracting fraud, without the temptation to practise it; to initiate youth by mock encounters in the art of necessary defence, and to increase prudence without impairing virtue. (*Rambler*, III: 22–23)

The difference between the alternatives is not of the order of a difference between alternative modes of desire but between desire and fear. It thus constitutes the narrative neither as a comic triumph of the self over the other, nor as a tragic defeat in which victory belongs to the other, but rather as a didactic overturning in which the self finally acknowledges the power of alterity but learns to avoid its snares. This can best be understood not as a mimesis that "shows all that presents itself without discrimination," but as a disjunctive activity that settles "boundaries," and affirms differences. It is significant in this connection that Johnson employs allegorical personifications such as "Treachery," "Innocence," "Virtue," and "Vice" to describe this disjunctive activity. If "allegory," as Johnson argued, "is one of the most pleasureable vehicles of instruction" (*Rambler*, I: 285), then his call for its use in comic romance constitutes a criticism of a mimesis that, through its willingness to allow reality to "present itself" to the reader without discrimination, fosters rather than dispels illusion.

Readers have often seen Johnson's call for a revision of comic romance as evidence of a conflict between mimetic and didactic ideals in his criticism, yet this conflict largely disappears when Johnson's program of reform is placed in the broader context of the difference between nonfictional and fictional prose genres. Johnson, fully as much as Sir Philip Sidney, is convinced that "poesy dealeth with the universal consideration" and "history" (understood in the broadest sense) with "the particular."[6] The issue is raised for Johnson because the comic romance emerged as a distinctive genre in the eighteenth century. The main problem here is that comic romance, unlike heroic romance, lacks all the formal properties of literary status and thus could be turned into a species of domestic history (or biography) in which the narrative purports to represent in vivid detail what actually happens in the world rather than what ought to happen. Thus one may want to think (and genuinely believe) that certain novels—Defoe's *Moll Flanders*, for instance, or Fielding's *Tom Jones*—are actual lives, that they describe the tribulations, reversals, and ultimate triumphs of real-world characters. But we are deluded—so the Johnsonian argument runs—if we fail to recognize that comic romance really has this power to introduce a confusion between fact and fiction or to undermine our sense of right and wrong. To this extent Johnson is surely justified in claiming that there should exist constraints on the conduct of fictive characters. It is by no means clear, moreover, that this characteristically Johnsonian program or something very much like it did not in fact become the basis for a reformulated version of the comic romance in the novels of Charles Dickens. In this version, the purgation of illusion through an encounter with alterity becomes a central feature of the narrative. At stake in comic romance is thus the difference between mimesis and allegory, even if Johnson did not explicitly recognize it as such, that is, between a mode that, by failing to impose discrimination upon what it presents to the reader, only confirms the self in its desires and one in which the self comes up against a repudiation of its wishes that makes us recognize the plenitude of the other model as a chimera. The difference in question also helps to account for the broader difference between genres in which the self is opposed to an other and genres that are no longer regarded as giving an adequate access to alterity. Hagstrum's comment that Johnson's "heart was not in his" attempts at generic criticism is valid only if one chooses to overlook this broad program of generic revaluation.[7] Both the extension of dialogic forms into fictional and nonfictional prose genres and the dismantling of the traditional hierarchy of genres are a response to a pervasive sense that the traditional literary kinds were no longer capable of adequately representing contemporary life. It is surely noteworthy, in this connection, that Johnson's definition of literature in the *Dictionary* as "learning; skill in letters" is broad enough to encompass both fictional and nonfictional genres. Indeed, it can even be argued that Johnson's ideas about literature have been crucial for subsequent developments in genre theory and not the least for his having anticipated the attention actually given to nonfictional as well as fictional genres in modern culture.

* * *

This aspect of Johnson's criticism needs stressing since so many readers have taken his generic criticism as just another version of neoclassicism, the idea that poems must be organized into a rigid and immutable hierarchy of literary forms. Where Johnson's judgments are most conservative, so this argument runs, he is conforming to a prescriptive theory of genre, relying on external rules, preconceived notions of form to which a writer must adhere. Yet it is precisely the absence of any sense of a deeply felt commitment to the traditional hierarchical system of generic classification that distinguishes Johnson's criticism from that of his closest critical contemporary, Sir

Joshua Reynolds. Most critics would agree that the traditional ordering of history painting, landscape, portraiture, and still life remains in full force in Reynolds's *Discourses*, even if that ordering no longer held the same importance in contemporary art. In Johnson's criticism, on the other hand, no such comparable system of ranking can be said to exist. Out of a traditional inventory that would include epic, tragedy, comedy, satire, pastoral, and lyric, Johnson allows only comedy and satire to retain their traditional positions. Pastoral is totally rejected, and tragedy is seen as having entered into a post-Addisonian state of decline. This typology still bears a resemblance to the highly charged value system developed by Reynolds, but Johnson—in opposition to Reynolds—proposes in *Idler*, number 45, that history painting should be demoted in importance in relation to portraiture. In a similar fashion, while Johnson believed that "the first praise of genius is due to the writer of an epick poem," he obviously regarded the stock topoi and props of the heroic genre to be worn out: "even war and conquest, however splendid, suggest no new images; the triumphal chariot of a victorious monarch can be decked only with those ornaments that have graced his predecessors" (*Lives*, I: 425). Johnson finds no comparable sense of exhaustion in the lyric and indeed he even distinguishes between "the ease and airiness of the lighter" and "the vehemence and elevation of the grander ode" (*Lives*, III: 419). Yet there is no sense that Johnson ever departed from the traditional opinion, advanced from the time of Catullus onward, that the lyric was an essentially nugatory and minor genre.

There may be a number of reasons why Johnson devoted so much more attention to pastoral poetry than to the other neoclassical genres, one of which was that his critique cast doubt upon the pretensions of pastoral at a time when it was still in vogue. Johnson's attack upon this vogue not only includes his adverse judgments of particular poems in the *Lives of the Poets* but also his theoretical speculations in *Rambler*, numbers 36 and 37, and his essay on Virgil's *Pastorals* in *Adventurer*, number 92. In its broadest sense, Johnson's critique of pastoral derives from the dialogism that informs his view of other genres. In Johnson's opinion, pastoral

> exhibits a life, to which we have been always accustomed to associate peace, and leisure, and innocence: and therefore we readily set open the heart, for the admission of its images, which contribute to drive away cares and perturbations, and suffer ourselves, without resistance, to be transported to elysian regions, where we are to meet with nothing but joy, and plenty, and contentment; where every gale whispers pleasure, and every shade promises repose. (*Rambler*, III: 195)

In contrast to the promise of eternal pleasure and repose offered by pastoral, dialogic forms of narrative and drama are temporal and thus inherently agonistic. The desires they project are either deferred or disrupted by the opposition of another self whose wishes the protagonist must also take into account. The give-and-take of the dialogic situation emphasizes in turn that the pastoral unity of desire and its object is narcissistic and illusory rather than an evocation of something that actually exists. In Johnson's dialogic conception of poetry, it is not permanence that takes precedence over temporality but reality that precedes and thus fissures illusion.

There was, of course, a contrary trend in eighteenth-century theory and practice to this poetry of pastoral illusion. A poetry whose aim was the realistic depiction of rural life afforded an alternative to a poetry whose goal was the evocation of a "Golden World."[8] Johnson's attitude toward this alternative was decidedly ambivalent: while he redefines pastoral in terms of a poetry of country life in *Rambler*, number 37, his strictures on pastoral in *Rambler*, number 36, appear to be committed to a complete repudiation of the theoretical premises on which the entire genre was based. Critics who advocated a more realistic and familiar kind of pastoral poetry assumed that the plenitude they denied as desire could be recuperated as fact. By capturing the vivid particularity of individual scenes and prospects, the pastoral poet could more than compensate for a failure to recreate Arcadia or the "Vale of Tempe." In *Rambler*, number 36, Johnson contests the epistemology upon which this exchange depends. The range of images available to the poet is so "narrow," he believes, that not even a densely specific description of country life can escape the destructive repetition of original and copy (*Rambler*, III: 197). In the context of this imagistic poverty, the literal imitation of rural life turns out to be a reduplication of the rhetorical imitation of the Elysian Fields. What is noteworthy about this argument is its rigor. At its deepest level, *Rambler*, number 36, probes not only the error behind the belief that the landscape affords an abundance of images to the poet but also the philosophical confusion—a confusion between metaphysics and epistemology—which produced that error. Philosophic understanding assumes not only that nature, strictly speaking, is "inexhaustible," but also that "its general effects on the eye and on the ear are uniform, and incapable of much variety in description" (*Rambler*, III: 197). Nature is thus both a metaphysical excess transcending mind and an epistemological deficiency falling below it, so that the quest for variety, asserted as a theoretical possibility in Imlac's dissertation on poetry, is seen here as a futile one. Pastoral, because of the uniformity and generality of its "occasions," can only blur the differences that arise in more "complicated transactions"; in contrast, drama brings out the kind of difference that "produces perplexities, terrors, and surprises" (*Rambler*, III: 198).

This account of the tedium elicited by the epistemological poverty of pastoral fails, however, to explain a crucial aspect of its importance as a genre. This is the persistent appeal the pastoral dream has exerted upon generations of readers. Johnson's assumes that this appeal is a delusive construct, the product of an obsessive, monologic quest for origins and presence. Indeed, the very universality of this quest is proof of the secondary, derivative nature of the poetry that seeks to satisfy it. Nothing less than a futile, essentially repetitive effort to recover a vanished joy and contentment can explain the seemingly countless number of pastoral imitations. Johnson emphasizes the compensatory nature of these imitations, all of which deliberately exploit

> that secondary and adventitious gladness, which every man feels on reviewing those places, or recollecting those occurrences, that contributed to his youthful enjoyments, and bring him back to the prime of life, when the world was gay with the bloom of novelty, when mirth wantoned at his side, and hope sparkled before him. (*Rambler*, III: 197)

Here pastoral appears as a version of that joy and plenty which the adult mind seeks to recover in childhood. The mature mind, to be sure, acknowledges the real world of which the child is unaware but is still governed by the desire to idealize, to recreate the plenitude it has lost. Johnson differs from early eighteenth-century antipastoralists like Swift in insisting that this desire is a universal, constitutive aspect of human experience, yet he, nonetheless, insists that it is still an attempt to cancel out a reality that is admitted to be there—hence it reveals itself and the poetry it engenders to be regressive and factitious. Johnson thus repudiates pastoral, but his repudiation is necessarily more somber and equivocal than that of Swift.

As Johnson continues his critique of pastoral in *Rambler*, number 37, he shifts his attention from nature to art, from epistemology to genre. Here Johnson defends the realistic version of pastoral, but in a form that finds little room for natural description. The locus for his highly qualified support of a certain kind of regional and topographical poetry can be found in Johnson's definition of pastoral. Although Johnson relies on the seemingly irreproachable authority of Virgil in formulating this definition, it turns out to be implicated in a strategy that submits the relation of cause and effect to an ironic reversal: a pastoral is "a poem in which any action or passion is represented by its effects up on a country life" (*Rambler*, III: 201). Here rural life is no longer seen as the source of joy and plenitude but is reduced instead to the site of effects generated by a subject, or in the course of an "action or passion" produced by a subject.[9] What Johnson accomplishes by this definition of a genre that no longer claims unmediated access to, or even identity with, a sensuous plentitude is to open up a gap between desire and fact. Pastoral is no longer associated with a nostalgic craving for origins and presence but is now explicitly mimetic in aim. It is, therefore, a genre that must be evaluated by its claim to truth. But the "truth" of pastoral is at least partly narrative and dramatic, the truth of other literary genres. This truth, in turn, is seen to be prior to the nostalgic fiction of innocence and ceases to be a reversion to some original bucolic state of nature.

The specific outcome of this redefinition of pastoral in terms of truth hinges upon Johnson's subversion of the traditional pastoral conventions, which he now derisively terms "fictions." Throughout the essay, Johnson uses the term fiction in two interrelated senses: to designate what lacks a specific, extratextual referent and to refer to a wholly "incredible" or "absurd" state of illusion. Johnson's attitude toward pastoral fiction is evident in his attack upon the "rustick dialect" that many poets have tried to invent in order to return to an age of innocence before time and history. The peculiar choice of "a mingled dialect which no human being has ever spoken" to represent the mind's encounter with corruptions in church and state reflects upon the implausibility of the pastoral project. It aspires toward the condition of a discourse prior to the experience of complexity and artifice, but its uneasy and glaring juxtaposition of this "barbaric dialect" with the "elegance" of the poet's "thoughts" undermines this aspiration. The problem facing poems that mix incongruous elements is not confined to style, moreover, but is reduplicated at the level of subject matter, in the mingling of pagan and Christian deities. In contrast to some Renaissance commentators, Johnson refuses to concede Theocritus and other pastoral poets access to an ancient (and syncretistic) wisdom prior to Christian revelation.[10] Instead he assumes a radical historical "change" that rendered the ancient mythology, like the ancient language of pastoral, wholly "incredible." This change exposes the fictionality of pastoral truth, a fictionality that extends, retroactively, to the earliest instances of the genre.

Repudiating these timeworn fictions leads Johnson to reject the-Golden Age pastoral altogether. In place of a poetry that transports the reader to an Elysian world of piping goatherds and melancholy shepherds, Johnson proposes a regional poetry of rural life. To the charge that such a poetry would have to be committed to the representation of rudeness and ignorance, Johnson holds that "pastoral admits all ranks of persons, because persons of all ranks inhabit the country" (*Rambler*, III: 203). But implicit in the reversal embodied in this chiasmus is the conviction that pastoral must be committed to the attainment of knowledge rather than the fulfillment of desire. The representation of rural life necessarily excludes images that are not drawn from "rural objects" (*Rambler*, III: 203–4), and it must not suggest that the knowledge behind its descriptions is other than it is:

> it is therefore improper to give the title of pastoral to verses, in which the speakers, after the slight mention of their flocks, fall to complaints of errors in the church, and corruptions in the government, or to lamentations of the death of some illustrious person, whom when once the poet has called a shepherd, he has no longer any labour upon his hands, but can make the clouds weep, and lilies wither, and the sheep hang their heads, without art or learning, genius or study. (*Rambler*, III: 204–205)

Here the willingness of the poet to allow himself to be deflected from the labor of representation into a monological "complaint" or "lamentation" turns out to repeat certain aspects of the pastoral desire and thus to suggest the delusiveness of the kind of art that seeks to achieve a mastery without learning or effort.

Behind Johnson's critique of pastoralism lies a model of art that resists any attempts to dispense with the demands of representation and truth. The precise terms of this critique can better help one to understand Johnson's relation to traditional neoclassical theories of genre. This relation cannot be understood, needless to say, in terms of a commitment to a universal and fixed canon of literary kinds. Yet Johnson's judgments make it clear that he cannot be assimilated to that line of generic thought which sharply distinguishes neoclassical hierarchies from present systems of classification. These latter take it for granted that genre theory is actively concerned with description, not prescription, and with description, moreover, as an elaborate, all-inclusive synchronic system in which no literary form is left out. In this respect, his thinking has closer affinities with theories that examine genres in terms of their popular consensual appeal, but which also require that the relative merit of different kinds of poems must be arrived at through a critical analysis of the arguments advanced in support of individual genres and not just allowed to emerge in accordance with the broad popular taste of the audience. What emerges from this reading of Johnson is his principled refusal to entertain values other than those arrived at by subjecting genres to a rigorous critique of their grounding suppositions, especially those which fail to satisfy a need for variety or go against reason, consistency, and plain good sense. To this extent at least, he belongs in the company of the neoclassicists: those critics who set out to determine the relative merits of each literary form in terms of some kind of normative standard of value.

The problem of pastoral as a poetic genre whose suppositions are radically at odds with what should be its aspirations continued to preoccupy Johnson's mind. In *Adventurer*, number 92, he devotes an entire essay to a survey of Virgil's ten pastorals. Here the oppositions between variety and monotony, between truth and fiction repeat the themes of *Rambler*, numbers 36 and 37. Johnson, as might be expected, treats Virgil with unfailing respect, but his interpretation actually puts the significance of Virgil's achievement as a pastoralist in question. By insisting, for example, upon the "absurdity" of the poetic mythologies of the fourth, fifth, and sixth eclogues, Johnson refuses to concede to Virgil a fictive solution to the problem of monotony he sees as inherent in the genre—and where Virgil is not inventive, he is seen as imitative, given to transparently derivative adaptations of other texts. Johnson discovers evidence of this imitativeness not only in Virgil's generalized indebtedness to Theocritus but also in the fact that the seventh eclogue virtually reduplicates the theme of the third and that the eighth is little more than a translation of a Grecian original.

These criticisms reformulate the claim encountered in Johnson's earlier discussion of pastoral: namely, that the derivative nature of the genre is not incidental but is a constitutive aspect of its structure, a poverty of form that corresponds to the poverty of its subject matter. In the first and tenth pastorals—the only pastorals of Virgil that Johnson singles out for special praise—he finds this poverty incorporated in a positive way within the very world of each poem. Although the first and tenth eclogues are not exempt from the monologic simplicity inherent in the genre, their existentially innocent protagonists are clearly bound to the pathos of life. Far from being exempt from the hostility and indifference of the world, they give voice to the themes of frustrated love and human misery. In the tenth pastoral, for example, "the complaint of Gellus disappointed in his love, is full of such sentiments as disappointed love naturally produces; his wishes are wild, his resentment is tender, and his purposes are inconstant" (*Idler, Adventurer*, 420). Somewhat paradoxically, the reader's pleasure appears to derive not from a stoicism that proclaims the mind's superiority to the world but rather from the supplementary beauty of its versification. Yet in the very dissociation of sound from sense, these poems give material expression to the gap between desire and fulfillment that they thematize in the predicaments of their principal characters.

Thus it would be wrong to see Johnson's view of pastoral as wholly negative, still less a critique that denies to pastoral all power to move.

Johnson's emphasis on artifice and fiction must be seen as part of an ongoing engagement with neoclassical theory and practice. But it is important to note that it is not rhetoric but nature and reason that provide Johnson with his norms. When he later turns his attention to Milton's *Lycidas* in the *Lives*, he holds out against the formalist desire to view the poem as a self-enclosed structure of conventions, exempt from real pathos. The monologic nature of Milton's fiction, as Johnson envisages it, is a measure of the distance that separates it from a natural antistoic poetry of pain and suffering. The priority of representation over fiction finds its equivalent in the priority of the pastoral hero, whose mode of perception is that of pathos and immersion in temporal existence, over the implicitly heroic figure of *Lycidas* who seems, through soliloquy, to have confronted the issues of existence and thus to have triumphed over them. A poet who has experienced genuine grief will not, Johnson holds, run "after remote allusions and obscure opinions" (*Lives*, I: 163). Unlike Milton, who sees his persona as dialectically transcending pagan suffering and becoming the Christian shepherd-poet of the conclusion, Johnson sees the poet-swain as confronting an irreducibly temporal destiny that restricts the power of pastoral to provide a catharsis of the pain of existence.

The very notion of temporal destiny bespeaks a certain realism in the quest for pastoral truth. Yet it would be wrong to see in Johnson's theory a complete break with the tradition that gives pastoral access to a fictionalized ideal. Although the emphasis of Johnson's account of Virgil's first and tenth eclogues falls upon suffering, it also praises "the description of Virgil's happiness in his little farm":

> Happy old man! then still thy farms restor'd,
> Enough for thee, shall bless thy frugal board.
> What tho' rough stones the naked soil o'erspread,
> Or marshy bulrush rear its wat'ry head,
> No foreign food thy teeming ewes shall fear,
> No touch contagious spread it's influence here.
> Happy old man! here 'mid th'accustom'd streams
> And sacred springs, you'll shun the scorching beams;
> While from yon willow-fence, thy pasture's bound,
> The bees that suck their flowery stores around,
> Shall sweetly mingle, with the whispering boughs,
> Their lulling murmurs, and invite repose:
> While from steep rocks the pruner's song is heard;
> Nor the soft-cooing dove, thy fav'rite bird,
> Mean while shall cease to breathe her melting strain,
> Nor turtles from th'aerial elm to plain. Warton.
>
> (*Idler, Adventurer*, p.424)

This description is not of a piece of wild country but of a landscape whose nature has been improved and idealized by art. It reminds one of the rustic farm in Gray's *Elegy in a Country Churchyard* or of the village green in Goldsmith's *The Deserted Village*, and not, as one might expect, of similar scenes in Crabbe's *The Village*. In such descriptions, the claim to truth is validated by the existence of an external referent but is nonetheless augmented by an appeal to a power that can impose its desire on the world of fact. Since this appeal relies on an effort to cancel out a reality that is implicitly still acknowledged to be there, it can be viewed as sentimental. Johnson, like Gray or Goldsmith, may see through this appeal, but at least in this one respect is still committed to a pastoral art defined in terms of illusion.

What does seem certain is that Johnson's critique of pastoralism has implications beyond the realm of generic criticism or of the rules of composition as customarily understood. It has to do with a way of seeing and interpreting the world, and of expressing that interpretation in a coherent way, a way that Rosalie Colie traces back to certain theorists in the Renaissance.[11] This conception of literary form prevents generic identification from becoming purely taxonomic, making it contingent upon formal properties to which prescriptive rules apply. Yet it also prevents generic classification from becoming purely descriptive, a mode of reading that accepts literary kinds at face value and makes no attempt to discriminate between them. For Johnson, it is essential that the various forms of literature be subject to a rigorous evaluation of their truth-claims, access to alterity, and resistance to illusion. Only thus can one avoid the twin temptations of a rationalist criticism devoid of human consequence and a species of historical criticism that renounces all pretension to evaluation and judgment.

* * *

Johnson's critique of the "sacred poem," like his critique of pastoral, can help one gain a better understanding of his approach to genre studies in general. A major literary genre in the seventeenth century, the sacred poem once again began to exert an important influence from the middle of the eighteenth century onward. A genre that existed outside the conventional hierarchy of literary kinds, the sacred poem was initially ignored or distrusted by neoclassical critics like Nicholas Boileau but then favorably regarded by writers such as John Dennis and Robert Lowth who helped to define a new poetry of the religious sublime.[12] A work such as Lowth's *Lectures on the Sacred Poetry of the Hebrews* (1753), while not explicitly devoted to poetic theory, lays the scholarly groundwork for the metaphysical legitimizing of a poetics based on the presence of the divine in the landscape. The large number of romantic poems concerned with what Abrams has called natural supernaturalism needs no comment. Sacred poetry is the traditional literary genre most germane to natural supernaturalism, considered as a poetic of the religious sublime.[13] Johnson's particular judgments are directed at Watts and such seventeenth-century poets as Donne, Cowley, and Waller, yet his criticism of "poetical devotion," like his criticism of pastoral, affords a striking contrast to the trend in preromantic aesthetics toward the affirmation of a poetic discourse that transcends temporality.

For Johnson, the sacred poem resembles the pastoral in a number of ways, not the least of which is the "paucity" of the topics it offers the poet for amplication. Inasmuch as these topics are, for the most part, fixed and "universally known," they are not susceptible to a differential play of ideas and images. It is this play that makes dialogue and disputation possible and that prevents the poet from withdrawing into a monological world of pious exhortation. Instead of being asked to adjudicate between differences in perspective and interpretation, the reader is invited to contemplate the paraphrase of topics that, inasmuch as they are accepted by all, cannot be made to differ from themselves. Sacred poetry, moreover, seems to lack any basis for conflict in Johnson's opinion. Any ultimate opposition between man's will and God's will appears to be unthinkable, and, in any case, would elevate man into a "higher state" than poetry—with its studied cadences and artfully chosen tropes and figures—is capable of sustaining. Johnson gives as two of his definitions of the term "presence" in the *Dictionary*: "state of being in view of a superior" and "approach, face-to-face, to a great personage." Johnson obviously regards the "presence" engendered by this kind of unmediated "face-to-face" encounter with the divine as incompatible with representation. The majestic terror it obviously inspires differs from natural supernaturalism in being epic and apocalyptic rather than sublime: more akin to an encounter with Christ the Judge of Romanesque art than to a sobering awareness of the spirit that pervades all things.

It is here that one can locate a major point of difference between Johnson's thinking and the interests of present-day critical theory. He offers a singularly impressive example of the way criticism can fix its sights on the most severely orthodox tenets of Christian belief and yet refuse to grant religious verse any special dispensation. This example is all the more worthy of attention in view of the rift between thinkers like William Empson, committed to preserving what they see as the emancipatory promise of English poetry in its resistance to a narrowly doctrinal reading, and those critics who find no difficulty in assimilating poetry to the mysteries of Christian revelation. To Johnson, such quarrels would appear to be misconceived in so far as they ignore the special character of scriptural language. Hence the main object of his argument: to show that religious language, because of its proximity to revelation, is inherently ill-adapted to the requirements of poetry. Johnson, in Hagstrum's apt formulation, conceived of religious discourse as "colorless, general, austere, and inscrutable."[14] These attributes point to a fundamental unity that, because it is self-sufficient and self-identical, is amenable to citation but not to amplification by the poet. By contrast, topics drawn from the realms of nature and life are inevitably fissured, enmeshed in a world of differences that makes invention, elaboration, and drama or narrative possible. The contrast between these two realms of discourse is elaborated most fully in the "Life of Waller" in which Johnson assumes that the value of a rule, here a negative rule or prohibition, resides not in particular examples, but rather in a condition that may be defined in general: namely that the divine, being fully present to itself, differs from nature and life, which are inherently divided and thus impure. In the case of the latter, mimesis functions as a necessary supplement, intended to display "those parts of nature which attract" and to conceal "those which repel, the imagination" (*Lives*, I: 292). But when this kind of mimesis is applied to religious topics, it can only "corrupt," Johnson argues, for it introduces something alien into what is meant to be viewed as integral and, in some sense, indivisible.

There is thus no room here for the verses of Donne, Herbert, and Crashaw, of Watts and Smart. Johnson's theory envisages a wholly self-sufficient, self-enclosed domain of language, generated by a transcendental signified and manifested in the vocabulary of superlatives traditionally utilized to describe the properties of the Creator:

> whatever is great, desireable, or tremendous, is comprised in the name of the Supreme Being. Omnipotence cannot be exalted; Infinity cannot be amplified; Perfection cannot be improved. (*Lives*, I: 292)

This argument is susceptible to two possible interpretations. The reader who rightly expects to experience "the enlargement of his comprehension or the elevation of his fancy" from poetry cannot demand this from a poetry that seeks to praise the Supreme Being, for, if he understands what is comprehended in the name of the Supreme Being, he will have already achieved such enlargement and elevation. Yet the argument could be also taken to imply that a finite mind can never expect to achieve such an expansion from what is implied in the name of the Supreme Being because it is incapable conceiving or imagining the infinite. Any idea purporting to be an idea of God is too great for "the wings of wit," as Johnson puts it in the "Life of Milton." It follows that our names for the infinite cannot constitute a plenitude. As intentional signs, they are never simply self-identical but are always appellations of something that lies beyond our grasp; when these names point to what "cannot be described," there is no actual access of knowledge or contact with reality. Hence, the mind, instead of rising to the ideality, only sinks back into itself.

Whether or not the mind is capable of comprehending the ideas that lie beyond the epithets traditionally employed to describe divinity, it is clear that this discourse is conceived of as being "uniform," integral, and sufficient unto itself. Its stylistic features imply that it is timeless, anonymous, and above all categorical; it is neither falsifiable, nor open to qualification. Not only literal appellations but also the "ornaments of figurative diction" are repelled by such a discourse. As a supplement intended to remedy what is divided and deficient, the "tropes and figures" of poetry cannot improve what is already "simple" and absolute or add variety to what is unitary. On this point, Johnson is following a venerable tradition; as Angus Fletcher observes, "the oldest term for ornamental diction" is "*kosmos*." In keeping with this definition, Marsilio Ficino opposes God to "the world" in his commentary on Plato's *Symposium*, contending that the term world "means ornament composed of many, whereas God must be completely simple."[15] This is the hierarchic opposition to which Johnson seeks to do justice in his critique of devotional poetry. The structure of divine discourse, implying absolute permanence, renders all alteration, substitution, inversion, and addition impossible. In Coleridgean terms, it is a language of abstract notions that cannot be translated into a picture language.

In the background of this argument one detects not only Johnson's antipathy to all forms of religious paraphrase and amplification but also his sense of the necessity of representing something palpable and therefore of submitting poetry to the actual. For Johnson, the proper object of a religious poet's descriptions is "not God, but the works of God." This does not mean that the poet cannot "praise the Maker for his works" (*Lives*, I: 291), but it does mean that he cannot praise the Maker *in* his works. Implicit in this distinction is a questioning of the assumption on which preromantic interpretations of the religious sublime as the union of finitude and infinity based themselves. The figures of epideictic rhetoric are verbal figures; they acknowledge, in their own insufficiency, the separation of the mind from its object.

It is thus possible to see the enterprise in which Johnson is engaged as one side of a debate that was to persist into the nineteenth century. Hazlitt's view that poetry "has something divine in it, because it raises the mind and hurries it into sublimity by conforming the shows of things to the desires of men" is probably behind his criticism of Johnson's "general indisposition to sympathize heartily and spontaneously with works of high-wrought passion or imagination" or to follow "the flights of a truly poetic imagination."[16] Hazlitt's charge is valid inasmuch as Johnson's criticism explicitly denies to poetry the power to transcend the separation of fiction from reality and to impose its desires on the world of fact. Indeed, it maintains that the mind must resist this seduction into illusion. To believe that the mind can be "hurried into sublimity" is for Johnson to ignore its estrangement from God and the world. It is because Johnson believes in the fact of this estrangement that he approaches pious meditation, like love poetry, as a performative rather than a constative or fictive genre:

> the employments of pious meditation are Faith, Thanksgiving, Repentance, and Supplication. Faith, invariably uniform, cannot be invested by fancy with decorations. Thanksgiving, the most joyful of all holy effusions, yet addressed to a Being without passions, is confined to a few modes, and is to be felt rather than expressed. Repentance, trembling in the presence of the judge, is not at leisure for cadences and epithets. Supplication of man to man may diffuse itself through many topics of persuasion; but supplication to God can only cry for mercy. (*Lives*, I: 292)

It is Johnson's assumption that in such "employments" we are not contriving fictions but performing such acts as giving thanks, asking forgiveness, and so forth. But just as theological discourse must be assumed to be simple and self-identical, so such prayers must assume an ideal continuity between intention and meaning, enthusiasm and expression. To express and achieve the conviction of sincerity, a work must strive to overcome the fact that it is only an imitation of a supplicant's speech act. As a living utterrance, it must issue forth from a violently agitated mind: enthusiasm is what ensures a swift transition between what nature prompts and the poet writes.

Yet inasmuch as such a work is addressed to a force that it can never master, it can never be present to itself as a fulfilled and actual intentionality, adequate to its desires or fears. It is probably in this sense that "repentance" is too agitated "for cadences and epithets." Arising as it does out of the distance between desire and its object, it can never be a means of closing that gap. Even though the "cry of mercy—a moment of absolute prostration before something that transcends and humiliates the temporal self—may release the individual from the prison-house of the ego, it will necessarily be devoid of any kind of expressive power in the romantic or postromantic sense. The passion to which John Ruskin refers when he complains that "all the work of Pope, Goldsmith, and Johnson is in sententious pentametre; in which emotion, however on sufferance admitted, never leads or disturbs the verse, nor refuses to be illustrated by ingenious metaphor" is a passion that derives its expressive force from the fact that it disrupts but does not destroy the fabric of the poetry. There is nothing of this balance between emotion and reason in Johnson's conception of sacred poetry. The fact that Johnson composed devotional verse in Latin in his old age or was moved to tears by the *Dies Irae, Dies Illa* doesn't necessarily invalidate this conception.[17] By insisting that the only power sacred poetry possesses is the knowledge of its own weakness, Johnson, in effect, leaves the sublime to the detached spectator of Burkean terror. His recuperation of the asserted limitation of devotional discourse takes the form of a reassertion of human imagination as sympathy.

* * *

There is much in Johnson's treatment of "Sacred verse" that might lead one to regard it as a particularly narrow form of neoclassicism, a series of interdictions designed to prevent poetry from advancing truth-claims or engaging with issues beyond a limited realm of everyday experience. Yet there is one area that Johnson exempts from these interdictions—religious controversy. Since religious controversy assumes the prior existence of disagreement and debate, Johnson distinguishes it from a monologic poetry of pious meditation or prophecy. As compared with Prior's *Solomon*, Dryden's *Religio Laici* and *The Hind and the Panther* afford little of the easy satisfaction to be had from didactic compositions that put forth the absolute judgments of a solitary sage. In this sense, they answer to the demand that individual utterances be shown as enmeshed in a world of controversy outside the speaker's intentions or control—hence Johnson's suggestion that there is something inherently unstable in this kind of verse. "Argumentative" rather than "poetical" in subject matter, it is unable to find its proper stylistic level with any degree of certainty. Introducing a mixture of the "familiar" and the "solemn," the "humorous" and the "grave," it is necessarily divided from itself as well as from the discourse to which it is responding (*Lives*, I: 442).

What is admirable in Dryden's controversial poems is equally admirable in the theodicies of Blackmore and Thomson. The openly professed dichotomy between subject and ornament is the reflection of a dichotomy between reason and revelation that prevents either kind of poetry from seeking to acquire the kind of privileged status—the authority of revealed truth—that would place them in competition with religious discourse. This is not the case, however, with the biblical epic. Johnson believes that the attempt to expand on the events of sacred history, like the attempts to amplify the topics of pious meditation, is inherently transgressive. But once again, there are aspects of his criticism that suggest a very different reading, one more alert to the possibilities of scriptural amplification. Because of his admiration for *Paradise Lost*, he found it impossible to equate Milton's epic with Cowley's *Davideis*. Johnson's discussion of *Davideis*, although obviously influenced by his low estimate of the quality of Cowley's verse, is based on the contention that it is impossible, if not licentious, to recreate the incidents of scriptural history:

> Sacred History has been always read with submissive reverence, and an imagination over-awed and controlled. We have been accustomed to acquiesce in the nakedness and simplicity of the authentick narrative, and to repose on its veracity with such humble confidence as suppresses curiosity. We go with the historian as he goes and stop with him when he stops. All amplification is frivolous and vain; all addition to that which is already sufficient for the purposes of religion, seems not only useless but in some degree profane. (*Lives*, I: 49–50)

Johnson's very phraseology, in its dissociation of scriptural history from its customary effects on the common reader, suggests, however, that another solution might be possible. Unlike Cowley, Milton is seen as possessing the capacity to take "the few radical positions which the Scriptures afforded him" and expand them "to so much variety, restrained as he was by religious reverence from licentiousness of fiction"(*Lives*, I: 183). Indeed, Johnson seems more than ready to concede that *Paradise Lost* is an instance of the very "*merveilleux Chretien*" whose possibility he repudiated in the "Life of Cowley": Milton's epic "contains the history of a miracle, of Creation and Redemption; it displays the power and mercy of the Supreme Being; the probable is therefore marvellous, and the marvellous is probable" (*Lives*, I: 174). Johnson still maintains that poets go wrong when they attempt to transcend the limits of contingent and time-bound human understanding. But here his language contrives to suggest the opposite through its fusion into paradox of terms that were kept separate in the commentary on *Davideis*. The effect of this paradox is to complicate Johnson's attitude of scepticism to the point where Milton's epic begins to take on something of the characteristic of revealed truth.

But this shift in allegiances looks less drastic if one recalls what Johnson has to say about sacred history in the "Life of Milton." For the conjunction of the marvellous and the probable is usually seen as a dynamic process, one that permits the reader to participate in the mysteries of the faith. But Johnson's critique of the Christian epic goes along with a deep scepticism with regard to our accessibility to ancient biblical history. In much the same way that the scriptural characters and events of *Davideis* are beyond the ken of its readers, so the Adam and Eve of *Paradise Lost* are in "a state which no other man or woman can know—from which it follows that the union between the marvellous and the probable is effectively severed. For modern Miltonists, ironically, it is these characters which present interpretation with its greatest challenge and which thus give rise to the subtlest form of moral-psychological commentary. Johnson, by contrast, writes self-consciously as an outsider, one for whom the meaning of revealed religious truth is a matter for pious reverence, humble admiration, and unquestioned acquiescence in what the mind cannot possibly hope to understand. Thus there operates a kind of compensatory mechanism whereby Milton's exceptional achievement is thus not really an exception but only the sort of exception that demonstrates the rule.

As has been suggested, this reading has a certain *prima facie* plausibility if one assumes—like Johnson—that the authenticity of scriptural narrative—the truth of those events set down under the guidance of divine inspiration—runs directly counter to reason and human sympathy alike. One would then have to agree with Johnson that Adam and Eve dwelled in a uniquely privileged realm where ordinary standards of human behavior and motivation don't apply. In this respect they bear a distinct resemblance to the allegorical agents that Johnson also criticizes. Johnson's censure of these agents is perhaps understood as an extension and deepening of Addison's *Spectator*, number 315, on Milton's "Allegory of Sin and Death." Both regard allegory as constituted by "allegorical agents" that refer to abstract ideas. Like Addison, Johnson was unwilling to allow allegorical machinery to become anything more than a decorative frame for whatever human action takes place:

> the employment of allegorical persons always excites conviction of its own absurdity; they may produce effects but cannot conduct actions: when the

phantom is put in motion it dissolves; thus Discord may raise a mutiny; but Discord cannot conduct a march, nor besiege a town. (*Lives*, III: 233)

It seems apparent that the overtly allegorical figure for Johnson is an empty figure in which the failure to inspire credibility announces a fundamental impotence. Thus he, like Addison, believes that the animation it supposes is a natural impossibility. Unlike the disguised allegorical figures that Johnson seems to be proposing for comic romance, the overtly allegorical figure has "no real existence" and thus cannot participate in any action in which events are connected from the first cause to the last effect "by a regular and unbroken concatenation." The only possibility available to the poet, therefore, is to establish a marginal region in which allegorical personages will exist as spectators rather than as "actants" or direct plot agents ("thus fame tells a tale, and Victory hovers over a general, or perches on a standard"). In this way, the allegorical figure stands in relation to the action not as a part of the whole but as a retrospective or reflective sign. It is important to emphasize, moreover, that Johnson never envisages a purely "poetical" or "aesthetic" reading in which the referential determination of the sign might be suspended. A loss of faith in the credibility of the allegorical figure does not exempt allegorical discourse from referential determination, since this loss, like the conviction it displaces, is governed by norms of truth and "absurdity" that are necessarily referential.[18]

To some readers, this argument may seem to offer further evidence of the narrowness of Johnson's critical assumptions. Yet what is at stake here—and what links Johnson's concerns with modern-day issues—is the insistence that questions of truth and absurdity not be overridden by an appeal to some alternative form of fabling or fiction outside and above the contingencies of lived experience. For Johnson, such a realm cannot be indifferent to matters of probability and *vraisemblance*. Johnson is not concerned, like some modern theorists, to establish the veracity of the statements made by characters or by the narrators of fictional texts.[19] What is a matter of concern to him is the veracity of the characters themselves. Such a concern, moreover, is not an isolated aspect of Johnson's estimate of *Paradise Lost*. It is clearly related to his interest in Milton's "delight" in sporting in "the wide regions of possibility." Johnson willingly grants Milton's right to imagine such regions. What he is attempting to establish are the criteria by which one can decide what is acceptable in these regions and what is not. Since the exploded mythology of the pagans is no longer a subject of belief, it is no longer a viable subject for invention in Johnson's opinion. On the other hand, "new modes of existence" inspired by sacred scripture are acceptable even though they go beyond what is humanly knowable. Yet Johnson believes that it is wrong to regard these modes of existence as exempt from the limits of human understanding. This error comes about through Milton's apparent failure to recognize that as a medium poetry can only be the material embodiment of perceptible images—hence Johnson's criticism of Milton's attempt to describe "what cannot be described, the agency of spirits" (*Lives*, I: 184). Because Milton failed to respect the differing claims of philosophy and poetry, he was unable to avoid a fundamental "confusion of spirit and matter." Where philosophy demands "pure spirit," poetry requires "animated body" and the two cannot be allowed to become bound up in a shuttling exchange of reciprocal definition that nowhere permits any rigorous demarcation between them.

It is important to emphasize at this point that Johnson's caveats concerning the "absurdity" of allegorical personages and the confusion of matter and spirit are possible only if he takes Milton's attempt to sport in the wide regions of possibility seriously. He obviously sees nothing but error and delusion in the idea that fabling must somehow be exempt from all rational sense-making norms. Yet in order to avoid arriving at an empiricist reduction of knowledge that would limit poetry only to what is actual, Johnson appears, in the "Life of Milton," to be working out another articulation in place of the conventional opposition between fiction and truth, illusion and reality. One senses in Johnson's use of the verb "sport" an avoidance of the more grandiose claims of the religious sublime and a countervailing sense that *Paradise Lost*, like *The Rape of the Lock*, is justified by a theory of art as play. But unlike theorists of the religious sublime, Johnson also seeks to account for the inconsistencies that a scrupulous critic cannot overlook, the opposition between what Johnson calls "possibility" on the one hand and "absurdity" on the other. The need for this new articulation was undoubtedly called for by Johnson's acknowledgement of the greatness of *Paradise Lost*. It seeks to arrive at a new tentative definition of the relation between sublimity and mimesis, imagination and reality.

No matter how one chooses to view Johnson's critique of allegorical persons and spirits, therefore, what emerges from his detailed reservations concerning *Paradise Lost* can by no means be seen as an attempt to judge the poem in terms of a narrow and rigid conception of the epic genre. Rather it is more likely an attempt to come to terms with the recognitions about the poem reached by enthusiasts of the religious sublime. But if Johnson approaches the perspective of some of Milton's enthusiasts at certain points, he does so only insofar as he locates this perspective within a larger framework of values. Johnson's insight into the importance of dramatic incident and dialogue marks the point at which he begins to diverge from Milton's defenders. For Johnson, the possible world constructed by the Miltonic imagination is completely independent of the actual world. Its appeal to the reader is therefore necessarily limited. Like the astronomer who recovered his sanity in *Rasselas* by returning to society, Johnson's common reader escapes madness by placing himself in transactions in which he discovers his differences with others and himself. In thus shifting from a subject to a reader-centered view of genre, Johnson decisively challenges not only the new poetry of the religious sublime but also the traditional hierarchy and system of literary kinds. Biography replaces history as the model for sympathetic identification and provides the rationale for a much more inclusive idea of genre that includes autobiography, biography, travel literature, and the personal letter. Inherently monologic subjects like descriptive, didactic, pastoral, and sacred verse are correspondingly devalued in importance. In all these respects, Johnson's idea of genre resembles the ideas of Bakhtin, with the important difference that Johnson does not make the novel but a much broader variety of fictional and nonfictional mimetic prose forms the center of its focus.[20]

8
Language as the Dress of Thought

Johnson's ideas about poetic language might seem to hold little interest for anyone concerned with issues in present-day literary criticism. Most readers will have a vague sense of Johnson as an exacting critic of linguistic impropriety, a thinker in the broad tradition of rationalistic neoclassicism, for whom prose sense was the foundation of all language, including the language of poetry. This impression comes chiefly from recent Anglo-American critics, among them Leavis who described Johnson's method as "the method of prose-statement, the only use of language that Johnson understands."[7] Leavis's observation was the outgrowth of a perspective that takes it for granted that poetry possesses a richness and complexity of verbal resources that distinguish it sharply from ordinary language and that any critic who fails to recognize this difference is simply benighted. The paradigm case for Leavis was Johnson's well-known criticism of the excesses of Shakespeare's style. What Leavis expressly objects to is Johnson's doctrine of verbal decorum, his belief that where "the language" of Shakespearean drama "is intricate . . . the equality of words to things is very often neglected" (*Shakespeare*, VII: 73).

This chapter takes the view that Johnson's writings are by no means so straightforward in their account of the workings of language. In fact, as I shall argue, they stand in a distinctly ambivalent relation to the neoclassical tradition that Leavis censures. This will mean reading Johnson with an eye to some observations that commentators have generally overlooked or have chosen to disregard as irrelevant to his critical concerns. Of course it is widely acknowledged that Johnson's attitude toward language is closely bound up with his general outlook. This may be why Johnson's distinction between "pious meditation" and "poetry" is perhaps the best place to begin a reconsideration of what is at stake not only in his theory of genres but also in his observations about poetic language. What sets these two realms apart is the notion that "the ideas of Christian theology" are a source of divinely sanctioned meaning and truth, guaranteed and authenticated by the self-present wisdom of the deity who inspired them. Transcending the vagaries of linguistic figuration, these ideas are not susceptible to change or corruption and thus cannot be amplified or embellished: "to recommend them by tropes and figures," Johnson insists, "is to magnify by a concave mirror the sidereal hemisphere" (*Lives*, I: 292–93). But this attitude goes beyond his dealings with questions about the value of devotional poetry and biblical paraphrase to produce what might be characterized as a dualistic view of language in general. For if ordinary language is treated as an inherently unstable, inadequate medium, always dependent upon transient associative linkages between meanings, concepts, and images—then it is hard to see how any kind of natural discourse, including the discourse of poetry, could lay claim to the simplicity and permanence characteristic of revealed truth. It was Cowley's failure to have recognized this fact that discloses him, in Johnson's opinion, to be a naïve poet. Cowley "seems not to have known, or not to have considered, that words being arbitrary, must owe their power to association, and have the influence, and that only, which custom has given them" (*Lives*, I: 58).

This aspect of Johnson's thought needs to be stressed since it leads him to formulate what is, in effect, a poststructuralist thesis. That is, Johnson assumes the existence of an alteration that, from the start, prohibits the full attainment of immediate self-present meaning in language, whether it be the language of prose or poetry. Like Locke and other advocates of the plain style, Johnson is firmly committed to the virtues of clarity, propriety, and consistency. But this commitment is severely curtailed by his belief that words are only arbitrary signs. In a sense, "custom" and "association" function in Johnson's censure of Cowley very much in the same way that the notion of "iterability" functions in Derrida's commentary on J. L. Austin's theory of speech acts. Derrida argued that the "iterability" which marks all utterances is such as to bar any firm distinction between those which are uttered in present good faith and those which possess only a preestablished, conventional sense.[2] Johnson's understanding of associationism, like Derrida's conception of iterability, refers to the possibility, even the inevitability, that words will be repeated and used in different senses on different occasions. Poetic texts are constrained by the fact that they embody conventional usages and tokens of utterance that are always in existence before the poet comes to use them. This associationism or power of acquiring meanings is evidence that poetic language cannot be confined to the unique, self-present moment of the poet's initial utterance. They partake of the "custom" or distancing from origin that marks all language insofar as it precedes and possibly even subverts the poet's intention.

What Johnson describes in Cowley's poetry, then, is something like the structure of iterability that Derrida locates in ordinary language. Of course, it might be argued that Johnson's argument depends upon that nostalgia for a lost or displaced origin which—according to Derrida—is the hallmark of Western metaphysics. It operates most often in alliance with a logocentric prejudice that elevates speech as the bearer of authentic meaning and relegates writing to a secondary, instrumental position. In Johnson's version of this distinction, sacred discourse occupies a place analogous to the primacy accorded to speech by philosophers, for whom it possesses the virtue of close proximity to living, self-present ideas, while ordinary language is relegated to the unreliable, purely derivative position of writing. But this analogy won't quite fit, since Johnson's distinction involves making a special case of the very limited realm of theological language, while regarding all other forms of language, whether oral or written, as inherently flawed by their reliance on mere verbal signs. Thus, even though associationism is not, like iterability, the absolutely generalized possibility of repetition, it also "breaches, divides, expropriates the 'ideal' plenitude of intention and meaning" and of all correspondence between intention and expression in prose or poetry.[3] The "accidental and colloquial senses" it engenders are, in Johnson's opinion, "the disgrace of language, and the plague of commentators" (*Shakespeare*, VII: 338). These senses alter the semantic determination of words, sometimes even cutting them off, at a certain point, from their "original" meanings and contexts. What this means, in practical terms, is that a poet like Cowley is forced to adopt the point of view of the reader, is forced to recognize that

> as the noblest mien or most graceful action would be degraded and obscured by a garb appropriated to the gross employments of rustics and mechanics, so the most heroic sentiments will lose their efficacy, and the most splendid ideas drop their magnificence, if they are conveyed by words used commonly upon low and trivial occasions, debased by vulgar mouths, and contaminated by inelegant applications. (*Lives*, I: 58–59)

This is not merely a warning against stylistic impropriety. It is also an argument against the metaphysical centrality and primacy of self-present meaning in all human discourse. To function at all, sentiments and ideas must depend upon the necessity of citing or repeating previously given "applications" or usages.

To some extent the tone of these remarks can be explained by Johnson's acute sense of incongruity, his rejection of inflated rhetoric in whatever context, or his disdain of vulgar, inelegant language. But the difficulty extends well beyond the offending passages that Johnson cites in the "Life of Cowley." If words can never be trusted, if they cannot be restricted to a poet or speaker's initial intention, then it would be impossible for Johnson to assert, as did La Bruyère, that "among all the different modes in which a single thought may be expressed, only one is correct."[4] Any such argument would amount to the claim that there is only one single way of establishing a strict correspondence between thought and expression. It could even be seen as approximating an incarnationalism in which language, as the unique expression of an authentic self-present intention, is viewed as resistant to linguistic alteration or paraphrase. For Johnson, however, there is no such clear-cut distinction to be drawn between a uniquely appropriate expression and other, more corrigible alternatives. The writing of "every work of imagination," he argues in one context, "may be varied a thousand ways with equal propriety" (*Rambler*, III: 127). This is not inconsistent of course with the contention that the poet should strive for a strict propriety between sentiment and sociolect. But it drastically modifies the neoclassical ideal of correctness—so deeply entrenched in eighteenth-century criticism since the time of Boileau and Pope. In Johnson's liberalized interpretation of this ideal, the most basic elements of a poem—its words and phrases—are, in principle, as open to revision and alteration as its thoughts and sentiments. The privilege accorded to the plain style gives way to a perspective that allows for the possibility of a wide variety of styles.

In Johnson, this leads to the well-known censure of Swift's familiar, "easy" manner of writing. Obviously Johnson is far from condemning Swift's prose style outright, but he does insist that good prose—as some proponents of the doctrine of propriety would have it—need not aim at a zero-degree of figuration. Here the chief point to be remarked is that Johnson contemptuously rejects the norm of perfect communicability—so beloved by Locke and proponents of the plain style as well as the notion that there is a single, uniform standard of style to which all writers should conform. This is why it would be hard to imagine Johnson subscribing, except as a miminal requirement, to Adam Smith's contention that "the perfection of style consists in expressing in the most concise, proper, and precise manner the thought of the author, and that in the manner which best conveys the sentiment, passion, or affection with which it affects—or he pretends, it does affect—him, and which he designs to communicate to his reader."[5]

Of course this argument cannot be pushed too far. Johnson is very far from agreeing with Leavis that the doctrine of propriety is nothing more than a pedestrian hindrance to unclouded critical perception. In fact, there is nothing to suggest that he does not subscribe to the neoclassical doctrine that language is the dress of thought. In a sense, the reader's comprehension of the propriety or impropriety of the relation between a word or phrase and its corresponding sentiment is what identifies it as "poetic" or nonpoetic. So described, Johnson's ideal of linguistic decorum might well seem to resemble one prominent strain of present-day structuralist thought, the semiotic theory of Riffaterre. In his *Semiotics of Poetry*, Riffaterre argues that a word or phrase comes to function as a "poetic sign" when it refers to a "preexistent word group" that is nowhere located in the text.[6] In effect, Johnson is making a similar distinction when he opposes language to thought. Johnson, it is true, never locates this thought in an existing verbal configuration, since—unlike Riffaterre—he holds out, as has been seen, the possibility at least that the sentiments of a poem—for example, the sentiments of Gray's *Elegy in a Country Churchyard*—can be original and thus not wholly derivable from a common cultural code or body of opinion.

Where Johnson differs sharply from Riffaterre lies in the fact that he views the poem as an empirical (and perishable) phenomenon rather than as an ideal construct that can account for all of the connotations of its words. When Riffaterre writes that "the characteristic feature of the poem is its unity," he is not relying upon external information about the customary association of words but rather asserting a general (and metaphysical) principle.[7] For Johnson, however, nothing is less certain than the unity of a poem in this sense; the functioning of associationism prohibits in practice, if not in theory, the attainment of the textual autonomy that such a theory purports to demonstrate. The much-maligned observations on Macbeth's invocation to night in *Rambler*, number 168, are evidence of this difference. A postromantic criticism that defends the "creativity" of this passage in terms of an ideally reconstructed polysemia can only succeed by sealing off the text from the dissemination of meanings brought about by perpetual alterations in usage. Johnson recognizes the "force" of Shakespeare's poetry in the passage but claims that it is not powerful enough to prevent the reader from reacting to the contemporary associations of the words. He insists that "words which convey ideas of dignity in one age, are banished from elegant writing or conversation in another, because they are in time debased by vulgar mouths, and can be no longer heard without the involuntary recollection of unpleasing images" (*Rambler*, V: 127). No criticism that seeks to take into account the presence of a historically differentiated reader can afford to ignore such linguistic changes. The limitation of a criticism that focuses solely on Shakespearean creativity is that, while it demonstrates the authority of the verbal icon, what it establishes is only the autonomy of the text's language, not the interaction of that language with other languages outside the text.

Johnson differs from Riffaterre in another sense inasmuch as he never suggests that the establishing of a correspondence between words and thoughts rather than words and things necessarily violates mimesis. What chiefly distinguishes Riffaterre's theory from an older tradition of rationalistic decorum is his argument that poetic texts deviate from the norm of mimesis in referring to a preexistent realm of codified, conventional, publicly available meanings. Riffaterre's theory rests on the claim that such texts depart from the canons of mimesis, the norms of a language's referential function, because at significant points they are "ungrammatical," that is to say, they pursue a logic of self-reference.[8] There is of course no evidence that Johnson ever considered such an argument. Yet it would be equally wrong to suppose that he subscribed to a simple copy theory in which the sign is seen as representing an idea which in turn is seen as representing a perceived thing. Johnson's contention that "words are but the signs of ideas," dependent for their existence upon custom rather than their natural affinity to "the things which they denote" effectively forecloses this as a straightforward possibility (*Works*, II: 37). Instead Johnson, especially in his annotations of Shakespeare's plays, is likely to focus on just those passages that strike the reader as corrupt, that possess some apparently confused significance, yet that cannot easily be reduced to some preexistent set of historical codes, conventions, or signifying structures. Associationism thus leads criticism to a point where commentary no longer has anything useful to say and where meaning can only be established conjecturally, through a patient yet hypothetical reconstruction of linked usages and applications.

It is at this point that the neoclassical doctrine of propriety really does become important in Johnson's argument, operating as a sort of countervailing force. Propriety, for Johnson, is what holds out against the dispersive, disseminating tendencies of language. This is why he praises Dryden, whom he obviously regards—in opposition to Cowley—as a highly self-conscious poet, for Dryden's achievement in introducing a "propriety in word and thought" into English poetry (*Lives*, I: 420). Yet there is no suggestion, once again, that Johnson believes that Dryden's system of "poetical diction" can ever really overcome the arbitrary nature of the sign. Indeed, what Johnson calls poetical diction is only a system of relations among signifiers, not a union of signifiers and signifieds. In this sense, it is opposed to romantic criticisms of the "artificiality" of eighteenth-century poetic diction. The latter repudiates any commitment to a prior system of differing terms, insisting that poetic language must be grounded in a naturalized fusion of word and idea. This organicist conception of language, in which names correspond initimately with the meanings they signify, reabsorbs image into thing. In Johnson's argument, on the other hand, this unity could only be characteristic of the language of God, not the languages of men. Poetic diction functions in ordinary language as a differential interplay between several pairs of opposites—generality/particularity, familiarity/novelty, grossness/ refinement—that restrict and define the propriety of words through a process of comparison and contrast. According to Johnson,

> there was . . . before the time of Dryden no poetical diction; no system of words at once refined from the grossness of domestick use and free from the harshness of terms appropriated to particular arts. Words too familiar or too remote defeat the purpose of a poet. From those sounds which we hear on small or on coarse occasions, we do not easily receive strong impressions, or delightful images; and words to which we are nearly strangers, whenever they occur, draw that attention on themselves which they should transmit to things. (*Lives*, I: 420)

What Johnson is insisting upon here is a firm distinction between the individual poem and the general system of words from which it is derived. This system, he reasons, should underlie and preexist any possible text, since words can be expected to draw attention to "things" rather than themselves only when they conform to a prearticulated system of verbal relations.

This argument might seem to come into conflict with Johnson's acute sensitivity to linguistic change. Any prearticulated vocabulary of poetic terms will inevitably be subject to the same erosion as language in general. But there is no suggestion, in Johnson's argument, that the system of poetic diction devised by Dryden and subsequently elaborated by Pope should not be revised or transformed as altered linguistic circumstances warrant. If there is one principle that sustains Johnson's praise of Dryden's invention of a system of poetical diction, it is the notion of a perpetually shifting disparity between words and their meanings. The effect of such a principle is to challenge the notion that there is one unique or permanent system of poetic signs. Both normative and deviant usages are caught up in a differential play that initiates, but also displaces, the egregious, unintentional kinds of verbal impropriety that Johnson enumerates in the "Life of Cowley" and in a brief discussion of Dryden's *Annus Mirabilis*. Nor does it preclude criticism of the self-consciously "cumbrous splendour" he finds in the odes of Collins, Gray, and Akenside. Yet, since the possibility of the mock-heroic, the burlesque, and the parodic, as well as serious forms of moralized landscape, sentimental effusion, and loco-descriptive poetry, are also dependent upon a formalized distance between word and idea, poetic diction draws attention to the element of fiction and artifice in literary language. Indeed, poetic diction is akin to representation in one sense, since it depends, like mimesis, upon the absence of what it purports to convey; the term "poetic diction" itself implies a recognition not only of the resemblance but also of a regulated difference between thoughts and the words in which they are robed.

It is plain enought to see how this argument might lend support to Leavis's strictures about Johnson's critical prejudices. Johnson's notion of poetic diction could well be seen as yet another sign of what Leavis terms Johnson's chronic incapacity to appreciate the creative uses of language, the power of poetry to reach a realm of complexity beyond any such prearranged system of words. But this would be to discount what is most distinctive and important in Johnson's argument. For his point is that we couldn't talk of creativity unless we first possessed this more basic grasp of what makes words work in our language. And this principle lends support for the kind of linguistic relativism espoused by Johnson, namely the argument that "all polished languages have different styles." Johnson takes this as a ground for asserting the impossibility of a total translation:

> when languages are formed upon different principles, it is impossible that the same modes of expression should always be elegant in both. While they run on together, the closest translation may be considered as the best; but when they divaricate, each must take its natural course. Where correspondence cannot be obtained, it is necessary to be content with something equivalent. (*Lives*, I: 422)

What can only be translated with certainty are the sentiments or images, the sense of a translation, for when languages are "formed on different principles," Johnson insists, their styles become, strictly speaking, untranslatable. At most, the translator can "exhibit his author's thoughts in such a dress of diction as the author would have given them, had his language been English."[9] Translation is thus an intrastylistic movement, assuring the transport of a signified from one system of signifiers to another. Yet this intrastylistic movement is not tantamount to stylistic license. In so far as possible, the most prominent features of an author's style are to be preserved: "rugged magnificence is not to be softened, hyperbolical ostentation is not to be repressed; nor sententious affectation to have its point blunted" (*Lives*, I: 423). Indeed, the very necessity of trying to preserve the main features of an author's style begins to place poetry outside the circle of what can be translated. This point is made by Johnson in a conversation with Boswell: "Johnson. 'You may translate books of science exactly. You may also translate history, in so far as it is not embellished with oratory, which is poetical. Poetry indeed, cannot be translated. . .'"[10] Doubtless, Johnson's argument is partly for dramatic emphasis, but it indicates the outer limits of a theory of language as the dress of thought. Translation must at times seek to preserve not only the substance but also the style with which substance, at least in the case of poetry, appears to have an internal and essential link.

To this extent, Johnson is aware of the peculiar difficulties that the tropes and figures of rhetoric put in the way of any serious attempt to translate poetry from one language to another. But there is another, equally important, reason why poetry cannot be translated, one that preserves a sense of the disparity between words and meanings. Johnson concedes in *Rambler*, number 94, that the fancy can occasionally act to naturalize the relation between the two: "It is scarcely to be doubted, that on many occasions we make the musick which we imagine ourselves to hear; that we modulate the poem by our own disposition, and ascribe to the numbers the effects of the sense" (*Rambler*, IV: 136). Such instances, however, are invariably subjective and ephemeral and thus do not alter the fundamental disjunction between words and ideas. To the extent that each language has its own distinctive configuration of sounds, therefore, this disjunction would render the translation of any poem virtually impossible. Translation is deflected from its aim by a disparity that prevents the sound from becoming an echo to the sense. Johnson's arguments against Pope's theory of "representative harmony" are too familiar to bear repetition here. What should be emphasized is Johnson's insistence upon the ease by which "resemblance in the mind" may govern "the ear." Even this kind of resemblance, moreover, is essentially "technical and nugatory" and thus is "not to be rejected and not to be solicited." Concrete phonic material can only be bestowed on meanings through "duration and different degrees of motion" and even these means are uncertain and ambiguous. The independence in principle of sound from sense would thus seem to be the essence or telos of language. What Johnson calls "the music of metre" would derive its validity as music from that which is in essence independent of meanings: the choice of "the flowing and the sonorous words," the variation of "pauses," the adjustment of the "accents," the diversification of the "cadence," and the "smoothness" of the "metre" (*Lives*, I: 466). At this point, mimesis as well as propriety can simply drop out of the picture, since they extend, as we have seen, to prose as well as poetry, to nonfictional as well as fictional genres. For if the "music of metre" is the criterion by which "poetry has been discriminated in all languages," Johnson argues, then it is verbal music that most fully manifests the essence of what we call poetry.

* * *

There are other reasons for regarding Johnson's relation to rationalistic neoclassicism as ambivalent. His contention that every text can be varied in a thousand ways with equal propriety is a case in point. It represents not only an attack on the doctrine of correctness but also a principled refusal to go along with the full implications of the neoclassical theory of decorum. The hierarchical stratification of styles into elevated, middle, and low was a natural extension of this theory, but for Johnson this hierarchy of styles has nothing like the sacrosanct authority and wisdom it holds for other critics. Johnson clearly accepted the conventions of this theory: he described Milton's "natural port," for example, as "gigantick loftiness" (*Lives*, I: 177), praised *Religio Laici* as an instance of "the middle kind of writing which, though prosaick in some parts, rises to high poetry in others, and neither towers to the skies nor creeps along the ground" (*Lives*, I: 442), and characterized the "diction" of Butler's *Hudibras* as "grossly familiar" and its "numbers" as "purposely neglected" (*Lives*, I: 217). Such precise discriminations, along with the insistence on a rigid separation of styles, have often been seen as characteristic of "authoritarian" cultures, which mark the boundary between a sanctioned language and any discourse that differs from it.[11] In criticism this authoritarianism takes the familiar form of holding that genres, metaphors, or styles should not be mixed and that decorum or propriety should be observed in character. Johnson, though praised for acknowledging Shakespeare's violation of decorum in character, is often seen as preserving and perpetuating the traditional neoclassical doctrine of the separation of styles.[12]

It is possible, however, to detect another strain in Johnson's criticism, one that calls this doctrine of separation of styles into question. Johnson, as has already been seen, clearly encourages the reader to cultivate an awareness of the individual styles of particular poets: Milton, Young, and Thomson are praised for achieving what Johnson describes, in the case of Milton, as a "uniform peculiarity of *Diction*, a mode and cast of expression which bears little resemblance to that of any former writer" (*Lives*, I: 189). Yet the very distance between an author's style and the language of common usage creates its own difficulties: upon analysis, a "uniform peculiarity of *Diction*" will often discompose itself into heterogeneous elements or reveal itself as contaminated by what is alien and parasitic. Thus Young has "the trick of joining the turgid and the familiar" (*Lives*, III: 398), while Milton is described as being "desirous to use English words with a foreign idiom," so that "the disposition of his words is . . . frequently Italian, perhaps sometimes combined with other tongues" (*Lives*, I: 190). The bewitchment of judgment that Johnson occasionally attributes to the specialized language of poetry can result from a specialized idiom with unexamined bases in alien vocabularies. This makes it all the more important to give credit to verbal parodies in which the impurities of a grand style are exposed to hearty laughter and derision. Johnson sees John Philips's *The Splendid Shilling* as performing just such a salutary exercise:

> to degrade the sounding words and stately construction of Milton, by an application to the lowest and most trivial things, gratifies the mind with a momentary triumph over that grandeur which hitherto held its captives in admiration; the words and things are presented with a new appearance, and novelty is always grateful where it gives no pain. (*Lives*, I: 317)

Philips's travesty, Johnson implies, forces the reader to confront all the faults that the seductive power of Milton's verse had formerly concealed from him: "whatever there is in Milton which the reader wishes away, all that is obsolete, peculiar, or licentious is accumulated with great care by Philips" (*Lives*, I: 318). To the extent that it directs the reader's attention to these deficiencies, *The Splendid Shilling* promotes a healthy distrust of Milton's self-conscious virtuosity of style.

Here again, there is a useful comparison to Bakhtin's theory of genres, a theory that assumes that the authority of an elevated style like Milton's is vulnerable to the mimicry of what Bakhtin calls its laughing, parodic double.[13] For Johnson—as for Bakhtin—this indicates the importance of the mock-heroic as a mode that exploits the primary conventions of serious genres to create replicas based on an entirely different level of style and culture. This parodic reduction is made possible by the heterogeneity that marks apparently uniform styles, splitting them into incongruous mixtures of high and low, grave and humorous. The term Johnson frequently employs to describe such mixtures is "peculiar," but this word can be used as a sign of either praise or blame. Thus while Johnson chastises Dryden for mingling the "sublime" and the "ridiculous" in *Annus Mirabilis*, he sees the "peculiar" strength of Juvenal's style as its "mixture of gaiety and stateliness, of pointed sentences, and declamatory grandeur" (*Lives*, I: 447). Such a mixture is not merely a reflection of the predilections of the individual poet. It is also evidence of the mixture of high and low elements within the language of any given culture. Thus in praising Dryden's poetic diction, Johnson observes that

> every language of a learned nation necessarily divides itself into diction scholastick and popular, grave and familiar, elegant and gross; and from a nice distinction of these different parts arises a great part of the beauty of style. But if we except a few minds, the favourites of nature, to whom their own original rectitude was in the place of rules, this delicacy of selection was little known to our authors: our speech lay before them in a heap of confusion, and every man took for every purpose what chance might offer him. (*Lives*, I: 420)

By "delicacy of selection," Johnson is not referring to an activity that would seek to erase the internal divisions within a language. For otherwise there would be no resisting the claim that Johnson's conception of style is negative, "less important for what it recommends than for what it forbids."[14] To avoid this conclusion, one has to recognize that this theory, far from striving to fashion a single, homogeneous style, actually acknowledges the stratification within a single language and thus seeks to select words from different levels without blurring them or merging them into a confused heap. It is true that such diversity is not meant to exceed the boundaries of a specifically literary language. Hence, it tries to exclude words that are "too familiar" or "too remote," not to speak of terms which, like the excretory vocabulary of Pope and Swift, are deemed gross and offensive. And it encompasses the rule that "all appropriated terms of art should be sunk in general expressions" (*Lives*, I: 433). Yet, even as it holds that "poetry is to speak a universal language," it also insists that within such a language "different colours" must be "joined to enliven one another" (*Lives*, I: 420).

It may be asked how Johnson's ideas, thus construed, could possibly serve as an antidote or corrective to a neoclassical theory of the strict separation of styles. Certainly Johnson—in contrast to Bakhtin—finds no room for a violent clash between the sociolects of rival cultural groups. Yet, in so far as he concentrates on variety, he also leads us to consider style as an "arrangement" in which diverse elements are incorporated into a system of differential relations. By itself, a style based on philosophic or popular terms is deficient; it is not until both are united in a dynamic mixture that sets one off against the other that they can achieve their actual potency. Nor should this style be thought of as excluding all terms drawn from the arts and sciences. Johnson censures Dryden for including some nautical terms in *Annus Mirabilis,* but he also chastises Dryden for employing a footnote to explain longtitude rather than integrating his knowledge in the poem itself:

> it had better become Dryden's learning and genius to have laboured science into poetry, and have shewn, by explaining longtitude, that verse did not refuse the ideas of philosophy. (*Lives*, I: 434)

These are demanding but elastic standards. A poem that attempted to live up to such norms would be required to incorporate within itself a good deal that is weighty and philosophical.

It is surely significant in this connection that Johnson's own prose attempts to encompass the union of popular and philosophic terms that he believed could be incorporated into verse. In what must be an unformulated law of the popular tradition of commentary on Johnson, he was accused of the very same corruptions for which he reproached Milton and Gray. Thus Robert Burrowes criticized Johnson for preferring the "remote word of Latin derivation to the received English one" and for bringing in "the whole vocabulary of natural philosophy, to perplex and encumber familiar English writing."[15] Such apparent incongruities are usually put down to the fact that Johnson was completing the first edition of the *Dictionary* at the same time that he was introducing complex Latinate words into the *Rambler* and *Idler* series. Yet Burrowes's censure is similar to Johnson's own, earlier description of Sir Thomas Browne's style as "a mixture of heterogeneous words, brought together from distant regions, with terms originally appropriated to one art, drawn by violence into the service of another." Johnson praises Browne for many "forcible expressions, which he would never have found, but by venturing to the utmost verge of propriety; and flights which would never have been reached, but by one who had very little fear of the shame of falling" (*Works*, XII: 303). What has prevented Johnson's style from being recognized as a similar assemblage of divergent words and daring flights is that it does not represent the introduction of popular idioms and locutions into an elevated form but rather the reverse—the reinsertion of the tropes and figures of an elevated manner into what had become an easy, familiar style of writing. This countermovement has all too often been seen as a reinvention of the high style rather than what it actually represents: a calculated mixture of heterogeneous or incongruous elements. Johnson's distinctive style, with its fondness for Latinisms and homely but unsettling metaphors, amounts to a renunciation of the strategies by which prose seeks to repress elements supposedly extraneous to it.

There is thus, I would suggest, a very real affinity between Bakhtin's theory and Johnson's practice of stylistic critique. Both start out from the belief that prose or verse can accommodate what is seemingly extrinsic to it. In place of a doctrine that adheres to the ideal of style as pure, homogeneous, and uniform, Johnson in effect affirms a norm that conceives of style as a heterogeneous mixture of differing elements. Johnson's lack of enthusiasm for conventional standards of stylistic propriety can be seen, for instance, in his summary judgment that the Earl of Roscommon is "elegant but not great; he never labours after exquisite beauties, and he seldom falls into gross faults" (*Lives*, I: 239). Of John Sheffield, he similarly writes, "he had the perspicuity and elegance of an historian, but not the fire and fancy of a poet" (*Lives*, II: 177). And in appraising Swift's poetry, he observes, "the diction is correct, the numbers are smooth, and the rhymes exact. There seldom occurs a hard-laboured expression or a redundant epithet; all his verses exemplify his own definition of a good style, they consist of 'proper words in proper places'" (*Lives*, III: 65). Although Johnson's Longinian alternative to the ideal of elegant decorum exemplified in these poets is far from being totally elastic, it is broad enough to include copious authors who—like Shakespeare, Bacon, or Browne—employ all the resources of language; there are places in the *Dictionary* where Johnson introduces and thus acknowledges Shakespearean, Baconian, and Brownean words. Johnson is convinced, in any case, that one function of style is to transform a disordered multiplicity into a focused drama in which contrasting elements are articulated into a distinct system. Although this norm can hardly be said to dissolve all distinction between the proper and the improper, it extends the boundary of propriety to encompass words that many of Johnson's contemporaries clearly found cumbersome, difficult, or simply bewildering.

* * *

There is another objection that has been frequently directed not only against Johnson but also against other eighteenth-century poets and critics in general. This is the claim that they privileged a poetry of statement over a poetry of suggestion. In a fairly typical formulation of this argument, F. W. Bateson argued that

> the Augustan achievement was by shearing words of their secondary and irrelevant associations to release the full emphasis of their primary meanings. The connotations, instead of blurring the denotations, reinforced them. The poetry of Dryden and Pope differs therefore from early and later English poetry in that it is not a poetry of suggestion but of statement.[16]

This amounts to a highly refined and sophisticated variation of the conventional nineteenth-century charge that the eighteenth-century is an age of prose. It measures Johnson as a critic who, in the words of Hazlitt, is "a judge of poetry as it falls within the limits of prose."[17] The argument, however, runs into problems as soon as one examines more closely how the opposition between statement and suggestion actually figures in Johnson's criticism. It is basic to Johnson's outlook that poetry is always exposed to secondary and irrelevant associations inasmuch as it is necessarily immersed in a larger world of customary and transient usage. Johnson takes account of "primary meanings" only as a kind of ideal limit, presumed to exist but strictly inaccessible to the poet, since the words commonly employed embody meanings that are independent of the way they are used. The fundamental opposition for Johnson is the opposition between image and concept. This creates a system of values in which fancy is privileged over understanding, the sensory over the intelligible, the picture over the idea. Thus he criticizes Cowley as noted, for attempting "rather to impress sentences upon the understanding than images on the fancy" (*Lives*, I: 59) and holds that Dryden's general fault in *Annus Mirabilis* is "that he affords more sentiment than description, and does not so much impress scenes upon the fancy, as deduce consequences and make comparisons" (*Lives*, I: 431).

This distinction is at the heart of Johnson's philosophy of language. It leads him to reduce didactic poetry to a minor genre that must generate a verbal efflorescence, a prodigal expenditure of ornament, if it is not to appear cold and frigid. Certainly Johnson is opposed to any theory which holds that didactic poetry can dispense with the tropes and figures of rhetoric. He insists, as has been noted, that *An Essay on Man* owes its distinction not to the novelty of its thoughts but to the "dazzling splendour" of its imagery and the "seductive powers" of its eloquence. "Disrobed of its ornaments,"

Pope's argument cannot subsist by "the powers of its naked excellence" (*Lives*, III: 243). Johnson is obviously critical of what he calls Pope's "thoughts," but his line of reasoning implies that these "thoughts" necessarily depend for their effectiveness upon the figurative language in which they are tricked out. Certainly there is small warrant for the belief, in Johnson's opinion, that poetic language manifests its ideas simply and immediately, that the mind can plunge straight to the doctrine illustrated. Johnson put the case most succinctly in his estimate of Cowley:

> Truth indeed is always truth, and reason is always reason; they have an intrinsick and unalterable value, and constitute that intellectual gold which defies destruction: but gold may be so concealed in baser matter that only a chymist can recover it; sense may be so hidden in unrefined and plebeian words that none but philosophers can distinguish it; and both may be so buried in impurities as not to pay the cost of their extraction. (*Lives*, I: 59)

This disturbing possibility—that "truth" (fact) and "reason" (value) may be so embedded in "baser matter" that only a philosopher can distinguish them—is enough to shake the opposition between ordinary language and logic. The very entangling of this argument in a play of metaphors appears to demonstrate the possible heterogeneity of poetical discourse, its potentiality for corruption, and the absence of any certain means by which words and ideas can be sorted out.

It may be objected that Johnson's example is only an extreme case, an account of a confusion between words and ideas that would only hold good for exceptionally obscure sentences and passages. There is still ample room for contexts in which language functions as a perfectly transparent medium, allowing the common reader to comprehend fully the ideas embedded in it. These contexts display the characteristic energy of a poetry of statement, the energy of a discourse that asserts its own propriety, the propriety of its primary, literal sense against all secondary, metaphoric senses. But this argument fails to consider how the literal and the metaphoric are related elsewhere in Johnson's writings. One could, for example, draw attention to Johnson's contention, in the *Preface to the Dictionary*, that "the exuberance of signification" is such that it is scarcely possible "to ascertain all the senses of words." Johnson, it is true, never abandons a belief in the original propriety of language. Every word, in theory at least, has a single, primitive, literal sense. But this sense has value only insofar as it can be discovered and, in all too many instances, Johnson believes, it has been erased, "driven out of use by its metaphoric senses." What this means for the lexicographer is that it will be impossible to dominate language from the inside, as it were, by using a genetic, linear model of signification. Such an etymological model may recognize that a word has many senses, but it will still fail because the "kindred senses may be so interwoven, that the perplexity cannot be disentangled, nor any reason assigned why one should be ranged before the other" (*Works*, II: 48). It is by the genetic priority of one sense to another, moreover, that the difference between primary and secondary meanings is maintained, yet "when the radical idea branches out into parallel ramifications, how can a consecutive series be formed of senses in their nature collateral?" Further, the concept of sense, whether primary or secondary, presupposes the notion of a distinct, unitary meaning, a nuclear entity that can be distinguished from all other entities, yet "the shades of meaning sometimes pass so imperceptibly into each other, so that though on one side, they apparently differ, yet it is impossible to mark the point of contact." Finally, in order for a meaning to be susceptible of definition, it must be capable of calling forth a corresponding name, yet the correspondence between signifiers and signifieds is by no means complete, for "ideas of the same race, though not exactly alike, are sometimes so little different, that no words can express the dissimilitude, though the mind easily perceives it, when they are exhibited together" (*Works*, II: 48). On this account, there is no properly lexicographical method by which primary and secondary senses can easily be distinguished. To overcome Johnson's objections, one would have to assume that the senses aimed at through words are not only independent of the medium that transports them but also can be confirmed by appealing to a realm of essences, necessary attributes, eternal ideas, or whatever. Yet it is precisely the absence of any such realm of universal truths that renders the distinction between proper and metaphoric, primary and secondary, denotative and connotative, problematic in Johnson's lexicography.

There is a similar problematic in Johnson's *Preface* to Shakespeare. Here it is the nature of textual corruption—the errors of unskillful copyists and overconfident editors—that provides the occasion for a series of arguments concerning the relation between truth, error, and human understanding. The latter part of the *Preface* leaves no doubt that Johnson is firmly committed to a position that questions the very possibility of reaching back to the primary intention of the author. Thus

> an emendatory critic would ill discharge his duty, without qualities very different from dulness. In perusing a corrupted piece, he must have before him all possibilities of meaning, with all possibilities of expression. Such must

> be his comprehension of thought, and such his copiousness of language. Out of many readings possible, he must be able to select that which best suits with the state, opinions, and modes of language prevailing in every age, and with his author's particular cast of thought, and turn of expression. Such must be his thought, and turn of expression. Conjectural criticism demands more than humanity possesses, and he that exercises it with most praise has very frequent need of indulgence. *(Shakespeare,* VII: 94–95)

This follows directly from Johnson's conception of the privative character of language, its failure to convey primary, literal meanings through some erroneous perception, some lapse or defect in attention, brought about by reasons that excel any individual's power of comprehension. Thus, "the compleat explanation of an authour not systematick and consequential, but desultory and vagrant, abounding in casual allusions and light hints, is not to be expected from any single scholiast" (*Shakespeare*, VII: 103). Such a limitation comes about because of our not being aware of all of the possibilities of meaning that operate both within an order of thoughts and sentiments and in the realm of language. It is a case, once again, of figurative senses displacing a primary, literal sense, substituting a play of allusion that obeys distinctive laws and thus comes to take on a life of its own.

It would be a somewhat parochial line of approach which insisted that these questions be treated solely in the context of Johnson's activities as a lexicographer and editor and not as statements that might be expected to have any bearing on poetry. Indeed, there is at least one issue raised in Johnson's critique of an etymological model the *Preface to the Dictionary* that is paralleled in his criticism. This is his argument in the "Life of Denham" that the distinction between literal and figurative senses may be relative rather than absolute, a category of language rather than a category of thought. In his estimate of Denham's *Cooper's Hill*, Johnson observes that the most famous quatrain beginning "O could I flow like thee" may not be "perfect,"

> for most of the words, thus artfully composed, are to be understood simply on one side of the comparison, and metaphorically on the other; and if there be any language which does not express intellectual operations by material images, into that language they cannot be translated. (*Lives*, I: 78–79)

This passage has all too often been seen as evidence that Johnson subscribed to the view that figurative language should be asked to conform to a naïve ideal of "translatability," yet it can be argued that Johnson's emphasis actually falls upon the difference between languages.[18] The quotation is cited as a kind of test case, a poetical text that is almost but not quite, perfect because there might always be one language into which its figurative structures could not be transported. This is only raised as a possibility, to be sure, but it is a possibility that works to unsettle the conviction that the literal/metaphoric opposition is a given that exists prior to the existence of specific natural languages. This is a variant of the argument that "one language cannot communicate its rules to another" (*Lives*, I: 192)—different, it would seem, from Johnson's remarks on variations in metrical convention only in the tentativeness of the formulation. But once the possibility that there may be a language in which "intellectual operations" are not expressed by "material images" is admitted, then the entire chain of oppositions (thought/language, signified/signifier, literal/metaphoric, intelligible/material) is, in this one context at least, placed in question. If Johnson's thinking were in fact bound by a conviction of the superiority of the literal to the metaphoric, one might expect him at this point to embrace what might be regarded as one of the grounding principles of a poetry of statement, namely that the strength of Denham's passage resides in its literal denotative meaning and its preservation of this meaning from secondary, associative contamination. Yet Johnson actually praises the quotation for compressing "so much meaning" into "so few words" and for collecting "the particulars of resemblance" so "perspicaciously" (*Lives*, I: 79).

Johnson's praise of Denham's compression can easily be overlooked because he belongs in the company of those critics and theorists for whom interpretation is not the normal mode of critical activity and the elucidation of multiple meanings its most satisfying outcome. Johnson was capable of course of extracting a range of meanings from a passage in Shakespeare but only because that passage presented a particular difficulty to the editor, commentator, or common reader. Such readings are best understood as a modified version of the approach adopted by classical scholars to explain an obscure passage in Homer or Aeschylus. Johnson's most characteristic approach to texts that do not display this kind of obscurity is one that starts out from a generally held opinion on a passage or poem, and then proceeds inductively to confirm or modify that opinion in accordance with rules or principles related to the text in question. The most obvious heirs of this kind of thinking are those modern formalist or structuralist critics who see no virtue in multiplying ingenious interpretations but concentrate instead on the rules and devices governing the operation of a text. Johnson differs from these critics only because his criticism is neither systematic nor scientific in its pretensions.

Of course one could argue that a poetics of statement is precisely the consequence of this emphasis on principles and devices. Evidence of this poetics is to be found in Johnson's mistrust of language, his insistence on the need to protect oneself against the inadequacy and imprecision of the words one is required to use. But this argument fails to consider the peculiar line of thought that Johnson develops in his essay on "easy poetry" in *Idler*, number 77. Johnson defines easy poetry in the broadest possible terms, as "that in which natural thoughts are expressed without violence to the language" (*Idler, Adventurer*, 239). Easy poetry, which can accommodate itself to wit, humour, and sublimity, must exclude "daring figures," "transposition," "unusual acceptations of words," and "any license that would be avoided by a writer of prose." In this sense, Johnson's "easy poetry" bears a striking resemblance to the "natural way of writing" that eighteenth-century critics often attributed to sentimental ballads and popular songs—a mode of language in which there is virtually no evidence of figurative artifice.

Yet what is striking about easy poetry is the ease with which this supposedly natural mode can be displaced by its unnatural double. It is "the prerogative of easy poetry to be understood as long as the language lasts," yet it is all too often counterfeited by "modes of speech, which owe their prevalence only to modish folly, or to the eminence of those that use them" and thus "die away with their inventors," so that "their meaning, in a few years, is no longer known" (*Idler, Adventurer*, 241). Thus, while seeming to point to the mirage of a natural, literal diction, easy poetry actually affirms the rhetorical, figurative character of poetic discourse. The irony behind this line of reasoning becomes particularly evident in the concluding paragraph of the essay in which Johnson observes that "Waller often attempted but seldom attained" to easy poetry, while "poets, from the time of Dryden, have gradually advanced in embellishment, and consequently departed from simplicity and ease" (*Idler, Adventurer*, 242). This so-called advance is primarily evidence of the obstacles confronting any poet who seeks to achieve a simple, literal style:

> it is less difficult to write a volume of lines swelled with epithets, brightened by figures, and stiffened by transpositions, than to produce a few couplets graced only by naked elegance and simple purity, which require so much care and skill, that I doubt whether any of our authors has yet been able, for twenty lines together, nicely to observe the true definition of easy poetry. (*Idler, Adventurer*, 242)

Figurative language is thus seen as central to a discourse that can only with the greatest of difficulty deny or ignore its effects. The supposed simplicity praised by so many eighteenth-century critics is so far from being intrinsic to poetic composition that it can be maintained only for a few lines at a time. Whether Johnson was aware of the irony implicit in the reversal that occurs at the end of *Idler*, number 77, is difficult to say. If discourse is radically metaphorical, its meanings caught up in the seductions of artifice, then poetry is deluded in its search for a naturalness beyond the mazy detours of language.

* * *

So one cannot, after all, read Johnson as subscribing unequivocally to a poetry of statement. The closest that Johnson comes to endorsing such an ideal is to be found in his contention that "of sentiments purely religious, it will be found that the most simple expression is the most sublime" (*Lives*, I: 292). But this, once again, is marked off as a separate linguistic domain where ordinary expectations no longer hold good and truth is best conveyed in the plainest possible form. This kind of "simple expression" may even carry poetry to the point where it attains what Coleridge called a "balance or reconcilement of opposite or discordant qualities." There is in Johnson's opinion, however, a marked contrast between this peculiar, uniquely sanctioned variety of language and the language of most kinds of poetry. Indeed, what chiefly interests Johnson—writing from the standpoint of one for whom the end of poetry cannot be the fusion of opposites—is the difference between qualities. Hence his praise of the "violence" by which "the most heterogenous ideas" are "yoked together" in metaphysical conceits. Such conceits are only the most extreme instance of an activity that both combines and distinguishes opposites like identity and difference or same and other. These conceits, while inviting the reader to consider them as signs and to penetrate them, also assert themselves as pure artifice: their heterogeneity preserves the difference between what they yoke together; their presence entails the absence of what, eventually, they might signify. Hence, the difference between a Johnsonian and a Coleridgean perspective may be not so much between a poetry of statement and a poetry of suggestion as between a poetry that preserves and one that abolishes the distance between tenor and vehicle. T. S. Eliot wrote that "the force of Johnson's 'impeachment' of the metaphysical conceit lies in the fact that often the ideas are yoked but not united."[19]

Of course it is open to debate whether Johnson is actually impeaching the metaphysical conceit. Certainly there exists no basis for concluding that the difference that prevents the two terms of the conceit from fusing ever quite disappears in Johnson's account of metaphor. At one level, the "exemplification" that Johnson examines in his detailed criticism of the angel simile in Addison's *The Campaign* might appear to stand at the opposite extreme from the metaphysical conceit:

> the mention of another like consequence from a like cause, or of a like performance by a like agency, is not a simile, but an exemplification. It is not a simile to say that the Thames waters fields as the Po waters fields; or that as Hecla vomits flames in Iceland, so Aetna vomits flames in Sicily. When Horace says of Pindar, that he pours his violence and rapidity of verse, as a river swoln with rain rushes from the mountain; or of himself that his genius wanders in quest of poetical decorations, as the bee wanders to collect honey; he, in either case, produces a simile: the mind is impressed with the resemblance of things generally unlike, as unlike as intellect and body. (*Lives*, II: 129–30)

Where the conceit presupposes a violent yoking together that fails to find a real point of contact, the exemplification discovers an analogy in things already alike. Yet in his explanation of exemplification, Johnson, in keeping with the tendency of his thought, still privileges heterogeneity and difference. Thus he implies that the supposed analogy of an exemplification is undermined by the "almost identity," which introduces a margin of difference into things basically similar.[20] It follows that, even though an exemplification serves to connect the homogeneous, it also introduces a hidden distance so that the point of expected convergence never quite takes place: "a simile may be compared to lines converging at a point, and is more excellent as the lines approach from a greater distance: an exemplification may be considered as two parallel lines, which run on together without approximation, never far separated, and never joined" (*Lives*, II: 130). An exemplification functions something like the geometric comparison that Johnson uses: that is to say, it introduces the idea of a differential play that always prevents (or constantly defers) the expected coincidence of tenor and vehicle.

This geometry of parallel and intersecting coordinates, with its uncertain center, is central to Johnson's theory of metaphor. Compared to exemplification, the conceit introduces the distance that is necessary for an effective conjunction to take place. From the perspective of Johnson's analogy of approaching lines, this distance is the initial disparity by which images or concepts differ from one another and is, therefore, the condition of their successful convergence. This distance, Johnson implies, is not an actual, literal distance, much less a contradiction, but rather the index of an irreducible heterogeneity or multiplicity without which the "mind" could never be "impressed by the resemblance of things unlike, as unlike as intellect and body." It is what prohibits the possibility of an original, homogeneous unity that could first be divided and then subsequently reunited in a totality. Hence, the distance opened up by this difference permits the tenor and vehicle to enter into a relation without, however, permitting them to coincide. The very image of lines that move toward a convergence or perhaps back outward to the original point of division does not permit the structure of the conceit to be one of reconciling the two aspects it unites.

The intermediate figure of the simile might appear to overcome the distance that keeps tenor and vehicle from fusing in the conceit and example. Yet even though the terms of a simile may not be joined by force, they still cannot be said to merge. In his review of Warton's *An Essay on the Writings and Genius of Pope*, Johnson praised Pope's famous Alps analogy as "perhaps the best simile in our language; that in which the most exact resemblance is traced between things utterly unrelated to each other" (*Works*, II: 419). In the "Life of Addison," he declared: "a poetical simile is the discovery of a likeness between two actions, in their general nature dissimilar, or of causes terminating by different operations in some resemblance of effect" (*Lives*, II: 129).

What is particularly striking here is that two operations, which would be viewed in twentieth-century criticism as the radically contrasting modes of metaphor and metonymy, are subsumed to a common category. Hence, instead of organizing them into a hierarchical typology in which a totalizing metaphor is assumed to be superior to metonymic fragmentation, Johnson locates the two in a single operation, thus emphasizing their similarity, despite their difference. The consequence is a far more radical understanding of figurative language, one that can only find adequate scope in the notion of a more generalized "likeness" or "resemblance" which—inasmuch as it is not an identity—introduces a difference everywhere between tenor and vehicle, statement and expression.

Of course these distinction are not affirmed explicitly in Johnson's criticism, appearing as they do in the context of particular poems and passages. Johnson makes no attempt to undertake the study of metaphor in and for itself, if it can be put thus. The relevant entries in the *Dictionary* go no further than generally received usage. They do not fill the field whose limits and topography they mark. There is no evidence, for example, that Johnson's understanding of metaphor in the *Lives* is comprehended by his conventional definition of it in the *Dictionary* as "a simile comprized in a word" or that he preferred simile and allegory to metaphor. What is rather put forth in Johnson's scattered remarks in the *Lives* is an argument that locates the two terms within a larger tropological field in which neither term is allowed to dominate. Johnson's most extensive analysis of tropological displacement occurs in his discussion of the conceits in Cowley's *The Mistress*: "Love is by Cowley, as by other poets, expressed metaphorically by flame and fire; and that which is true of real fire is said of love, or figurative fire, the same word in the same sentence retaining both significations" (*Lives*, I: 41). The point of departure for Johnson's analysis of Cowley's conceits is *Spectator*, number 62, in which Addison distinguishes between true wit, mixed wit, and false wit. True wit, in Addison's view, consists in a resemblance of ideas, false wit in a resemblance of words (e.g., puns, quibbles, acrostics, rebuses), and mixed wit in a resemblance of both words and ideas. The duality of signification implicit in mixed wit is precisely what renders the dynamics of metaphor problematic for Johnson. What his reading assumes is that language should always be held accountable to some kind of truth-claim, even where it is overtly figurative. Hence, of those "conceits, Addison calls 'mixed wit'," Johnson writes, "wit consists of thoughts true in one sense of the expression, and false in the other." Johnson quotes several examples from Addison's essay, among them the following: "Upon the dying of a tree, on which had cut his loves, he observes that his flames had burnt up and withered the tree" (*Lives*, I: 41). Johnson is thinking here of the kind of hyperbolic conceit he describes elsewhere in the "Life of Cowley": a conceit in which the vehicle is obviously false ("his flames had withered the tree") even though the tenor is true (the tree on which he had carved his love's name had died). The problem for Johnson is that the employment of a conceit that can affirm a poetical fiction because it is hyperbolic rather than sublime is also an admission that this analogy is false rather than true because it cannot authenticate the claims made for love by its central point of comparison. Johnson believes that the artificiality of the hyperbolic conceit introduces into Cowley's amatory poetry an element of unintentional irony which inhibits the reader's response to what is natural (i.e., the representation of passion) in the verse. Such a conceit may "entertain" by its novelty, but "being unnatural . . . soon grows wearisome."

Clearly there is a sense in which this argument constitutes an outright repudiation of hyperbole—a trope that—like metaphor, simile, or irony—alters the meanings of words rather than simply reshaping—as figures do—their graphic or acoustic form. It was in this spirit that Johnson complained of Cowley's "enormous and disgusting hyperboles" and argued of the metaphysical poets that "their amplifications had no limits: they left not only reason but fancy behind them" (*Lives*, I: 27 and 21). Johnson is obviously unwilling to accept the sort of rationalization adopted, for instance, by La Bruyère who holds that "hyperbole expresses more than the truth that the mind may realize it better."[21] For Johnson—unlike La Bruyère—there is no question of locating rhetorical tropes in a privileged realm of poetical fiction where standards of truth don't fully apply. On the contrary, Johnson's judgment assumes that any adequate reading of a figurative expression must make every effort to explain its sense in rationally accountable terms. Only then will the critic be able to avoid the belief that tropes are fictive ornaments applied to a pre-existing structure of truth. Indeed, if this were the case, then one would have no choice but to conclude that figurative language is a mere surface embellishment, an ingenious but, in the end, secondary sugaring of the pill. Johnson's reluctance to accept this view of language may help to explain why he is so resistant to the kinds of dazzling verbal ingenuity which twentieth-century critics have found everywhere at work in early seventeenth-century poetry.

Johnson's sturdy rationalism, his resistance to the seductions of metaphor is most marked in contexts where he questions a well-known passage or poem. Thus he holds, for example, that the St. Cecilia's Day odes of both Dryden and Pope "end with the same fault; the comparison of each is literal on one side, and metaphorical on the other" (*Lives*, II: 228). What Johnson is objecting to here is a phrase like the "untuning of the sky," where the tenor embodies a literal, sacred truth "so awful that it can owe little to poetry." For Johnson, the most convincing metaphors are those which avoid such confusions by maintaining a firm sense of the ontological difference between the figural structures of metaphor and the mysteries of revelation. It is this distinction that Dryden and Pope most flagrantly transgress by refusing to separate the truths of Christianity from those other, less answerable truths of poetic figuration. In a sense, Johnson is seeking to preserve the word of God from the very same erosion that some modern critics have seen as threatening the words of poetry. For such rigorous New Critics as Brooks or Wimsatt, the "heresy of paraphrase" involved the notion that poetical language can somehow be restated—without alteration or dilution—in the form of rational prose discourse. Without actually using the term "heresy." Johnson applies the virtually same notion in the service of a higher Christian revelation. Poetry, as understood by critics like Wimsatt and Brooks, would surely have figured for Johnson as a warning example of the confusion that can occur when a secular form of language is treated as if it were equivalent to Holy Scripture. Johnson's determination to avoid this confusion takes the form of seeking to call religious language back to its authentic literal meaning. The purpose that words ought to serve in such contexts is to preserve and point to the sense alone that revelation confers upon them.

To read Johnson in the light of modern critical assumptions is, therefore, to face very directly the different set of priorities that he sought to impose upon the reader. The opposition between the sacred and the profane is reproduced in every phase of Johnson's critical writings, the design always being to insist that religion has access to truths that poetry can only obscure or vitiate by its dissimulating play with language and metaphor. This should not be taken to mean that figurative language is consigned in Johnson's poetics to a fictive realm, cut off from the cognitive or referential uses available to ordinary language. Rather, that it is only through the limitations of ordinary language that poetic tropes come into existence. For Johnson, metaphor is indeed a necessary component of poetry but only insofar as an underlying impoverishment makes figuration essential. The tenor, properly speaking, does not furnish matter for embellishment solely because it is the proper, literal term of a comparison. If it were truly proper, truly literal, it would, like the truths of revelation, be fully present to itself—i.e., it would figure forth what it represents or signifies and thus be resistant to figurative displacement. There is no doubt that this occasionally occurs in poetry: "the ideas of pursuit and flight," in one of many possible examples that Johnson might have cited, "are too plain to be made plainer" (*Lives*, III: 230). Yet insofar as a word lends itself to illustration and amplification by such figures as periphrasis or simile, or, at a different level of organization, to the tropological substitutions of metaphor and metonymy, it is because of the absence of any natural relation of resemblance, participation, or analogy between the signified and the signifier, that is, here, between thought and language, or further between what is represented and its representation by signs. Figurative embellishment is thus not a superimposition of what is inessential but a supplement for a deficiency. Its aim is to "show" forth "to the understanding" what requires further illumination, or to "display" to "the fancy" what demands greater enhancement (*Lives*, III: 229). It obviously allows for the kind of reversal from the positive to the negative pole of amplification that is characteristic of satire and burlesque. In the case of either illustration or amplification, however, the insufficiency of the word to make itself or its meaning fully present is what generates figurative reproduction, figurative resignification.

In the background of this argument, one detects not only Johnson's conviction that poetic language is in some sense inimical to religious mystery but also his distinctly Lockean sense of the dangers implicit in any use of language that fails to take into account the vague and imprecise meanings of many words. Johnson's attitude doubtless has much in common with the viewpoint of other eighteenth-century critics, but it is also consistent with a perspective that distrusts the wisdom and sufficiency of ordinary language. It takes for granted the inability of "truth" to manifest itself, to reproduce itself without assistance, without the reappropriation of language in its capacity to substitute one term for another. Although figurative language, as Johnson envisages it, maintains an affinity with ordinary usage in so far as it is an adornment or embellishment of a preexisting structure of "thoughts" or "sentiments," it must also be seen as a deepening of that usage. If tropological activity were unnecessary or merely ornamental, it would also suggest the existence prior to that activity of a unified, self-present and self-sustaining body of literal concepts and images. Figurative language, as Johnson understands it, denies the possibility that the tenor can serve as its own vehicle. It is a supplementary, ornamental mode that is indispensable to discourse precisely because of the inability of truth to embody itself as truth.

9
Conclusion

Johnson's notions about poetic language could easily be made the basis for a far more systematic and comprehensive program of interpretation than he ever envisaged. This program might be devoted to an analysis of the way the various tropes and figures work to redeem ordinary language from its natural imprecision and flaccidity. But, if such a program were to be faithful to Johnson's own purposes, it would not be primarily descriptive in the modern sense. Indeed the kind of semiosis that often seems to interest Johnson—the consideration of internal contradictions, unwitting incongruities, and downright absurdities—becomes important only at the stage where the merit of particular poems and passages comes into question. In short, he sees absolutely no virtue in the kind of intepretive approach that sees the poetry of the past as a kind of secular scripture. The issue for Johnson comes down to a matter of unprejudiced understanding, of rendering a balanced, fair-minded judgment of the works in question. Johnson's own judgments have notoriously been subject to continuous challenge and debate. But the burden of his criticism was always such as to place stress on the issue of evaluation: no amount of vague talk about tradition or a *consensus gentium* will suffice to clinch the case for the worth of a particular poem. Poetry is not being understood if the critic regards its texts as canonical in a scriptural sense, if he is not estimating the merits and demerits of each poem as it presents itself to him. In accord with this perspective, Johnson usually limits interpretation to textual criticism, that is, to the task of enhancing knowledge of the work, insofar as the language of a work is other than the critic thinks it ought to be.

This is the point where Johnson parts company with present-day defenders of formalist literary criticism. They would emphasize what Johnson so strenuously denies: the need to make interpretation, not personal judgment, the foundation of literary criticism. This practice can of course be traced back to T. S. Eliot who in a famous series of essays identified the proper interests of criticism with those of detailed exegesis. The subsequent development is sufficiently well known to bear repetition, from I. A. Richards's *Practical Criticism*—in which close reading is taken to be the touchstone of critical activity—to Leavis and the *Scrutiny* group, the American New Critics, and subsequent competing schools of critical discourse and debate. It has sometimes been argued that this whole complex phase in the history of criticism grows out of an earlier tradition of scriptural interpretation. Northrop Frye, a critic who was strongly opposed to making evaluation the basis of critical activity, has touched upon this aspect of modern literary criticism in *The Anatomy of Criticism* and elsewhere.[1] What chiefly interested Frye is the extent to which modern interpretive criticism derives in large part from techniques invented in scriptural exegesis. For Frye, such techniques are best understood as a secularized version of the approach adopted by biblical commentators when they read some passage from scripture allegorically, as fulfilling an Old Testament prophecy or as revealing hidden layers of meaning.

Johnson's distance from this tradition can be seen in the very different value he places upon biblical commentary. Indeed, he belongs in the company of those orthodox eighteenth-century Anglicans who viewed scriptural hermeneutics with distrust, contending that it had given rise in the past to many needless and futile disputes. This background is evident in Johnson's strictures on religious controversy in his sermons.[2] Johnson never advocates passive submission to authority, but his view of the relation between tradition and private judgment affords small room for exegetical liberty, restricting it to a cautious reexamination of the points laid down by earlier scholars. The same perspective is evident in Johnson's attitude toward interpretation. In *Rambler*, number 176, he condemns those critics who

> see with great clearness whatever is too remote to be discovered by the rest of mankind, but are totally blind to all that lies immediately before them. They discover in every passage some secret meaning, some remote allusion, some artful allegory, or some occult imitation which no other reader ever suspected; but they have no perception of the cogency of arguments, the force of pathetick sentiments, the various colours of diction, or the flowery embellishments of fancy; of all that engages the attention of others, they are totally insensible, while they pry into worlds of conjecture, and amuse themselves with phantoms in the clouds. (*Rambler*, V: 167)

What Johnson has in mind here is a certain form of divinatory textual exegesis that bears a close resemblance to scriptural hermeneutics. Hence his use of the term "telescope" to apply to those critics whose stock in trade it is—so Johnson argues—to produce all manner of subtleties from the literal sense of the text while failing to recognize what is apparent to everyone else. By such means, they are enabled to ignore both the logical and the rhetorical means by which the text manifests its power to interest and move our emotions.

This is where Johnson's practice might have a greater bearing on contemporary critical theory than has usually been supposed. His influence ought to be greatest on those critics whose work is directed "against interpretation," that is, against the view that the main object of criticism is the detailed reading of particular texts. For Johnson, this mode of hermeneutic exegesis is indistinguishable from other forms of adversarial criticism, all of which are intelligible as a species of oppressive monological discourse; "the critick's purpose is to conquer," Johnson writes in a typical passage, "the author only hopes to escape" (*Rambler*, V: 165). It is in this spirit that Johnson holds up the attacks of Dryden upon Settle, or of Dennis upon Pope, as examples of a "gothic" past of verbal violence and deluded righteousness. Criticism enters under an alien spell in so far as it breaks with orthodox intepretive restraints and enters into what he saw as a melancholy realm of interpretive license, partisan strife, and *ad* hominem satire. Johnson, as has been already seen, was more than ready to enter the lists, at least in matters of evaluation and judgment. But it is precisely his aim, throughout the *Lives*, to show how disagreements can be conducted through general principles, while nonetheless asserting that the imperatives of good taste and good manners can transcend such short-term disputes. Johnson's vocabulary of critical controversy—"brutal fury," "malice," "rage," "terrour"—provides an implicit link between "Criticism" and the misguided zeal and fanatacism that he strongly condemned in religious quarrels. This vocabulary gains an added resonance from the lengthy extracts that he published from the controversial criticism of Dryden and Dennis. Literary-critical controversy is consistently opposed to a canon of restraint and good taste; blind presumption and zeal to balanced judgment.

The consequence of this reaction is Johnson's view of literary exegesis as a matter of reconstructing difficult texts, that is, of providing emendations or readings that will best explain what an author might have meant in passages that seem confused or corrupt. This, in turn, requires that reason be allowed full scope for the exercise of a critical hermeneutics that derives its authority not from biblical commentary but from classical philology. Johnson makes his allegiance most explicit in the *Preface* to Shakespeare where he argues that

> conjectural criticism has been of great use in the learned world; nor is it my intention to depreciate a study, that has exercised so many mighty minds, from the revival of learning to our own age, from the Bishop of Aleria to English Bentley. (*Shakespeare*, VII: 109–10)

Yet Johnson—like several other eighteenth-century editors of Shakespeare—is keenly aware of the dangers of this kind of critical activity. For Johnson, such an activity is valid only to the extent that it keeps to a "middle way between presumption and timidity." Johnson's project in his edition of Shakespeare depends—as he sees it—upon his sticking to this middle way lest he fall into the kind of errors for which he reproaches earlier editors. To this extent, Johnson can be said to reveal the same doubts about the normative assumptions of emendatory criticism that he displays toward other kinds of criticism. Indeed, what he discovers on every page of previous editions, he declares, is the spectacle of "Wit struggling with its own sophistry, and Learning confused by the multiplicity of its views." There could thus be no question of criticizing earlier editors from a wholly enlightened point of view, since this would entail the implausible claim that "Wit" can achieve an order of knowledge ideally independent of the partiality that informs "sophistry." From this line of argument, it can be readily understood why Johnson often appears to treat the claims of conjectural criticism in the *Preface* as mere impositions of a will-to-power that masquerades in the guise of learning, science, and objectivity. It is precisely because of his desire to resist such impositions—such manipulative strategies designed to establish the superiority of one editor over earlier editors—that he also argues the case for a different order of inquiry, one that is attentive to philological scholarship, historical criticism, and the detailed comparison of different manuscripts. Indeed, he sees very clearly that conjectural criticism, if pursued in isolation from these other kinds of study, can easily lead to the same kind of interpretive excess that has characterized other schools of criticism.

This rejection of conjectural criticism in favor of a pared-down version of philological scholarship was of course nothing new in the history of Shakespearean commentary. Benjamin Heath and Sir Thomas Hamner had reacted against the excesses of William Warburton and Lewis Theobald for much the same reason. For Johnson, however, this meant that philological scholarship could never attain the same importance as the judgment of individual authors and works. The disagreement over obscure passages is for Johnson an index to which politics—the struggle for possession of critical texts—has displaced a possible realm of shared values, beliefs, and interests. Attempts to make emendations or explanatory notes the basis of Shakespearean criticism are denounced as a futile enterprise, an endeavor that has actually added "little" to Shakespeare's "power of pleasing" (*Shakespeare*, VII: 111). To erect textual criticism into an absolute is to fall into an attitude that Johnson refuses to countenance. The only alternative, he argues, is an emphasis upon the opposite kind of criticism, one that seeks to discover why a poet has fallen from favor or, conversely, by what "peculiarities of excellence" an author has held the favor of others.

This is why Johnson raises issues that cannot be shunted aside by protesting that critical theory should have nothing to do with matters of value. Critics who take this line are ignoring the close relation between the kind of evaluative criticism advocated by Johnson and the process of canon formation, canon preservation, and canon revision. It is worth recalling that the same forces drawing Shakespearean plays into the body of works recognized as canonical also operated consciously or unconsciously, in Johnson's project in the *Lives*, marking the new valuation of individual authors in the emerging institution of English literature. The project proposed to Johnson by the London booksellers is directly related to an attempt to establish a canon of English authors and, at the same time, to make their works more readily available by bringing them out into the public domain. Moreover, it is in the realm of poetry—the genre perhaps most susceptible to revolutions in taste—that criticism is best placed to undertake this task. This is why a work like the "Life of Cowley" had a power to arouse interest—and to antagonize—beyond what might be expected from its stringent judgments on Cowley and the metaphysical poets. Boswell makes this point when he observes of the "Life of Cowley" that

> Johnson has exhibited [the Metaphysical Poets] at large, with such happy illustration from their writings, and in so luminous a manner, that indeed he may be allowed the full merit of novelty, and to have discovered to us, as it were, a new planet in the poetical hemisphere.[3]

In the formation of literary canon, we are constantly in the process of reviving interest in authors whose works may have been unknown or undeservedly forgotten and of revising our estimate of works whose importance may have been exaggerated. That is to say, the chief interest of evaluative criticism is to ascertain where renewed attention needs to be directed, or where the need to correct inflated reputations imposes a judgement counter to received or canonical ideas of the value of an author or poem.

Certainly Johnson is far from believing, as has sometimes been supposed, that the canon should be ossified into a fixed and timeless body of literary works. As Carey Kaplan and Ellen Cronan Rose have recently observed, Johnson "certainly did not see himself as freezing literature into monumental permanence."[4] Indeed, there are many intimations in the *Lives* that Johnson was far from satisfied by the current calendar of authors and works. His request to the booksellers to add the lives of Blackmore, Pomfret, Yalden, Watts, and possibly Thomson may be one indication of this dissatisfaction. It is worth recalling that there was a much broader representation in earlier collections. "Cibber's" (e.g., Robert Shiels's) 1753 *Lives of the Poets of Great Britain and Ireland to the Time of Dean Swift* encompasses more than two hundred poets, a significant number of whom are women. These include Katherine Philips, Aphra Behn, Anne Killigrew, Susanna Centlivre, Anne Finch, and Elizabeth Singer Rowe. By contrast, in the London booksellers' project, there are only forty-seven poets, all of whom are men. Johnson's suggested additions can hardly be said to alter the basic plan, but it may be a measure of the unease that he may have felt at such a drastically circumscribed list of authors.

To some extent, no doubt, this selection can be attributed to matters of editorial intention and publishing exigency. Where Shiels's vast project entailed only short notices and estimates, the London booksellers—acting in response to a rival project in Edinburgh—intended to include both lives and volumes of poetry. Indeed, the booksellers had originally planned to publish "an elegant and accurate edition of all the English poets from Chaucer to the present time," but almost immediately decided that such a project was too large and therefore should be limited to the era from 1660 to the present and exclude poets who were still alive. Yet while there is no doubt that Johnson accepted this limitation, there are other indications of his dissatisfaction with the current selection of poets. While the aim of Shiels's brief *Lives* was presumably to offer as fair an estimate as possible, his evaluations were either uniformly laudatory or silent on the merits of the poets in question. Johnson, it hardly needs to be said, was rigorous and unsparing in his judgments of poets and poems. His observations on the poetry of several authors, including Swift and Watts, for example, are so severe as to amount to an argument for a virtual dismissal of their claims to be included in any serious canon of English poetry. There is also evidence that Johnson changed his own mind about the merits of individual poets and poems. As Allen Reddick has pointed out, Johnson appears to have had a change of heart about the worth of Thomson's *Seasons*, eliminating many quotations drawn from Thomson's poem in the 1773 edition of *The Dictionary*.[5] In this respect Johnson stands at the opposite extreme from critics for whom the broadest possible coverage is the major goal and who, therefore, pay minimal attention to matters of value or of genuine popular appeal. To Johnson, on the contrary, such inclusiveness would appear, at best, a matter of special pleading and, at worst, a technique for evading the task of assessing the merits and demerits of individual poems.

It is also the case, however, that Johnson's criticism demands much more in the way of an awareness of the social, political, and material factors involved in the process of canonization than could ever be provided by a purely literary estimate. This can be seen not only in his quiet deflation of the attainment of poets whose past reputations may have partly been a result of their power and influence, e.g., Rochester, Dorset, and Roscommon. Of John Sheffield, for example, he observes:

> he is introduced into the late collection only as a poet; and, if we credit the testimony of his contemporaries, he was a poet of no vulgar rank. But favour and flattery are now at an end; criticism is no longer softened by his bounties or awed by his splendour, and being able to take a more steady view, discovers him to be a writer that sometimes glimmers, but rarely shines, feebly laborious, and at best but pretty. His songs are upon common topicks; he hopes, and grieves, and repents, and despairs, and rejoices, like any other maker of little stanzas: to be great he hardly tries; to be gay is hardly in his power. (*Lives*, II: 174–75)

It can also be found in his awareness of the plight of neglected or forgotten poets. In the case of Elkanah Settle, a poet who was not included in the *Lives*, Johnson argues:

> such are the revolutions of fame, or such is the prevalence of fashion, that the man whose works have not yet been thought to deserve the care of collecting them; who died forgotten in an hospital; and whose latter years were spent in contriving shows for fairs, and carrying an elegy or epithalamium, of which the beginning and end were occasionally varied, but the intermediate parts were always the same, to every house where there was a funeral or a wedding—might with truth had inscribed upon his stone 'Here lies the Rival and Antagonist of Dryden'. (*Lives*, I: 375)

There is no suggestion that Johnson views Sheffield or Settle as particularly unique or, indeed, as any different from other, similar instances of literary inflation or neglect. It is therefore one of the tasks of criticism to debunk overblown reputations and to rescue forgotten or unknown authors from oblivion and to reexamine anew the case for their inclusion in the canon. The latter follows directly from the Johnsonian principle that the disappearance of a once prominent author is not necessarily the result of some sort of impersonal, automatic process of correction and adjustment. Rather it takes its rise from a complex combination of factors that can include matters of power, rivalry, prejudice, and sheer chance.

To this extent, Johnson might be thought to approximate the position of critics who attribute the process of selection solely to the influence of power. But Johnson clearly differs from those critics in believing that power and influence are subject to temporal change and thus are limited by certain constraints, among which are tests that provide at least a background of shared consensual understanding against which to judge evidence of special pleading. This may have been one reason why Johnson so eagerly seized upon the opportunity presented to him by the London booksellers. For it then became possible for Johnson to argue his case in a popular form—in prefaces to volumes largely chosen by others—and thereby provide himself some defense against the charge—subsequently raised by Horace Walpole and others—of malicious or destructive intent. But—more importantly—this approach allowed him to acknowledge—tacitly at least—what some contemporary theorists have recognized as the existence of competing canons. The rival Edinburgh edition, *The British Poets* (1773–76), for example, was limited to fifteen poets and thus gave a much greater prominence to Milton's minor poems as well as to a line of poets that included Parnell, Thomson, Gray, Collins, Akenside, Shenstone, and Beattie. In a sense, Johnson's Lives could be said to offer the alternative of an outlook that shares the commitment of *The British Poets* to *Paradise Lost* and the poetry of Dryden and Pope but which also finds room for a clear recognition of the limitations of those poems that have gained prominence through the advocacy of certain groups. In which case, Johnson could suggest—at least to those readers capable of reading between the lines—that the interest of works as understood by current defenders were not identical with the interests of the general public as perceived through the power of an active intellect.

Hence, Johnson's pronounced scepticism with regard to literary fashions, movements, and other such dubious examples of literary pretension, adopted—he argues—solely with the purpose of persuading indifferent or credulous minds and lacking any evidence of real merit. Thus of *The Progress of Poesy* and *The Bard*, Johnson writes,

> some that tried them confessed their inability to understand them, though Warburton said that they were understood as well as the works of Milton and Shakespeare, which it is the fashion to admire. Garrick wrote a few lines in their praise. Some hardy champions undertook to rescue them from neglect, and in a short time many were content to be shewn beauties which they could not see. (*Lives*, III: 426)

Where the enthusiasts went wrong is in attempting to reconcile these beauties with the requirements of a broad reading public, one whose members cannot (or should not) be so easily imposed upon by such blatantly obvious persuasive techniques. In short, we may persuade many readers of the justness of our opinions, reversing or completely changing their initial response, however straightforward it may have been. But this approach is misguided—a potential source of error and delusion—in so far as it substitutes mere fashion for the much more difficult business of understanding what enables a poem to grasp and hold our interest. What makes it especially insidious or seductive is the scope this approach offers for new ways of admiring—ways that appear to contest a reader's original judgment, but that, in fact, involve some degree of mystification—some convenient departure from good sense—by which to head off any real questions as to the actual merits of the "beauties" involved and the personal interests of those who purport to explain them.

Of course it might be argued that what is involved here is simply a more common reference point, a sign that readers possess a shared basis of understanding and delight. If it is true that the genuine appreciation of poems depends upon a background of shared consensual values and interests, then the canon consists of only those texts that have somehow become genuinely and permanently popular. Hence only a few touchstones—e.g., *The Rape of the Lock*, *The Beggar's Opera*, or the *Elegy in a Country Churchyard*—would be worthy of serious critical attention. But while this argument possesses some validity, it fails to take into account Johnson's qualified praise of a much larger intermediate group that cannot be said to be popular in the same sense as Gray's *Elegy* yet that are still deserving of serious consideration. These include such poems as *Paradise Lost*, *Cooper's Hill*, *Mac Flecknoe*, *Absalom and Achitophel*, *Windsor Forest*, *Eloisa to Abelard*, *The Dunciad*, and, with further qualifications, even *Hudibras*, *The Seasons*, and *The Love of Fame*. Johnson never claims that these poems possess the immediate appeal of *The Rape of the Lock* or the *Elegy*, yet he assumes that they still retain an obvious power to move and interest the reader.

This estimate of the relative degree of popular and critical appeal is of course subject to dispute. Johnson's conviction that an audience is prevented by its own limited sphere of knowledge from entering into the imaginative universe of earlier eras is such that it leads him to qualify his judgments of such works as *Absalom and Achitophel* and *Hudibras*. That is to say, Johnson sometimes pitches his argument to the broadest level of general response and sees little hope of a better understanding of the allusions, the detailed particularities, or the essentially contingent character of works like *Hudibras*. It is here that William Hazlitt appears to offer a competing account of some of the same poets in his *Lectures upon the English Comic Writers*. Hazlitt's scope is of course much broader than that of Johnson, beginning with Shakespeare and encompassing fiction and drama as well as poetry. Yet Hazlitt's intention—especially in his chapters on Cowley and Butler—often appears aimed at reversing Johnson's reserved and measured judgments. Like Johnson, Hazlitt regards the pleasure of the text as a kind of limit point beyond which the critic cannot go. But he also claims that this limit point is implicit in the very nature of wit and humor and thus is capable of a much wider range of sympathetic identification than Johnson was willing to allow. Furthermore, Hazlitt assumes that this response has not been blocked—in whatever degree—by the workings of prejudice, fashion, or political difference. In effect, this argument reinstates, subject to some different qualifications, a whole range of authors that Johnson believed had virtually dropped out of sight.

For Johnson, such disagreements may give rise to a sobering reflection on the weakness to which all readers are prone when they try to give justifications for their preferences and judgments. But one must also recall Johnson's conviction that value judgments cannot be treated on a par with demonstrative science or elevated to a realm of canonical truth where questions of prejudice and error don't pertain. For it is precisely by virtue of what Johnson terms the "tentative" and "experimental" character of critical discourse—its power to restate, modify, or reject earlier judgments—that criticism is enabled to detect the sins of commission and omission in previous estimates of individual authors and works. This is simply a more rigorous way of making the point that the critic can only present an argument, and, what is equally important, engender counterarguments that take the opposite point of view for precisely the same reason. This applies in Johnson's case not only to the obvious instances—his notorious judgments on *Lycidas,* Gray's sister odes, or *Gulliver's Travels*—but also to Lives whose design on the reader is much less obvious but which anticipate a whole gamut of responses from endorsement to rejection. Of course, this should not be understood in terms of a species of critical relativism, a renunciation of the quest for reason and truth in matters of critical judgment. Nor can it be grasped solely by reference to that aspect of Johnson's thinking which equates criticism with the *libido dominandi*, the drive for mastery and power that Johnson sees as endemic to the human condition. On the contrary, what Johnson assumes is that the give-and-take of critical exchange provides the only means of resisting such a drive for power in so far as it forces critical thought to recognize the delusions of partiality, the naïveté and errors that result from its blindness to its own historically contingent character.

Now it may be argued—as it has by some scholars—that Johnson himself has a political agenda—a core set of conservative Tory and Anglican values—and thus shouldn't pose as the kind of public critic who is devoid of such prejudices and interests. But, once again, this ignores what is distinctive about Johnson's criticism: the fact that it may indeed have been put to such partial, self-interested, or prejudiced use, yet still provide a yardstick by which to measure these distortions of its own legitimate claims. Thus—to take what is the most obvious contemporary example—Johnson's *Lives* have a good deal to say about the emerging canon of English poetry, but which Johnson and the booksellers choose to understand as overlooking the poetry of women. This is where Johnson appears as a critic who probably read only male poets in his youth and who drew his illustrations for the *Dictionary* almost exclusively from male writers. To this extent there would be some warrant for a feminist reading that argued that Johnson—in spite of his manifest sympathies and encouragement for contemporary women writers—still pursued an exclusionary canon. But one should also take note of the other side of the argument: that Johnson's blind spots of partiality do come to light in the end, albeit often within the context of considerable debate and disagreement. Yet the reason why Johnsonian practice exhibits this self-correcting tendency—unlike more dogmatic or objective theories—is that its central assumptions incorporate within themselves the possibility of prejudice and error and thus are not tied down to some kind of stipulative meanings in accordance with "timeless" and "universal" standards of truth. The point is not to deny Johnson's own prejudices but to remark how his perspective is consistent with those who contest the notion of an enduring and immemorial cultural heritage. On this question, Johnson stands squarely against the assumption that a sacrosanct tradition of acknowledged "great works" can be given the same weight, the same veneration, as the authorized canon of Old and

New Testament books. For Johnson, on the contrary, the process of canonical revision and challenge is exactly what distinguishes English poetry from Holy Scripture—and he is certainly not inclined to blur the distinction between them, much less to argue that the literary canon should be placed on a par with the biblical canon.

It would be an exaggeration to hold that the issues in the current debate over the canon can be understood by going back to the practice of Johnson. Nonetheless, there are grounds for supposing that this is not an impossible claim; that Johnson was indeed the first and preeminent modern critic to raise questions about canon formation and canon revision that are still very much a part of contemporary critical discussion. One aspect of this practice that has been widely recognized—at least by admirers like Boswell—is Johnson's efforts to revive interest in the metaphysicals—a group of poets whose works had been virtually forgotten by Johnson's time. But one will misunderstand what that achievement amounts to if one does not see that many of Johnson's other "Lives"—his attempts to distinguish deserving from merely inflated reputations—were conducted in the spirit of an admittedly preliminary yet systematic attempt at canonical revision. The same applies to his insistence that a critic should have nothing to do with "the philosophical and religious tenets" of an author, but only with his "poetry." This principle is behind Johnson's resistance to any theory that would judge poetry mainly in terms of its doctrinal value. And it is here that contemporary critics might well examine the implications of Johnson's practice and its relation to the ongoing debates in contemporary critical thought.

Notes

Chapter 1. Introduction: Between Theory and Practice

1. Roland Barthes, "Criticism as Language," *Times Literary Supplement,* 27 September 1963, p. 740.
2. Mikhail Bakhtin, *Problems of Dostoevsky's Poetics*, trans. Caryl Emerson (Minneapolis: University of Minnesota Press, 1984); and his *The Dialogic Imagination: Four Essays*, trans. Caryl Emerson and Michael Holquist (Austin: The University of Texas Press, 1981).
3. William R. Keast, "Johnson's Criticism of the Metaphysical Poets," in *Eighteenth-Century English Literature: Modern Essays in Criticism*, ed. James L. Clifford (New York: Oxford University Press, 1959), p. 302.
4. Ibid.
5. Jean H. Hagstrum, *Samuel Johnson's Literary Criticism* (Chicago: University of Chicago Press, 1967), p. 59.
6. William Hazlitt, *Collected Works*, ed. A. R. Waller and Arnold Glover, 12 vols. (London: Dent, 1902), I: 177.
7. Leopold Damrosch, Jr., *The Uses of Johnson's Criticism* (Charlottesville: University of Virginia Press, 1976), p. 2.
8. Ibid., p. 3.

Chapter 2. Tradition and Critical Difference

1. See Bertrand Bronson, "The Double Tradition of Dr. Johnson," in his *Johnson Agonistes and Other Essays* (1951; Berkeley and Los Angeles: University of California Press, 1965), pp. 156–76, for an analysis of the popular tradition of Johnsonian commentary.
2. René Wellek, *The Attack on Literature and Other Essays* (Chapel Hill: University of North Carolina Press, 1982), p. 77.
3. W. R. Keast, "The Theoretical Foundations of Johnson's Criticism," in *Critics and Criticism*, ed. R. S. Crane, abr. ed. (Chicago: University of Chicago Press, 1957), pp. 169–87.
4. Arthur Sherbo, in his *Samuel Johnson: Editor of Shakespeare, with an Essay on The Adventurer,* vol. 42 of *Illinois Studies in Language and Literature* (Urbana: Univer-

sity of Illinois Press, 1956) seeks to disclose the extent of Johnson's indebtedness to earlier eighteenth-century editors of Shakespeare. Sherbo's study needs to be seen, in part at least, as a legacy of the eighteenth-century response to the obvious intertextuality of Johnson's edition. For a defense of Johnson against the general charge of plagiarism and specifically against Sherbo's charge of unacknowledged borrowings from Benjamin Heath's *Revisal of Shakespeare's Text* (1765), see Arthur M. Eastman, "In Defense of Dr. Johnson," *Shakespeare Quarterly* 8 (1957): 493–500. A broad assessment of Johnson's contribution to eighteenth-century scholarship and criticism can be found in David Nichol Smith, *Shakespeare in the Eighteenth Century* (Oxford: Clarendon Press, 1926), pp. 48–55 and passim.

5. John Wain, *Samuel Johnson: A Biography* (New York: McGraw-Hill, 1974), p. 347.

6. James Boswell, *Boswell's Life of Johnson*, ed. George Birkbeck Hill, rev. and enl. by L. F. Powell, 6 vols. (Oxford: Clarendon Press, 1936–64), V: 273. For similar sentiments, see *Life*, II, 61; III, 375; and V, 400.

7. *Boswell's Life of Johnson*, II: 335.

8. *Table Talk*, 1 Nov. 1833, in Samuel Taylor Coleridge, *Coleridge's Table Talk and Omniana* (London: Oxford University Press, 1917), p. 284.

9. Leslie Stephen, *The History of Rasselas with the Life of the Author* (London: A. L. Burt, n.d.), p. 149.

10. "Conversation"(1847), in Thomas De Quincey, *De Quincey as Critic*, ed. John E. Jordan (London: Routledge & Kegan Paul, 1973), p. 143.

11. *Boswell's Life of Johnson*, V: 17.

12. In his *Problems of Dostoevsky's Poetics*, Bakhtin holds that "language lives only in the dialogic interaction of those who make use of it. Dialogic interaction is indeed the authentic sphere where language *lives*. The entire life of language, in any area of its use (in everyday, business, scholarship, art, and so forth) is permeated with dialogic relationships" (p. 183).

13. [William Fitzthomas], *Cursory Examination of Dr. Johnson's Strictures on the Lyric Performances of Gray* (London, 1781); quoted from *Johnson: The Critical Heritage*, ed. James T. Boulton (London: Routledge & Kegan Paul, 1971), p. 292. See James E. Swearingen, "Johnson's Life of Gray," *TSLL* 14 (1972): 283–302, for an analysis of this issue. Swearingen argues that "Johnson speaks sharply with the intention of correcting a view that even Gray's warmest admirers would not regard as extreme" (p. 283). Lionel Basney, in "'Ah, ha!—Sam Johnson!—I see thee!' Johnson's Ironic Roles," *South Atlantic Quarterly* 75 (1976): 198–211, draws attention to Johnson's ability to enter into many public and private roles with both sympathy and irony. A general account of how Johnson's criticism functions as "a highly self-conscious form of conversation with others" can be found in William Bowman Piper's "Samuel Johnson as Exemplary Critic," *TSLL* 20 (1978): 457–73. Fredric Bogel, in "Johnson and the Role of Authority," in *The New 18th Century: Theory, Politics, English Literature*, ed. Felicity Nussbaum and Laura Brown (London and New York: Methuen, 1987), argues that Johnson "discloses the *inherently* dramatic or histrionic character of authority," revealing it to be "intrinsically divided by internal conflict and self-questioning" (p. 205).

14. Among scholars who have noticed Johnson's pervasive practice of responding to earlier biographers, see Benjamin Boyce, "Samuel Johnson's Criticism of Pope," *RES* 5 (1954): 37–46; F. W. Hilles, "The Making of the *Life of Pope*," in *New Light on Dr. Johnson*, ed. F. W. Hilles (New Haven: Yale University Press, 1959), 257–84; J. P. Hardy, *Samuel Johnson: A Critical Study* (London: Routledge & Kegan Paul, 1979), pp. 195–200; and Pat Rogers, "Johnson's *Lives of the Poets* and the Biographical Dictionaries," *RES*, n.s. 21 (1980): 40–71. Wayne Warnke, in "Samuel Johnson on Swift: the *Life*

of Swift and Johnson's Predecessors in Swiftian Biography," *JBS* 7 (1968): 56–64, contends that Johnson returned to the generally negative tone and attitude of Swift's earliest biographer, Lord Orrery, deemphasizing the more favorable estimates of Delany, Deane Swift, and Hawkesworth.

15. In using the phrase, Lawrence Lipking holds, in *The Ordering of the Arts in Eighteenth-Century England* (Princeton: Princeton University Press, 1970), that "too much has been suppressed" in a Johnsonian life: "there is no perpetual acknowledgement. Johnsonian commentary is not well documented, not consistent in its method, not always specific about the objects of its criticism" (p. 82).

16. William Kenrick, *Review of Johnson's Shakespeare* (1765), quoted in Boulton, ed., *Johnson: The Critical Heritage*, p. 179. Arthur M. Eastman, in "Johnson's Shakespeare and the Laity: A Textual Study," *PMLA* 55 (1950): 1112–21, makes a useful distinction between Johnson's *Preface* and *Notes*, which have been frequently reprinted, and his text, which was quickly superseded. Eastman argues that the numerous changes that Johnson introduced into the text of Shakespeare's plays were designed to make them more available to the common reader.

17. Walter Raleigh, *Six Essays on Johnson* (Oxford: Clarendon Press, 1910), p. 92.

18. *Boswell's Life of Johnson*, V: 35.

19. Ken Frieden, *Genius and Monologue* (Ithaca and London: Cornell University Press, 1985), p. 67.

20. Edward Young, *Conjectures on Original Composition* (London: Millar and Dodsley, 1759), p. 37; William Duff, *An Essay on Original Genius, and its various modes of exertion in Philosophy, and the Fine Arts, particularly in Poetry* (London: Printed for E. and C. Dilly, 1767), p. 176.

21. Sermon 1 in Samuel Johnson, *Sermons*, ed. Jean Hagstrum and James Gray (New Haven: Yale University Press, 1978), p. 3.

22. The argument developed in this part of the chapter is partly anticipated by Stephen Fix in "Distant Genius: Johnson and the Art of Milton's Life," *MP* 81 (1984): 244–64. Using *Lycidas, Comus, L'Allegro* and *Il Penseroso*, as well as *Paradise Lost*, as examples, Fix shows how Johnson develops an image of Milton as a man and a poet who self-consciously sets himself apart from others.

23. Hazlitt, *Collected Works*,V: 67.

24. See the excellent survey by Warren Fleischauer, "Johnson, *Lycidas* and the Norms of Criticism," in *Johnsonian Studies*, ed. Magdi Wahba (Cairo: privately printed, 1962), pp. 235–56.

25. Johnson's expectation that the focus of any elegy should be on the deceased is emphasized by Raleigh, in *Six Essays on Johnson*, p. 132, and James L. Battersby, in *Rational Praise and Natural Lamentation: Johnson, Lycidas, and Principles of Criticism* (Rutherford, N.J.: Fairleigh Dickinson University Press, 1980), p. 187. In view of Johnson's contention that "where there is fiction, there is no passion," Battersby is mistaken, in my opinion, in holding that "what is said of *Lycidas* would have been said of the poem if it had been only an 'imaginative' elegy" (p. 191).

26. Paul De Man, *Allegories of Reading: Figural Language in Rousseau, Nietzsche, Rilke, and Proust* (New Haven: Yale University Press, 1979), p. 249.

27. August Wilhelm von Schlegel, *Lectures on Dramatic Art and Literature* (1808); quoted in Boulton, ed., *Johnson: The Critical Heritage*, p. 196.

28. Matthew Arnold, "Johnson's *Lives of the Poets*" (1875), in his *Essays Religious and Mixed*, ed. R. H. Super (Ann Arbor: University of Michigan Press, 1972), p. 316. For a fascinating study of the way the cardinal oppositions of Romantic criticism (poetry versus prose, poetry versus versification) shape Arnold's view of Gray as an isolated figure, see Neil H. Hertz, "Poetry in an Age of Prose: Arnold and Gray," in *In Defense*

of Reading, A Reader's Approach to Literary Criticism, ed. Richard Poirier and Reuben Brower (New York: Dutton, 1962), pp. 57–75.

29. Samuel Taylor Coleridge, "Lecture on Style," in his *Coleridge's Essays & Lectures on Shakespeare & Some Other Old Poets & Dramatists* (London: Dent; New York: Dutton, 1907), p. 325.

30. Horace Walpole, "General Criticisms of Dr. Johnson's Writings" (ca. 1779), quoted in Bouton, ed., *Johnson: The Critical Heritage*, p. 325.

31. Edmund Gosse, *Leaves and Fruit* (New York, 1927), p. 361; quoted in William K. Wimsatt, Jr., *The Prose Style of Samuel Johnson* (New Haven: Yale University Press, 1941), p. 125.

32. John Dennis, *The Advancement and Reformation of Poetry*, I: 5, in his *The Critical Works*, ed. Edward Niles Hooker, 2 vols. (Baltimore: Johns Hopkins University Press, 1939), I: 215.

33. Young, *Conjectures upon Original Composition*, p. 60.

34. Samuel Johnson, *Rambler*, no. 125. On Johnson's scepticism concerning the absolute value of critical terms, see Keast, "The Theoretical Foundations of Johnson's Criticism," pp. 174–75.

35. Joseph Wood Krutch, *Samuel Johnson* (New York: Harcourt, Brace & Co., 1944), p. 473.

36. William Wordsworth, *Preface to the Lyrical Ballads* (1850), in his *The Prose Works*, ed. W. J. B. Owen and Jane Worthington Smyser, 3 vols. (Oxford: Clarendon Press, 1974), I: 135. For an argument that Johnson's view of the relation of poetry to prose is akin to Wordsworth's, see Donald Greene, "The Proper Language of Poetry: Gray, Johnson, and Others," in *Fearful Joy: Papers from the Thomas Gray Bicentenary Conference at Carleton University*, ed. James Downey and Ben Jones (Montreal and London: McGill-Queen's University Press, 1974), pp. 94–100.

37. Thomas Babington Macaulay, "Boswell's Life of Johnson," in his *Critical and Historical Essays*, 2 vols. (London: Dent; New York: Dutton, 1907), II: 555.

38. F. R. Leavis, "Johnson and Augustanism," in his *The Common Pursuit* (1952; London: Hogarth Press, 1984), pp. 104, 110, and 108. Leavis develops essentially the same argument in "Johnson as Critic," in his *Anna Karenina and Other Essays* (1933; New York: Simon and Shuster, 1969), pp. 197–218.

39. Jacques Derrida, *Of Grammatology*, trans. Gayatri Chakravorty Spivak (Baltimore: Johns Hopkins University Press, 1974), p. 202.

40. David Perkins, "Johnson on Metaphysical Poetry," *ELH* 20 (1953), p. 205.

Chapter 3. Author, Text, and Audience

1. M. H. Abrams, *The Mirror and the Lamp: Romantic Theory and Critical Tradition* (1953; New York: W. W. Norton, 1958), pp. 15–16.

2. Ibid., p. 19.

3. Hagstrum, *Samuel Johnson's Literary Criticism,* p. 37; Keast, "Johnson's Criticism of Metaphysical Poets," p. 302: Paul Fussell, *Johnson and the Life of Writing* (1971; New York: Norton, 1986), p. 48.

4. For an analysis of the way the subject persists in theories that supposedly banish it, see David Carroll, *The Subject in Question: The Languages of Theory and the Strategies of Fiction* (Chicago: University of Chicago Press, 1982), pp. 1–26 and passim. In this argument, I will be differing from Leopold Damrosch, Jr., who argues, in "Samuel

Johnson and Reader Response Criticism," *ECent* 21 (1980): 91–108, that Johnson, like Wordsworth, sees the poet as a man speaking to men and regards the author-reader relationship as "secure" because he assumes a stable, underlying reality. Johnson's conceptions of temporality and of the unstable identity of the subject, in my opinion, render both arguments questionable.

5. George Campbell, *The Philosophy of Rhetoric* (New York: Harper & Bros., 1850), p. 295.

6. Cleanth Brooks, *The Well-Wrought Urn: Studies in the Structure of Poetry*, (New York: Harcourt, Brace & Co., 1947), p. 150.

7. The notion of the author as an empirical subject was put forward by Jonathan Culler in "Changes in the Lyric," in *Lyric Poetry: Beyond New Criticism*, ed. Chaviva Hosek and Patricia Parker (Ithaca and New York: Cornell University Press, 1985), p. 49. I am indebted to Culler for the initial formulation of this idea.

8. Krutch, *Samuel Johnson*, p. 464.

9. Abrams disputes Krutch's contention that Johnson was sometimes led "to seek in poetry the personality of the poet," contending that Johnson makes a sharp distinction between life and art (*The Mirror and the Lamp*, pp. 232–34). See also Robert Folkenflik, *Samuel Johnson: Biographer* (Ithaca and London: Cornell University Press, 1978), pp. 118–29 and 140n.

10. Johnson's conception of the authorial subject thus stands apart from the two versions of romanticism, one spontaneous and unpremeditated, the other conscious and deliberate, put forward by A. O. Lovejoy in "On the Discrimination of Romanticisms," in his *Essays in the History of Ideas* (1948; New York: G. P. Putnam, 1960), pp. 228–53.

11. It is perhaps in this respect that Johnson differs most strikingly from Swift. Johnson's belief that delusion is an inseparable part of human experience may help to account for what Walter Jackson Bate has termed his *satire manque*. See W. J. Bate, "Dr. Johnson and *Satire Manqué*," in *Eighteenth-Century Studies in Honor of Donald F. Hyde*, ed. W. H. Bond (New York: Grolier Club, 1970), pp. 145–60. See also Morris Golden, *The Self Observed: Swift, Johnson, and Wordsworth* (Baltimore: Johns Hopkins University Press, 1972), pp. 67–70.

12. On the importance of the distinction between probable and demonstrative certainty in Johnson's criticism, see Keast, "The Theoretical Foundations of Johnson's Criticism," pp. 176–177. See also Hoyt Trowbridge, "Scattered Atoms of Probability," *ECS*: 5 (1971): 1–38.

13. For the opinion that Johnson was an "outright dissenter against the neoclassic rules," see William K. Wimsatt, Jr., ed., *Dr. Johnson on Shakespeare* (New York: Hill and Wang, 1960), p. 18.

14. On evidence of Johnson's doubts about the *consensus gentium*, see R. D. Stock, *Samuel Johnson and Neoclassical Dramatic Theory* (Lincoln: University of Nebraska Press, 1973), p. 22. W. J. Hipple detects a shift in the *Preface* to Shakespeare from a theory based on the *consensus gentium* to one based on philosophic principles (William Gerard, *An Essay on Taste*, ed. W. J. Hipple, Jr. [Gainesville, Fla.: Scholars Facsimiles, 1963], xxii). What Hipple's argument fails to take into account, in my opinion, is the extent to which the *consensus gentium* remains a mediating element between the text and critic in Johnson's writings.

15. Shirley White Johnston, in "The Unfurious Critic: Samuel Johnson's Attitudes toward his Contemporaries," *MP* 77 (1979): 22, argues that "Johnson's abstention from judicial criticism of contemporaries remains nearly absolute."

16. On Johnson's penchant for debunking overblown reputations, see Folkenflik, *Samuel Johnson: Biographer*, pp. 137–38; Mark Booth, "Johnson's Critical Judgments in *The Lives of the Poets*," *SEL* 16 (1976): 513; and Stephen Fix, "The Contexts and

Motives of Johnson's *Life of Milton*," in *Domestick Privacies: Samuel Johnson and the Art of Biography*, ed. David Wheeler (Lexington: University Press of Kentucky, 1987), pp. 107–32.

17. Murray Krieger, "Fiction, Nature, and Literary Kinds," in his *Poetic Presence and Illusion: Essays in Critical History and Theory* (Baltimore: Johns Hopkins University Press, 1979), p. 185.

18. Voltaire, *Oeuvres* (Paris, 1878), xvii and 397; quoted from Boulton, ed., *Johnson: The Critical Heritage*, p. 194. On Voltaire's commitment to the doctrine of the strict separation of styles, see Erich Auerbach, *Mimesis* (1946; New York: Doubleday Anchor, 1957), p. 362. This aspect of Bakhtin's thought can perhaps be best seen in his *The Dialogic Imagination*, pp. 3–40.

19. Samuel Johnson, "Preface to the *Characters of Shakespeare's Plays*," in his *Collected Works*, I: 177.

20. The dialectical reversal that Hazlitt draws attention to should not be confused with the "conception of polarity, inconsistency, or contradiction" that James L. Battersby accuses Oliver Sigworth, Paul Fussell, Arieh Sachs, and Murray Krieger of wrongly attributing to Johnson (*Rational Praise and Natural Lamentation*, pp. 13–136). Dialectical reversal is a structural principle in Johnson's writings and is in no way incompatible with rational consistency. It occurs, for instance, in the section on wit in the "Life of Cowley," in Imlac's dissertation on poetry in *Rasselas* as well as in many shorter passages in his critical and moral writings. See Robert DeMaria, Jr., "Johnson's Form of Evaluation," *SEL* 19 (1979): 501–14, for a discussion of the pervasive convention of "polarity" in Johnson's criticism.

Chapter 4. Presence and Representation

1. Henry Home, Lord Kames, *Elements of Criticism*, 3 vols. (Edinburgh: Millar and Bell, 1762), I: 110, 108, 111, and 118. Further citations to the *Elements of Criticism* in the text are to this edition.

2. Martin Heidegger, "The End of Philosophy and the Task of Thinking"; quoted in *Deconstruction in Context: Literature and Philosophy*, ed. Mark Taylor (Chicago: University of Chicago Press, 1986), p. 243.

3. Jean H. Hagstrum, *The Sister Arts: The Tradition of Literary Pictorialism and English Poetry from Dryden to Gray* (Chicago: University of Chicago Press, 1958), pp. 11–36 and passim.

4. Hugh Blair, *Lectures on Rhetoric and Belles Lettres*, 2 vols. (Carbondale: University of Southern Illinois Press, 1965), I: 360.

5. Joseph Addison, *The Spectator*, ed. Donald F. Bond, 5 vols. (Oxford: Clarendon Press, 1965), III: 547 and 580. All citations to *The Spectator* in the text are to this edition.

6. Edmund Burke, *A Philosophical Enquiry into the Origin of our Ideas of the Sublime and the Beautiful*, ed. J. T. Boulton (London: Routledge & Kegan Paul; New York: Columbia University Press, 1958), p. 175.

7. See, e.g., Monroe C. Beardsley, *Aesthetics from Classical Greece to the Present: A Short History* (New York: Macmillan, 1966); Harold Osborne, *Aesthetics and Art Theory: An Historical Introduction* (New York: E. P. Dutton, 1970); and René Wellek, *A History of Modern Criticism: 1750–1950. Volume 1* (New Haven: Yale University Press, 1955).

8. Smith, *Shakespeare in the Eighteenth Century*, p. 72, and Sherbo, *Samuel Johnson, Editor of Shakespeare*, p. 58. Hagstrum, in *Samuel Johnson's Literary Criticism*,

emphasizes that Johnson's critique of dramatic illusion is related to "his lifelong opposition to the imagination as an instrument of delusion" (p. 92). See also Damrosch, *The Uses of Johnson's Criticism*, pp. 110–12.

9. On this point, see Stock, *Samuel Johnson and Neoclassical Dramatic Theory*, pp. 97–99. William Edinger is mistaken, in my opinion, in arguing in a review of Stock's work *(MP* 72 (1975): 429) that Johnson distinguishes in the *Preface* to Shakespeare between delusion and dramatic illusion and thus does not deny the existence of the latter. The reader of *Macbeth* who "looks round alarmed, and starts to find himself alone" is not necessarily deceived or a captive to illusion but may rather be akin to the "mother" who "weeps over her babe when she remembers that death may take it from her."

10. On the dilemma posed by an emphasis on the spectator's consciousness of his own safety, see France Ferguson, "The Sublime of Edmund Burke, or the Bathos of Experience," *Glyph* 8 (1981): 70–71.

11. Wellek, *A History of Modern Criticism*, pp. 79–82.

12. David Nichol Smith, ed., *Eighteenth-Century Essays on Shakespeare*, 2d ed. (Oxford: Clarendon Press, 1963), p. 45.

13. Sir Joshua Reynolds, *Discourses on Art*, ed. Robert R. Wark (New Haven and London: Yale University Press, 1975), pp. 238 and 232.

14. David Hume, *A Treatise on Human Nature*, ed. Ernest G. Mossner (Harmondsworth: Penguin Books, 1969), p. 173.

15. Hume, *A Treatise on Human Nature*, pp. 170–71.

16. Duff, *An Essay on Original Genius*, p. 171.

17. This shift is described in the context of eighteenth-century philosophy by Anthony J. Tillinghast, "The Moral and Philosophical Basis of Johnson's and Boswell's Ideas of Biography," in *Johnsonian Studies*, ed. Magdi Wahba (Cairo, 1962), pp. 122–24. Folkenflik, in *Samuel Johnson, Biographer*, p. 27, denies the existence of such a shift, contending that Johnson was referring to both biography and autobiography when he used the term biography in *Rambler*, no. 60.

18. Hume, *A Treatise on Human Nature*, p. 307.

19. John Locke, *An Essay Concerning Human Understanding*, ed. Alexander Campbell Fraser (first publ. 1894; New York: Dover, 1959], I. 2. 20. 16, I: 306–7; Edmund Burke, *A Philosophical Inquiry*, p. 33; Hume, *A Treatise on Human Nature*, pp. 300.

20. Michel Foucault, *The Order of Things: An Archaeology of the Human Sciences* (New York: Vintage Books, 1973), p. 49.

21. Dennis, *The Critical Works,* I: 218.

22. Samuel Taylor Coleridge, *Collected Letters of Samuel Taylor Coleridge*, ed. Earl Leslie Griggs, 6 vols. (Oxford: Clarendon Press, 1959), IV: 1010.

23. Agostino Lombardo, "The Importance of Imlac," trans. Barbara Arnett Melchiori, in *Bicentenary Essays on Rasselas*, ed. Magdi Wahba (Supplement to *Cairo Studies in English*, 1959), p. 41.

Chapter 5. Recollection, Curiosity and the Theory of Affects

1. Alexander Pope, *An Essay on Criticism*, ll. 301–2, in his *The Poems of Alexander Pope*, ed. John Butt (New Haven: Yale University Press, 1963), p. 153.

2. Biographical preface of John Scott (of Amwell), *Critical Essays of Some of the Poems of Several English Poets* (1785), p. liii; quoted in Damrosch, *The Uses of Johnson's Criticism*, p. 3–4.

3. For accounts that define the opposition between the general and the particular in terms of a Platonic aesthetic, see Louis I. Bredvold, "The Tendency toward Platonism in Neo-classical Esthetics," *ELH* 1 (1934): 91–119; and Wellek, *A History of Modern Criticism, Volume 1*, p. 85. Walter Jackson Bate, in *From Classic to Romantic* (Cambridge: Harvard University Press, 1946), pp. 59–79, followed this tradition, contending that Johnson's view of "general nature" is organized in terms of a series of hierarchical oppositions (probable versus marvellous, objective versus subjective, clarity versus obscurity, ideal reality versus defective accident, nature versus custom, rational versus emotional, society versus individual), but subsequently modified his argument in *The Achievement of Samuel Johnson* (New York: Oxford University Press, 1965), pp. 198–200. For Keast, on the other hand, Johnson's assumption is that "great writing must be both general and particular, true and striking, uniform and varied, familiar and novel" (rev. of Scott Elledge article in *PQ* 27 [1948]: 131). Recent accounts that view Johnson's notion of the terms "general" and "general nature" in Lockean, empirical terms include Hagstrum, *Samuel Johnson's Literary Criticism*, pp. 84–89; Lionel Basney, "'Lucidus Ordo': Johnson and Generality," *ECS* 5 (1971): 39–71; and Howard D. Weinbrot, "The Reader, the General, and the Particular: Johnson and Imlac in Chapter Ten of *Rasselas*," *ECS* 5 (1971): 80–96. John S. Boyd, S.J., in *The Function of Mimesis and Its Decline* (1967; New York: Fordham University Press, 1980), pp. 289–308, finds a synthesis of empirical and rational elements in Johnson's account of "general nature."

4. Reynolds, *Discourses*, XI: 200. On the relation between portraiture and inscription, see Jonathan Goldberg, "The Inscription of Character in Shakespeare," in his *Voice Terminal Echo: Postmodernism and English Renaissance Texts* (New York and London: Methuen, 1986), pp. 86–100; and David Marshall, *The Figure of Theater: Shaftesbury, Defoe, Adam Smith, and George Eliot* (New York: Columbia University Press, 1986), pp. 40–42.

5. Wimsatt, *The Prose Style of Samuel Johnson*, pp. 95–96.

6. See also *Rambler*, no. 145; *Adventurer*, nos. 115 and 119.

7. Boswells's *Life of Johnson*, V: 269.

8. Foucault, *Language, Counter-Memory, and Practice* (Ithaca, N.Y.: Cornell University Press, 1977), p. 182.

9. Robert DeMaria, Jr., "The Ideal Reader: A Critical Fiction," *PMLA* 93 (1978): 464, points to the idealizing function that the common reader sometimes plays in Johnson's criticism, describing it as "an allegorical, archetypal figure" like Everyman. DeMaria's argument is suggestive yet fails, it seems to me, to specify precisely what purpose this figure serves in Johnson's criticism.

Chapter 6. The Dialectic of Original and Copy

1. See, e. g., *Lives*, III:247, on Pope's *Imitations of Horace* (and, by implication, Johnson's own imitations of Juvenal), and *Lives*, III:332–33, on West's imitations of Spenser. On Johnson's distrust of the neoclassical theory of rhetorical imitation, see William Edinger, *Samuel Johnson and Poetic Style* (Chicago: University of Chicago Press, 1979), pp. 96–97. Hagstrum, in *Samuel Johnson's Criticism*, p. 97, draws attention to the importance Johnson attaches to the practice of imitation in the formation of a prose style.

2. In the *Dictionary*, Johnson gives the word "form" as one of his definitions of the term "mode." He defines "model" as "a copy to be imitated"; "originary" as "produc-

tive; causing existence"; and "original" as "first copy; archetype; that from which any thing is transcribed or translated." For discussions that emphasize the importance of intertextuality and imitation in Johnson's writings, see Paul Fussell, Jr., "Writing as Imitation: Observations on the Literary Process," in *The Rarer Action: Essays in Honor of Francis Fergusson*, ed. Alan Cheuse and Richard Koffler (New Brunswick, N.J.: Rutgers University Press, 1970), pp. 218–39; and Joel Weinsheimer, "Give Me Something to Desire: A Johnsonian Anthropology of Imitation," *PQ* 64 (1985): 211–23.

3. Hazlitt, *Collected Works*,VIII: 100–1.

4. Paul De Man, *Blindness and Insight: Essays in the Rhetoric of Contemporary Criticism*, 2d ed. (Minneapolis: University of Minnesota Press, 1983), p. 271.

5. For a study that interprets Johnson's attention to these controversies as evidence of his awareness of the writer as a professional man of letters, thus anticipating Alexandre Beljame's *Men of Letters and the English Public in the Eighteenth Century* (1881), see Harlan W. Hamilton, "The Relevance of Johnson's 'Lives of the Poets'," in *English Studies Today, Fourth Series* (Rome: Edizione di Storia e Litterature, 1966), pp. 339–55.

6. Damrosch, in *The Uses of Johnson's Criticism,* draws attention to Johnson's elaboration of the "paradox" that "everything Joseph Warton and others had said was perfectly true: Pope is, above all, cautious, correct, and uniform; yet these qualities are somehow combined with an aspiring genius of a kind Warton would not recognize in him" (p. 207). See also Hardy, *Samuel Johnson: A Critical Study*, pp. 194–200.

7. On the influence of Burke's conception of the sublime and the beautiful on the Johnsonian opposition between the great and the little, see Scott Elledge, "The Background and Development in English Criticism of the Theories of Generality and Particularity," *PMLA* 62 (1947): 147–82.

8. See Hagstrum's discussion of Johnson's employment of these categories in "The Beautiful, the Pathetic, and the Sublime," in his *Johnson's Literary Criticism*, pp. 129–62. Arieh Sachs, in *Passionate Intelligence: Imagination and Reason in the Works of Samuel Johnson* (Baltimore: Johns Hopkins University Press, 1967), chap. 5, sees the general as being opposed in Johnson's writings to the narrow, the particular, and the limited in a moral and religious sense. Isobel Grundy, in *Samuel Johnson and the Scale of Greatness* (Leicester: Leicester University Press, 1986), pp. 79–101, emphasizes the heroic and aesthetic dimension of this opposition in Johnson's criticism.

9. On this distinction, see Hagstrum, *Samuel Johnson's Literary Criticism*, pp. 134–35.

10. Claude Lévi-Strauss, *The Savage Mind* (1962; Chicago: University of Chicago Press, 1966), pp. 16–36.

11. John Constable, *Further Documents and Correspondence* (London: Tate Gallery and Suffolk Records Society, 1975), p. 35. The volume of Reynolds's *Works* in which the "business of the poet" passage is inscribed is dated 1822 or later. In this connection, William Youngren asserts that he has been unable to find "a single passage in which Johnson is held up to scorn by a contemporary as the adherent of an outmoded neo-Platonic or quasi-Aristotelian theory of art, nor one in which he accuses any of his contemporaries of promoting a new and dangerous tendency by insisting on particularity" (see his "Dr. Johnson, Joseph Warton and the 'Theory of Particularity'," *Dispositio* 4 [1979]: 167). Youngren demonstrates the closeness of Johnson's views of generality and particularity to those of Joseph Warton in *An Essay on Pope*. Edinger, in *Samuel Johnson and Poetic Style*, points out that Johnson's conception of species is not an "abstraction" but "a fully intelligible individual" (p. 89).

12. Gerard, *An Essay on Taste*, p. 48.

13. On the difference between the procedures of Linneaus and those of other eighteenth century naturalists, see Lorin Anderson, *Charles Bonnet and the Order of the*

Universe (Dordrecht, Holland: D. Reidel, 1982), p. 36; and James L. Larson, *The Representation of the Natural Order in the Work of Carl von Linne* (Berkeley: University of California Press, 1971), pp. 73–74.

14. Foucault, *The Order of Things*, pp. 119 and 151. Foucault departs from the conventional account of the opposition between Linnaeus and Buffon in contending that the procedures of both, in spite of the obvious differences, "rest upon the same epistemological base" (p. 144).

15. Alan T. McKenzie, "Logic and Lexicography: The Concern with Distribution and Extent in Johnson's *Rambler*," *ECent* 23 (1982): 49–63.

16. In a slightly broader context, Howard D. Weinbrot, in "The Reader, the General, and the Particular, " 80–96, holds that Imlac's views are not identical with Johnson's. Martin Kallich, "Samuel Johnson's Criticism and Imlac's Dissertation on Poetry," *JAAC* 25 (1966–67): 71–82; and Donald Siebert, "The Reliability of Imlac," *ECS* 5 (1971): 80–96, defend the older view that Imlac is a spokesman for Johnson's critical views. See Robert Folkenflik's contextual analysis of the "streaks of the tulip" passage in his "The Tulip and Its Streaks: Contexts of *Rasselas* X," *Ariel* (Calgary), 9, no. 2 (1978): 57–71.

Chapter 7. Redefining Genre

1. Keast, "The Theoretical Foundations of Johnson's Criticism," p. 182.

2. Ibid, p. 183.

3. For a useful survey of the treatment of these genres in the Renaissance, see Ann E. Imbrie, "Defining Nonfiction Genres," in *Renaissance Genres: Essays on Theory, History, and Interpretation*, ed. Barbara Kiefer Lewalski (Cambridge: Harvard University Press, 1986), 45–69.

4. The charge that Johnson is applying a naïve canon of "sincerity" to *The Mistress* or to Prior's amatory verse has been advanced by Cleanth Brooks and Robert Penn Warren, *Understanding Poetry*, rev. ed. (New York: Henry Holt, 1950), p. 471; Fussell, *Samuel Johnson and the Life of Writing*, pp. 53–61; and Oliver Sigworth, "Johnson's *Lycidas*: The End of Renaissance Criticism," *ECS* 1 (1967): 157–68. James L. Battersby, in *Rational Praise and Natural Lamentation*, holds that Johnson is not so much attacking insincerity as "inappropriateness" in "*expression*" (p. 190).

5. Hayden White, *Metahistory: The Historical Imagination in Nineteenth-Century Europe* (Baltimore: Johns Hopkins University Press, 1973).

6. Sir Philip Sidney, *Defence of Poesy*, ed. Dorothy M. Macardle (London: Macmillan, 1919), p. 17.

7. Hagstrum, *Samuel Johnson's Criticism*, p. 33.

8. On the double tradition of pastoral, see J. E. Congleton, *Theories of Pastoral Poetry in England, 1648–1798* (Gainesville: University of Florida Press, 1952); and H. M. Richmond, "Rural Lyricism: a Renaissance Mutation of Pastoral," *CL* 16 (1964): 193–210. See also Richard Kelly, "Johnson among the Sheep," *SEL* 8 (1968): 475–85, for an enumeration of the general principles Johnson employs in judging pastorals; and Victor Milne, "Reply to Oliver Sigworth," *ECS* 2 (1969): 300–2.

9. A similar argument concerning *Rambler*, number 37, has been advanced by Damrosch in *The Uses of Johnson's Criticism*, pp. 284–85.

10. Johnson explicitly acknowledges this tradition of commentary in *Adventurer*, number 92: "To search into the antiquity of this kind of poetry, is not my present purpose: that it has long subsisted in the east, the Sacred Writings sufficiently inform us;

and we may conjecture, with great probability, that it was sometimes the devotion, and sometimes the entertainment, of the first generations of mankind" (*Idler, Adventure*, 417–18).

11. Rosalie L. Colie, *The Resources of Kind: Genre Theory in the Renaissance*, ed. Barbara Kiefer Lewalski (Berkeley: University of California Press, 1973).

12. Nicholas Boileau, *Art Poetique*, Canto III. Cf. John Dennis, *The Advancement and Reformation of Modern Poetry* (1707); and Robert Lowth, *Lectures on the Sacred Poetry of the Hebrews* (first publ. in Latin in 1757), trans. G. Gregory (London, 1787).

13. On the link between the tradition of devotional poetry and the new vogue for the religious sublime, see David B. Morris, *The Religious Sublime: Christian Poetry in Eighteenth-Century England* (Lexington: University Press of Kentucky, 1972), pp. 104–54.

14. Hagstrum, *Samuel Johnson's Criticism*, p. 68. David B. Morris, in *The Religious Sublime*, pp. 209–21, offers a useful summary of Johnson's opinions concerning devotional poetry. See also, David R. Anderson's perceptive and thorough "Johnson and the Problem of Religious Verse," *The Age of Johnson* 4 (1991): 41–57.

15. Angus Fletcher, *Allegory: Theory of a Symbolic Mode* (Ithaca, N.Y.: Cornell University Press, 1964), p. 108. Marsilio Ficino, *Commentary on Plato's Symposium on Love*, trans. and ed. by Sears Jayne, 2d ed. (Dallas, Tex.: Spring Publishers, 1985), p. 38.

16. William Hazlitt, *Collected Works*,V: 3, VIII: 30, and I: 175.

17. John Ruskin, "The Elements of English Prosody," in *The Literary Criticism of John Ruskin*, ed. Harold Bloom (Garden City, N.Y.: Doubleday, 1965), p. 352. Hester Lynch Thrale Piozzi, *Anecdotes of Samuel Johnson*, in *Johnsonian Miscellanies*, ed. George Birkbeck Hill (Oxford: Clarendon Press, 1897), p. 284.

18. Edward A. Bloom, in "The Allegorical Principle," *ELH* 18 (1951): 183–84, holds that Johnson is consistently opposed to allegory, employing allegorical figures in his own essays only as personfied abstractions, not as plot actants. However, one must bear in mind that Johnson spoke favorably about allegory in the *Rambler* series (*Rambler*, IV: 285) and that his allegorical personifications do perform as characters in a narrative, even though they are never portrayed as interacting with nonallegorical personages. Vereen M. Bell, in "Johnson's Milton Criticism in Context," *ES* 49 (1968): 127–32, and Stephen Knapp, in *Personification and the Sublime, Milton to Coleridge* (Cambridge: Harvard University Press, 1985), pp. 57–65, trace Johnson's possible indebtedness to Dennis, Voltaire, and Addison in his criticism of allegorical agency.

19. For a survey of modern theories concerning the validity of statements in poetry, see Wallace Martin, *Recent Theories of Narrative* (Ithaca, N.Y.: Cornell University Press, 1986), pp. 181–86. On speculation concerning the invention of "possible worlds," see Thomas G. Pavel, *Fictional Worlds* (Cambridge: Harvard University Press, 1986).

20. See Bakhtin, "Epic and Novel," in *The Dialogic Imagination*, pp. 2–40.

Chapter 8. Language as the Dress of Thought

1. Leavis, "Johnson and Augstanism," p. 110.

2. Jacques Derrida, "Signature, Event, Context," in his *Margins of Philosophy*, trans. Alan Bass (Chicago: University of Chicago Press, 1982), pp. 307–30.

3. Jacques Derrida, "Limited, Inc.," *Glyph* 2 (1977): 200. Derrida, it should be noted, holds that "the value" of iterability "resides not in the indicative and variable examples (an absence that is real or factual, provisional or definitive, such as death for instance), but rather in a condition that may be defined in general" and thus as an a pri-

ori "structural possibility" (p. 194). For Johnson, associationism and custom, by contrast, are clearly empirical and a posteriori, yet are comprehensive enough to function in relation to the plenitude of intentional meaning in virtually the same way as iterability.

4. Jean de La Bruyère, *The Morals and Manners of the Seventeenth Century, Being the Characters of La Bruyère*, trans. Helen Scott (Chicago: McClurg, 1890), p. 8.

5. Adam Smith, *Lectures on Rhetoric and Belles Lettres*, ed. John Lothian (Carbondale: University of Southern Illinois Press, 1963), p. 51.

6. Michael Riffaterre, *The Semiotics of Poetry* (Bloomington: Indiana University Press, 1978), p. 2.

7. Ibid., p. 23.

8. Ibid., pp. 7–11 and passim. See also Riffaterre's "Interpretation and Descriptive Poetry: A Reading of Wordsworth's 'Yew Trees'," *New Literary History* 4 (1972): 229–56.

9. See, also, Johnson, *Idler*, number 69 (*Idler, Adventurer,* 217).

10. Boswell, *Boswell's Life of Johnson*, p. 742. Johnson makes a similar observation in a comment on Lord Hailes's translation of John Hale of Eton, ibid., pp. 1308–9.

11. Concerning the authoritarian aspects of the traditional hierarchy of styles, see Auerbach in "The Faux Devot," in his *Mimesis*, pp. 316–46; and Bakhtin in *The Dialogic Imagination,* pp. 41–83.

12. The claim that Johnson adhered to a strict separation of styles has been advanced by, among others, Wellek, *A History of Modern Criticism,* p. 90. John Barrell argues, with more plausibility, that Johnson's conception of stylistic propriety in the *Plan* and *Preface to the Dictionary* is governed by an opposition between the polite and the vulgar, yet also embodies elements that modify that opposition; see his *English Literature in History 1730–1780: An Equal Wide Survey* (New York: St. Martin's Press, 1983), pp. 152–61.

13. The notion of a "laughing, parodic double" is an especially important concept for Bakhtin: "it is as if such mimicry rips the word away from its object, disunifies the two, shows that a given straightforward generic word—epic or tragic—is one-sided, bounded, incapable of exhausting the object; the process of parodying forces us to experience those sides of the object that are not included in a given genre or style" (*The Dialogic Imagination*, p. 55).

14. Hagstrum, *Samuel Johnson's Literary Criticism*, p. 101. Even though Wimsatt, in *The Prose Style of Samuel Johnson*, effectively describes the heterogeneous elements of Johnson's prose, his analysis of Johnson's theory reaches the same conclusion as that of Hagstrum (see, especially, pp. 104–14.) William Edinger is also mistaken, in my opinion, in holding that Johnson's "critical remarks on the subject of levels of style reveal . . . a pronounced preference for the unspecialized language advocated by Cicero and Quintilian" and that Johnson "defends the advantages of simplicity and plainness" (*Samuel Johnson and Poetic Style*, pp. 174–75).

15. Robert Burrowes, "Essay on The Stile of Doctor Samuel Johnson" (1787), quoted in Boulton, ed., *Johnson: The Critical Heritage*, p. 328.

16. F. W. Bateson. *English Poetry and English Language* (Oxford: Clarendon Press, 1934), p. 58.

17. William Hazlitt, *Collected Works*, I: 174.

18. For the view that Johnson is advocating a naïve canon of translatability in this passage, see Allen Tate, "Johnson on the Metaphysicals," *Kenyon Review* 11 (1949): 379–83, and William Edinger, "Johnson on Conceit: The Limits of Particularity," *ELH* 39 (1972): 597–602.

19. Samuel Taylor Coleridge, *Biographia Literaria* (London: Dent; New York: Dutton, 1906), p. 166. T. S. Eliot, "Johnson as Critic and Poet," in his *On Poetry and Poets* (New York: Farrar, Strauss, and Cudahy, 1943), p. 60. Elsewhere in the same essay,

Eliot argues in a similar vein that Johnson "would not agree that, after the dissociation, they put the material together again in a new unity" (p.63). For an interpretation of Johnson's view of metaphor that emphasizes its rationalistic and neoclassical aspects, see Alex Page, "Faculty Psychology and Metaphor in Eighteenth-Century Criticism," *MP* 66 (1969): 237–47.

20. See Johnson's similar comments on exemplification in *Lives*, I: 20, I: 441, and III: 230. Johnson's explanation differs from Addison's in *Spectator*, number 62, in that it deals with exemplification "abstracted from its effects upon the hearer" and thus "more rigorously and philosophically." According to Addison, "it is necessary that the Ideas should lie too near one another in the Nature of Things; for where the Likeness is obvious, it gives no Surprize . . . . unless, besides this obvious Resemblance, there can be some further Congruity discovered in the two Ideas that is capable of giving the Reader some Surprize" (*Spectator*, I: 264). Joseph Priestley, in *A Course of Lectures on Oratory and Criticism* (London: J. Johnson, 1777), formulates a criticism of the angel simile in Addison's *The Campaign* that is broadly similar to Johnson's argument yet is considerably more diffuse in its presentation (p. 167).

21. La Bruyère, *The Characters of La Bruyère*, p. 23. On the traditional view of hyperbole as a figure that mediates between truth and falsehood, see Brian Vickers, "Donne's 'Songs and Sonnets' and the Rhetoric of Hyperbole," in *John Donne: Essays in Celebration*, ed. A. J. Smith (London: Methuen, 1972), pp. 142–48. In this connection, see also Donald Greene, "The Term 'Conceit' in Johnson's Literary Criticism," in *Evidence in Literary Scholarship: Essays in Memory of James Marshall Osborne*, ed. René Wellek and Alvaro Riveiro (Oxford: Clarendon Press, 1979), pp. 337–51. Greene identifies Johnson's observations on the conceit with his "fulminations against the obviously cerebral and contrived in Poetry" and holds that "the closest synonym in current English is 'gimmick' defined . . . as 'tricky device, esp. one adopted for the purpose of attracting attention or publicity'" (pp. 347–48). Here I would hold that Johnson also occasionally uses the term conceit in a positive sense, as, for instance, when he reproaches Swift for the absence of "sparking conceits" in his prose.

Chapter 9. Conclusion

1. Northrop Frye, *The Anatomy of Criticism: Four Essays* (1957; New York: Atheneum, 1966), pp. 86–91; see also his essays on "Allegory" in *Princeton Encyclopedia of Poetry and Poetics*, ed. Alex Preminger (Princeton: Princeton University Press, 1965), pp. 12–15, and his "Literary Criticism," in *The Aims and Methods of Scholarship in Modern Languages and Literatures*, ed. James Thorpe (New York: Modern Language Association, 1963), pp. 65–66.

2. See, e.g., Sermons 7 and 11, in Johnson, *Sermons*, pp. 83 and 117.

3. Boswell, *Boswell's Life of Johnson*, IV: 38.

4. Carey Kaplan and Ellen Cronan Rose, *The Canon and the Common Reader* (Knoxville: University of Tennessee Press, 1990), p. 26.

5. Allen Reddick, *The Making of Johnson's Dictionary, 1746–1773* (Cambridge and New York: Cambridge University Press, 1990), pp. 132, 136, and 139.

Bibliography

Abrams, Meyer H. *The Mirror and the Lamp: Romantic Theory and Critical Tradition.* 1953. New York: W. W. Norton, 1958.

Addison, Joseph. *The Spectator*. Edited by Donald F. Bond. 5 vols. Oxford: Clarendon Press, 1965.

Anderson, David R. "Johnson and the Problem of Religious Verse." *The Age of Johnson* 4 (1991): 41–57.

Anderson, Lorin. *Charles Bonnet and the Order of the Universe*. Dordrecht, Holland: D. Reidel, 1982.

Arnold, Matthew. "Johnson's *Lives of the Poets*." In *Essays Religious and Mixed*, edited by R. H. Super. Vol. 8 of his *The Complete Prose Works*. Ann Arbor: University of Michigan Press, 1972.

Auerbach, Erich. *Mimesis*. 1946. New York: Doubleday Anchor, 1957.

Bakhtin, Mikhail. *The Dialogic Imagination: Four Essays*, translated by Caryl Emerson and Michael Holquist. Austin: The University of Texas Press, 1981.

———. *Problems of Dostoevsky's Poetics*. Translated by Caryl Emerson. Minneapolis: University of Minnesota Press, 1984.

Barrell, John. *English Literature in History 1730–1780: An Equal Wide Survey*. New York: St. Martin's Press, 1983.

Barthes, Roland. "Criticism as Language." *Times Literary Supplement* (27 September 1963): 740.

Basney, Lionel. "'Ah, ha!—Samuel Johnson—I see thee!' Johnson's Ironic Roles." *South Atlantic Quarterly* 75 (1976): 198–211.

———. "'Lucidus Ordo': Johnson and Generality." *Eighteenth-Century Studies* 5 (1971): 39–71.

Bate, Walter Jackson. *The Achievement of Samuel Johnson*. New York: Oxford University Press, 1965.

———. *From Classic to Romantic*. Cambridge: Harvard University Press, 1946.

———. "Dr. Johnson and *Satire Manqué*." In *Eighteenth-Century Studies in Honor of Donald F. Hyde*, edited by W. H. Bond. New York: Grolier Club, 1970.

Bateson, F. W. *English Poetry and English Language*. Oxford: Clarendon Press, 1934.

Battersby, James L. *Rational Praise and Natural Lamentation: Johnson, Lycidas, and Principles of Criticism*. Rutherford, N.J.: Fairleigh Dickinson University Press, 1980.

Beardsley, Monroe C. *Aesthetics from Classical Greece to the Present: A Short History.* New York: Macmillan, 1966.

Bell, Vereen M. "Johnson's Milton Criticism in Context." *English Studies* 49 (1968): 127–32.

Blair, Hugh. *Lectures on Rhetoric and Belles Lettres.* 2 vols. Carbondale: University of Southern Illinois Press, 1965.

Bloom, Edward A. "The Allegorical Principal." *ELH* 18 (1951): 163–90.

Bogel, Fredric. "Johnson and the Role of Authority." In *The New 18th Century: Theory, Politics, English Literature*, edited by Felicity Nussbaum and Laura Brown. London and New York: Methuen, 1987.

Booth, Mark. "Johnson's Critical Judgments in *The Lives of the Poets.*" *Studies in English Literature* 16 (1976): 505–15.

Boswell. James. *Boswell's Life of Johnson.* Edited by George Birkbeck Hill; revised and enlarged by L. F. Powell. 6 vols. Oxford: Clarendon Press, 1936–64.

Boyce, Benjamin. "Samuel Johnson's Criticism of Pope." *Review of English Studies* 5 (1954): 37–46.

Boyd, John S. *The Function of Mimesis and Its Decline.* 1967. New York: Fordham University Press, 1980.

Bredvold, Louis I. "The Tendency toward Platonism in Neo-classical Esthetics." ELH 1 (1934): 91–119.

Bronson, Bertrand. *Johnson Agonistes and Other Essays.* 1951. Berkeley and Los Angeles: University of California Press, 1965.

Brooks, Cleanth, *The Well-Wrought Urn: Studies in the Structure of Poetry.* New York: Harcourt, Brace & Co., 1947.

Brooks, Cleanth and Warren, Robert Penn. *Understanding Poetry.* Revised edition. New York: Henry Holt, 1950.

Burke, Edmund. *A Philosophical Enquiry into the Origin of our Ideas of the Sublime and the Beautiful.* Edited by James T. Boulton. London: Routledge & Kegan Paul; New York: Columbia University Press, 1958.

Campbell, George. *The Philosophy of Rhetoric.* New York: Harper & Bros., 1850.

Carroll, David. *The Subject in Question: The Languages of Theory and the Strategies of Fiction.* Chicago: University of Chicago Press, 1982.

Coleridge, Samuel Taylor. *Biographia Literaria.* London: Dent; New York: Dutton, 1906.

———. "Lecture on Style." In his *Coleridge's Essays & Lectures on Shakespeare & Some Other Old Poets & Dramatists.* London: Dent; New York: Dutton, 1907.

———. *Coleridge's Table Talk and Omniana.* London: Oxford University Press, 1917).

———. *Collected Letters of Samuel Taylor Coleridge.* Edited by Earl Leslie Griggs. 6 vols. Oxford: Clarendon Press, 1959.

Colie, Rosalie. *The Resources of Kind: Genre Theory in the Renaissance.* Edited by Barbara Kiefer Lewalski. Berkeley: University of California Press, 1973.

Congleton, J. E. *Theories of Pastoral Poetry in England, 1648–1798.* Gainesville: University of Florida Press, 1952.

Constable, John. *Further Documents and Correspondence.* London: Tate Gallery and Suffolk Records Society, 1975.

Culler, Jonathan. "Changes in the Lyric." In *Lyric Poetry: Beyond New Criticism*, edited by Chaviva Hosek and Patricia Parker. Ithaca and New York: Cornell University Press, 1985.

Damrosch, Leopold, Jr. "Samuel Johnson and Reader Response Criticism." *Eighteenth Century: Theory and Interpretation* 21 (1980): 91–108.

———. *The Uses of Johnson's Criticism.* Charlottesville: University of Virginia Press, 1976.

De Man, Paul. *Allegories of Reading: Figural Language in Rousseau, Nietzsche, Rilke, and Proust.* New Haven: Yale University Press, 1979.

———. *Blindness and Insight: Essays in the Rhetoric of Contemporary Criticism.* 2d edition. Minneapolis: University of Minnesota Press, 1983.

DeMaria, Robert Jr. "The Ideal Reader: A Critical Fiction." *Publications of the Modern Language Association* 93 (1978): 463–74.

Dennis, John. *The Advancement and Reformation of Poetry.* In his *The Critical Works,* edited by Edward Niles Hooker. 2 vols. Baltimore: Johns Hopkins University Press, 1939.

De Quincey, Thomas. *De Quincey as Critic.* Edited by John E. Jordan. London: Routledge & Kegan Paul, 1973.

Derrida, Jacques. *Of Grammatology.* Translated by Gayatri Chakravorty Spivak. Baltimore: Johns Hopkins University Press, 1974.

———. "Signature, Event, Context." In his *Margins of Philosophy,* translated by Alan Bass. Chicago: University of Chicago Press, 1982.

Duff, William. *An Essay on Original Genius, and its various modes of exertion in Philosophy and the Fine Arts, particularly in Poetry.* London: Printed for E. and C. Dilly, 1767.

Eastman, Arthur M. "In Defense of Dr. Johnson." *Shakespeare Quarterly* 8 (1957): 493–500.

———. "Johnson's Shakespeare and the Laity: A Textual Study." *Publications of the Modern Language Association* 55 (1950): 1112–21.

Edinger, William. "Johnson on Conceit: The Limits of Particularity." *ELH* 39 (1972): 597–602.

———. *Samuel Johnson and Poetic Style.* Chicago: The University of Chicago Press, 1979.

Eliot, T. S. "Johnson as Critic and Poet." In his *On Poetry and Poets.* New York: Farrar, Strauss, and Cudahy, 1943.

Elledge, Scott. "The Background and Development in English Criticism of the Theories of Generality and Particularity." *Publications of the Modern Language Association* 62 (1947): 147–82.

Ferguson, Frances. "The Sublime of Edmund Burke, or the Bathos of Experience." *Glyph* 8 (1981): 62–78.

Ficino, Marsilio. *Commentary on Plato's Symposium on Love.* Translated and edited by Jayne Sears. 2d edition. Dallas, Tex.: Spring Publishers, 1985.

Fix, Stephen. "The Contexts and Motives of Johnson's *Life of Milton.*" In *Domestick Privacies: Samuel Johnson and the Art of Biography,* edited by David Wheeler. Lexington: University Press of Kentucky, 1987.

———. "Distant Genius: Johnson and the Art of Milton's Life." *Modern Philology* 81 (1984): 244–64.

Fleischauer, Warren. "Johnson, *Lycidas* and the Norms of Criticism." In *Johnsonian Studies,* edited by Magdi Wahba. Cairo: privately printed, 1962.

Fletcher, Angus. *Allegory: Theory of a Symbolic Mode*. Ithaca: Cornell University Press, 1964.

Folkenflik, Robert. *Samuel Johnson: Biographer*. Ithaca and London: Cornell University Press, 1978.

———. "The Tulip and Its Streaks: Contexts of Rasselas X." *Ariel* (Calgary) 9, no. 2 (1978): 57–71.

Frieden, Ken. *Genius and Monologue*. Ithaca and London: Cornell University Press, 1985.

Frye, Northrop. "Allegory." In *Princeton Encyclopedia of Poetry and Poetics*, edited by Alex Preminger. Princeton: Princeton University Press, 1965.

———. *Anatomy of Criticism: Four Essays*. 1957. New York: Atheneum, 1966.

———. "Literary Criticism." In *The Aims and Methods of Scholarship in Modern Languages and Literatures*, edited by James Thorpe. New York: Modern Language Association, 1963.

Foucault, Michel. *Language, Counter-Memory, and Practice*. Ithaca and London: Cornell University Press, 1977.

———. *The Order of Things: An Archaelogy of the Human Sciences*. New York: Vintage Books, 1973.

Fussell, Paul. *Samuel Johnson and the Life of Writing*. 1971. New York: W. W. Norton, 1986.

———. "Writing as Imitation: Observations on the Literary Process." In *The Rarer Action: Essays in Honor of Francis Fergusson*, edited by Alan Cheuse and Richard Koffler. New Brunswick, N.J.: Rutgers University Press, 1970.

Gerard, William. *An Essay on Taste*. Edited by W. J. Hipple, Jr. Gainesville, Fla: Scholars Facsimiles, 1973.

Goldberg, Jonathan. *Voice Terminal Echo: Postmodernism and English Renaissance Texts*. New York and London: Methuen, 1986.

Golden, Morris. *The Self Observed: Swift, Johnson, and Wordsworth*. Baltimore: Johns Hopkins University Press, 1972.

Greene, Donald. "The Proper Language of Poetry: Gray, Johnson, and Others." In *Fearful Joy: Papers from the Thomas Gray Bicentenary Conference at Carleton University*, edited by James Downey and Ben Jones. Montreal and London: McGill-Queen's University Press, 1974.

———. "The Term 'Conceit' in Johnson's Literary Criticism." In *Evidence in Literary Scholarship: Essays in Memory of James Marshall Osborne*, edited by René Wellek and Alvaro Riveiro. Oxford: Clarendon Press, 1979.

Grundy, Isobel. *Samuel Johnson and the Scale of Greatness*. Leicester: Leicester University Press, 1986.

Hagstrum, Jean H. *Samuel Johnson's Literary Criticism*. Chicago: University of Chicago Press, 1967.

———. *The Sister Arts: The Tradition of Literary Pictorialism and English Poetry from Dryden to Gray*. Chicago: University of Chicago Press, 1958.

Hamilton, Harlan W. "The Relevance of Johnson's 'Lives of the Poets'." In *English Studies Today, Fourth Series*. Rome: Edizione di Storia e Litterature, 1966.

Hardy, J. P. *Samuel Johnson: A Critical Study*. London: Routledge & Kegan Paul, 1979.

Hazlitt, William. *Collected Works*. Edited by A. R. Waller and Arnold Glover. 12 Vols. London: Dent, 1902.

Heidegger, Martin. "The End of Philosophy and the Task of Thinking." In *Deconstruc-*

tion in Context: Literature and Philosophy, edited by Mark Taylor. Chicago: University of Chicago Press, 1986.

Hertz, Neil H. "Poetry in an Age of Prose: Arnold and Gray." In *In Defense of Reading, A Reader's Approach to Literary Criticism*, edited by Richard Poirier and Reuben Brower. New York: Dutton, 1962.

Hilles, F. W. "The Making of the Life of Pope." In *New Light on Johnson*, edited by F. W. Hilles. New Haven: Yale University Press, 1959.

Hume, David. *A Treatise on Human Nature*, edited by Ernest G. Mossner. Harmonsdworth, Middlesex: Penguin Books, 1969.

Imbrie, Anne E. "Defining Nonfiction Genres." In *Renaissance Genres: Essays on Theory, History, and Interpretation*, edited by Barbara Kiefer Lewalski. Cambridge: Harvard University Press, 1986.

Johnson, Samuel. *Johnson: The Critical Heritage*. Edited by James T. Boulton. London: Routledge & Kegan Paul, 1971.

———. *Dr. Johnson on Shakespeare*. Edited by William K. Wimsatt, Jr. New York: Hill and Wang, 1960.

———. *Sermons*. Edited by Jean Hagstrum and James Gray. Vol. 14 of the *Yale Edition of the Works of Samuel Johnson*. New Haven: Yale University Press, 1978.

Johnston, Shirley White. "The Unfurious Critic: Samuel Johnson's Attitudes toward his Contemporaries." *Modern Philology* 77 (1979): 18–25.

Kallich, Martin. "Samuel Johnson's Criticism and Imlac's Dissertation on Poetry." *Journal of Aesthetics and Art Criticism* 25 (1966–67): 71–82.

Kaplan, Carey, and Rose, Ellen Cronan. *The Canon and the Common Reader*. Knoxville: University of Tennessee Press, 1990.

Kames, Lord, Henry Home. *Elements of Criticism*. 3 vols. Edinburgh: Millar and Bell, 1762.

Keast, William R. "Johnson's Criticism of the Metaphysical Poets." In *Eighteenth- Century English Literature: Modern Essays in Criticism*, edited by James L. Clifford. New York: Oxford University Press, 1959.

———. "The Theoretical Foundations of Johnson's Criticism." In *Critics and Criticism*, edited by R. S. Crane. Abridged edition. Chicago: University of Chicago Press, 1957.

Kelly, Richard. "Johnson Among the Sheep." *Studies in English Literature* 8 (1968): 475–85.

Knapp, Stephen. *Personification and the Sublime, Milton to Coleridge*. Cambridge: Harvard University Press, 1985.

Krieger, Murray. "Fiction, Nature, and Literary Kinds." In his *Poetic Presence and Illusion: Essays in Critical History and Theory*. Baltimore: Johns Hopkins University Press, 1979.

Krutch, Joseph Wood. *Samuel Johnson*. New York: Harcourt, Brace & Co., 1944.

La Bruyère, Jean de. *The Morals and Manners of the Seventeenth Century, Being the Characters of La Bruyère*. Translated by Helen Scott. Chicago: McClurg, 1890.

Larson, James L. *The Representation of the Natural Order in the Work of Carl von Linne*. Berkeley: University of California Press, 1971.

Leavis, F. R. "Johnson and Augustanism." In his *The Common Pursuit*. 1952. London: Hogarth Press, 1984.

———. "Johnson as Critic." In his *Anna Karenina and Other Essays*. 1933. New York: Simon and Shuster, 1969.

Lévi-Strauss, Claude. *The Savage Mind.* 1962. Chicago: University of Chicago Press, 1966.

Lipking, Lawrence. *The Ordering of the Arts in Eighteenth-Century England.* Princeton: Princeton University Press, 1970.

Locke, John. *An Essay Concerning Human Understanding.* Edited by Alexander Campbell Fraser. 2 vols. 1894. New York: Dover, 1959.

Lombardo, Agostino. "The Importance of Imlac." Translated by Barbara Arnett Melchiori. In *Bicentenary Essays on Rasselas*, edited by Magdi Wahba. Supplement to *Cario Studies in English*, 1959.

Lovejoy, A. O. "On the Discrimination of Romanticisms." In his *Essays in the History of Ideas.* First published 1948. New York: G. P. Putnam, 1960.

Macaulay, Thomas Babington. "Boswell's Life of Johnson." In his *Critical and Historical Essays.* 2 vols. London: Dent; New York: Dutton, 1907.

McKenzie, Alan T. "Logic and Lexicography: The Concern with Distribution and Extent in Johnson's *Rambler.*" *Eighteenth Century: Theory and Interpretation* 23 (1982): 49–63.

Marshall, David. *The Figure of Theater: Shaftesbury, Defoe, Adam Smith, and George Eliot.* New York: Columbia University Press, 1986.

Martin, Wallace. *Recent Theories of Narrative.* Ithaca and London: Cornell University Press, 1986.

Milne, Victor. "Reply to Oliver Sigworth." *Eighteenth-Century Studies* 2 (1969): 300–2.

Morris, David. *The Religious Sublime: Christian Poetry in Eighteenth-Century England.* Lexington: University Press of Kentucky, 1972.

Osborne, Harold. *Aesthetics and Art Theory: An Historical Introduction.* New York: E. P. Dutton, 1970.

Page, Alex. "Faculty Psychology and Metaphor in Eighteenth-Century Criticism." *Modern Philology* 66 (1969): 237–47.

Pavel, Thomas G. *Fictional Worlds.* Cambridge: Harvard University Press, 1986.

Perkins, David. "Johnson on Metaphysical Poetry." *ELH* 20 (1953): 200–17.

Piper, William Bowman. "Samuel Johnson as Exemplary Critic." *Texas Studies in Language and Literature* 20 (1978): 457–73.

Piozzi, Hester Lynch Thrale. *Ancedotes of Samuel Johnson.* In *Johnsonian Miscellanies*, edited by George Birkbeck Hill. Oxford: Clarendon Press, 1897.

Pope, Alexander. *The Poems of Alexander Pope*, edited by John Butt. New Haven: Yale University Press, 1963.

Priestley, Joseph. *A Course of Lectures on Oratory and Criticism.* London: J. Johnson, 1777.

Raleigh, Walter. *Six Essays on Johnson.* Oxford: Clarendon Press, 1910.

Reddick, Allen. *The Making of Johnson's Dictionary, 1746–1773.* Cambridge and New York: Cambridge University Press, 1990.

Reynolds, Sir Joshua. *Discourses on Art.* Edited by Robert R. Wark. New Haven and London: Yale University Press, 1975.

Richmond, H. M. "Rural Lyricism: A Renaissance Mutation of Pastoral." *Comparative Literature* 16 (1964): 193–210.

Riffaterre, Michael. "Interpretation and Descriptive Poetry: A Reading of Wordsworth's 'Yew Trees'." *New Literary History* 4 (1972): 229–56.

———. *The Semiotics of Poetry*. Bloomington: Indiana University Press, 1978.

Rogers, Pat. "Johnson's *Lives of the Poets* and the Biographical Dictionaries." *Review of English Studies* n. s. 21 (1980): 40–71.

Ruskin, John. "The Elements of English Prosody." In his *The Literary Criticism of John Ruskin*, edited by Harold Bloom. Garden City, N.Y.: Doubleday, 1965.

Sachs, Arieh. *Passionate Intelligence: Imagination and Reason in the Works of Samuel Johnson*. Baltimore: Johns Hopkins University Press, 1967.

Shakespeare, William. *Eighteenth-Century Essays on Shakespeare*. Edited by D. Nichol Smith. 2d edition. Oxford: Clarendon Press, 1963.

Sherbo, Arthur. *Samuel Johnson: Editor of Shakespeare, with an Essay on The Adventurer. Illinois Studies in Language and Literature*, Vol. 42. Urbana: University of Illinois Press, 1956.

Sidney, Sir Philip. *Defence of Poesy*. Edited by Dorothy M. Macardle. London: Macmillan, 1919.

Siebert, Donald. "The Reliability of Imlac." *Eighteenth-Century Studies* 5 (1971): 80–96.

Sigworth, Oliver. "Johnson's *Lycidas*: The End of Renaissance Criticism." *Eighteenth-Century Studies* 1 (1967): 157–68.

Smith, Adam. *Lectures on Rhetoric and Belles Lettres*. Edited by John Lothian. Carbondale: University of Southern Illinois Press, 1963.

Smith, David Nichol. *Shakespeare in the Eighteenth Century*. Oxford: Clarendon Press, 1926.

Stephen, Leslie. *The History of Rasselas with the Life of the Author*. London: A. L. Burt, n. d.

Stock, R. D. *Samuel Johnson and Neoclassical Dramatic Theory: The Intellectual Context of the Preface to Shakespeare*. Lincoln: University of Nebraska Press, 1973.

Swearingen, James E. "Johnson's Life of Gray." *Texas Studies in Language and Literature* 14 (1972: 283–302.

Tate, Allen. "Johnson on the Metaphysicals." *Kenyon Review* 11 (1949): 379–83.

Tillinghast, Anthony J. "The Moral and Philosophical Basis of Johnson's and Boswell's Ideas of Biography." In *Johnsonian Studies*, edited by Magdi Wahba. Cairo: Privately printed, 1962.

Trowbridge, Hoyt. "Scattered Atoms of Probability." *Eighteenth-Century Studies* 5 (1971): 1–38.

Vickers, Brian. "Donne's 'Songs and Sonnets' and the Rhetoric of Hyperbole." In *John Donne: Essays in Celebration*, edited by A. J. Smith. London: Methuen, 1972.

Wain, John. *Samuel Johnson: A Biography*. New York: McGraw-Hill, 1974.

Warnke, Wayne. "Samuel Johnson on Swift: the *Life of Swift* and Johnson's Predecessors in Swiftian Biography." *Journal of the Bibliographical Society* 7 (1968): 56–64.

Weinbrot, Howard D. "The Reader, the General, and the Particular: Johnson and Imlac in Chapter Ten of *Rasselas*." *Eighteenth-Century Studies* 5 (1971): 80–96.

Weinsheimer, Joel. "Give Me Something to Desire: A Johnsonian Anthropology of Imitation." *Philological Quarterly* 64 (1985): 211–23.

Wellek, René. *The Attack on Literature and Other Essays*. Chapel Hill: University of North Carolina Press, 1982.

———. *A History of Modern Criticism: 1750–1950. Volume 1*. New Haven: Yale University Press, 1955.

White, Hayden. *Metahistory: The Historical Imagination in Nineteenth-Century Europe.* Baltimore: Johns Hopkins University Press, 1973.

Wimsatt, William K., Jr. *The Prose Style of Samuel Johnson.* New Haven: Yale University Press, 1941.

Wordsworth, William. *Preface to the Lyrical Ballads* (1850). In his *The Prose Works,* edited by W. J. B. Owen and Jane Worthington Smyser. 3 vols. Oxford: Clarendon Press, 1974.

Young, Edward. *Conjectures on Original Composition.* London: Millar and Dodsley, 1759.

Youngren, William. "Dr. Johnson, Joseph Warton, and the 'Theory of Particularity'." *Dispositio* 4 (1979): 163–88.

Index

PR 3537 .L5 H56 1994
HINNANT, CHARLES H.
"STEEL FOR THE MIND"

DATE DUE

Demco, Inc. 38-293